LADY UNKNOWN

With all good wishes

to Donnie McLeod

Edna Healey.

Angela Burdett-Coutts: a portrait in watercolour upon ivory by
William Ross, 1858.

Lady Unknown

The Life of
Angela Burdett-Coutts

Edna Healey

SIDGWICK & JACKSON

LONDON

First published in Great Britain in 1978
by Sidgwick and Jackson
Reprinted February 1978
Reprinted April 1978
Copyright © 1978 Edna Healey

ISBN 0 283 98339 6

Picture research by Philippa Lewis
Map by Dan Kitts

Printed in Great Britain
by Biddles Ltd, Guildford, Surrey
for Sidgwick and Jackson Limited
1 Tavistock Chambers, Bloomsbury Way
London WC1A 2SG

To my Mother

Contents

List of Illustrations

List of Illustrations

Preface

MANY YEARS ago we came to live on the Holly Lodge Estate, Highgate, in a house built with others in the grounds of what had once been the home of the nineteenth-century philanthropist, Baroness Burdett-Coutts. Intrigued by the old gardens, with their cedars and high rhododendrons, urns and crumbling summer houses, and by the strange, enclosed Victorian Gothic village that she built at the edge of her estate, I searched in vain for a full biography.

There was a short history of her philanthropy compiled by command of the Duchess of Teck in 1893. A biography written in old age by Mrs Patterson, a descendant of her sister, was tantalizingly incomplete, but it gave some indication of the extraordinary richness and variety of her life. Two selections of the letters to her by Charles Dickens have been published, one with an excellent biographical introduction by her former secretary, Charles C. Osborne.

Edgar Johnson's scholarly *The Heart of Charles Dickens* was of immense value and led me to the complete collection of Dickens's letters to Angela Burdett-Coutts in the Pierpont Morgan Library, New York.

Her friendship with Rajah Brooke, of Sarawak, and their correspondence has been dealt with in great detail by Dr Owen Rutter in his *Rajah Brooke and Baroness Burdett-Coutts*. Extracts from the Duke of Wellington's letters to her in *Wellington and His Friends* by the 7th Duke of Wellington directed me to the letters at Stratfield Saye among the archives of the present Duke of Wellington. For his kind help I am most deeply grateful. The advice and assistance of Mrs Joan Wilson, the archivist at Stratfield Saye, has been of immense value to me.

Apart from these and articles in newspapers and magazines, a chapter in *Noble Lives of Noble Women*, and scattered references in memoirs of the period there was little published biographical material. Yet this was the woman whom Queen Victoria had made a Baroness in her own right, the first woman so to be honoured, the first woman Freeman of the Cities of London and Edinburgh; whom Edward VII described as 'after my Mother the most remarkable woman in the country'.[1]

After her death her husband had hoped to write her biography, but faced with what he described as a house as full of documents as the Records Office, his courage failed. Her own modesty and reticence discouraged biographers in her lifetime, and she outlived most of her friends and was therefore able to destroy most of her letters to them. Dickens, with her consent, burned most of her letters with those of his other friends in a great bonfire at Gad's Hill. So that, although there are in existence hundreds of letters to her from famous people of the nineteenth century, comparatively few of her own still remain. And these are in a handwriting that is almost deliberately obscure.

So began my absorbing search for sources in public and private archives. Nothing in this biography has been invented. Wherever possible I have given exact references, although sometimes this has not been possible, the evidence has often been a scrap of paper in an old tin box.

I have to acknowledge the gracious permission of H.M. the Queen for the use of material in the Royal archives. I am indebted to Sir Robin Mackworth-Young and his staff at Windsor Castle for their generous help.

I am deeply indebted to Lord Latymer, Mr David Money-Coutts and the Directors of Coutts and Co. for the use of material in their archives. I am most particularly grateful for the unfailing kindness and competent assistance of their archivist Miss Veronica Stokes, who also helped me to compile the family tree. The Earl of Harrowby has most kindly allowed me to see the family records at Sandon Hall. For his help and the pleasure of working in his well-ordered muniment-room I am most grateful.

My warmest thanks are due to Mrs Betty Coxon, daughter of Mrs Patterson and direct descendant of Sir Francis Burdett. She has helped me from the first and placed her mother's material at my disposal. Mr Ashmead Burdett-Coutts of Cape Town has most generously lent me letters from the archives of the Baroness's husband's family which are in his possession. He and his sister Whimbrell gave me from the first invaluable help and encouragement. To them I am most profoundly grateful.

I have to thank the librarians and staffs of the British Library, Lambeth Palace Library and the Bodleian Library, Oxford, and the Keeper of the Muniments at Westminster Abbey. The Librarian of Highgate Literary Institute gave me kind assistance at the beginning of my research. The

Librarians of the Public Libraries of Camden, Westminster, Edinburgh, Manchester, Carlisle, Brighton, Tunbridge Wells and Torquay gave me much assistance. In Torquay the local historian, Miss Hilda Walker, was particularly helpful, as were the former owners of Rosetor Hotel (the old Ehrenberg Hall).

Miss Pillars and the staff at Dickens House have been most helpful. For access to the unpublished letters of Charles Dickens in the Pierpont Morgan Library, New York, I am most grateful. The Editors of the Pilgrim Edition of the *Letters of Charles Dickens* have kindly given me permission to publish short extracts of those letters.

To the authorities of the following institutions I express my gratitude for permitting me to make use of the letters in their possession: Kunsthaus, Zurich; Musée des Beaux-Arts, Paris; The Henry E. Huntington Library, California. The Director of the Folger Museum, Washington, kindly allowed me to see the First Folio Shakespeare which had belonged to the Baroness and is now in their possession. The Director of the Museum at the Château de Chantilly was most helpful and discovered letters from the Baroness to the Duc d'Aumale concerning her lease of the Château.

I am deeply grateful to the High Commissioners of Canada and Australia and to their Excellencies the Ambassadors of France and Belgium for the valuable assistance given me by their Librarians.

Sir Anthony Wagner has kindly allowed me to see his collection of letters from Henry Wagner to the Baroness. Mr Laurence Irving directed me to his grandfather's manuscripts in the keeping of the Theatre Museum, London. His *Life of Sir Henry Irving* has been of great interest, to him and to the museum staff I am most grateful.

I have to thank the executors of the late Reginald Colby, who have allowed me to see his unfinished biography of the Baroness. The late Mrs Twining, wife of the Reverend Twining, Vicar of St Stephen's from 1889, wrote an interesting unpublished biography and journal, now in the Westminster City Libraries, Archives Department.

Her Royal Highness Princess Alice, Queen Victoria's granddaughter, graciously described for me the Baroness as she remembered her; she still wears the opal ring the Baroness gave her as a little girl.

Mrs Willard, daughter-in-law of the head gardener at Holly Lodge vividly remembered her father-in-law's accounts of the Baroness at Holly Lodge. Mr Sapsford-Chalklin kindly furnished me with interesting information about his grandfather, John Sapsford. I am most grateful to the Reverend Davidson, vicar of St Stephen's Church, and his wife for all

12

their help. I am grateful to the many scores of people who have sent me family or personal reminiscences; they are too numerous to mention individually.

I am greatly indebted to Lord Briggs, not only for his kindness in reading the manuscript and for his helpful comments, but also because I have found no better guide to the Victorian world.

My thanks to Mr Gary Clendennen, whose wide knowledge of the letters of David Livingstone has been of great value.

Mr Henry Fry and Mrs Willard of the Trade Union, Labour, Co-operative Democratic History Society gave me some interesting material on Sir Francis Burdett for which I am grateful.

I am deeply grateful to my editor, Margaret Willes, for her friendly and constructive criticism; to John Goldsmith without whose skilful surgery this book would be three times too long, to Lindsay Duguid who copy-edited my typescript, and to Philippa Lewis, the picture editor who discovered the early photographs. I am indebted to Patricia Watts-Jones who not only typed but who, by her cheerful good humour, has been my constant support. My thanks to Donna Barker, Christine Scott and Susan Whippey who also helped with the typing.

My warmest thanks are due to Lady Elwyn-Jones (Pearl Binder) who made me start this book. To my husband and family who kept me at it with loyal and loving encouragement, I give my love and heartfelt thanks.

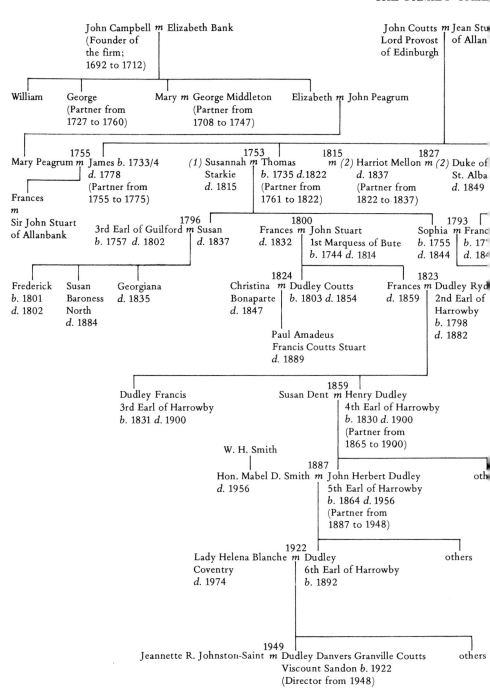

ELA BURDETT-COUTTS

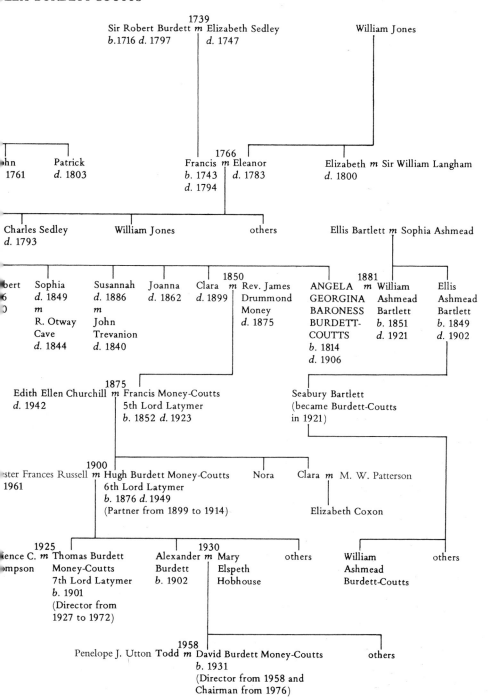

1739
Sir Robert Burdett *m* Elizabeth Sedley
*b.*1716 *d.* 1797   *d.* 1747

William Jones

1766
Francis *m* Eleanor
b. 1743   *d.* 1783
d. 1794

Elizabeth *m* Sir William Langham
d. 1800

ohn   Patrick
1761   *d.* 1803

Charles Sedley
d. 1793

William Jones   others

Ellis Bartlett *m* Sophia Ashmead

1850
bert   Sophia   Susannah   Joanna   Clara *m* Rev. James
6   *d.* 1849   *d.* 1886   *d.* 1862   *d.* 1899   Drummond
0   *m*   *m*   Money
       R. Otway   John   *d.* 1875
       Cave   Trevanion
       d. 1844   *d.* 1840

1881
ANGELA   *m* William   Ellis
GEORGINA   Ashmead   Ashmead
BARONESS   Bartlett   Bartlett
BURDETT-   *b.* 1851   *b.* 1849
COUTTS   *d.* 1921   *d.* 1902
b. 1814
d. 1906

1875
Edith Ellen Churchill *m* Francis Money-Coutts
d. 1942   5th Lord Latymer
                          b. 1852 *d.* 1923

Seabury Bartlett
(became Burdett-Coutts
in 1921)

1900
ster Frances Russell *m* Hugh Burdett Money-Coutts   Nora   Clara *m* M. W. Patterson
1961   6th Lord Latymer
                         b. 1876 *d.* 1949
                         (Partner from 1899 to 1914)

Elizabeth Coxon

1925
ience C. *m* Thomas Burdett
ompson   Money-Coutts
            7th Lord Latymer
            b. 1901
            (Director from
            1927 to 1972)

1930
Alexander *m* Mary   others
Burdett   Elspeth
b. 1902   Hobhouse

William   others
Ashmead
Burdett-Coutts

1958
Penelope J. Utton Todd *m* David Burdett Money-Coutts   others
                           b. 1931
                           (Director from 1958 and
                           Chairman from 1976)

CHAPTER ONE

The Double Inheritance

1814–37

IN THE early hours of 20 June 1837 Victoria, granddaughter of George III, became Queen of England. Two months later Angela, youngest daughter of Sir Francis Burdett MP and granddaughter of Thomas Coutts the banker, stood with her family in a darkened London room and heard the level voice of the lawyer reading the will that declared her heiress to one of the greatest fortunes of the century. Her grandfather's half-share in his highly successful bank, his houses and most of his priceless possessions were now hers.

An unknown girl who had always shunned the limelight was suddenly exposed to its glare. The newspapers gloated – it was a fortune, they reported, of £1,800,000. The *Morning Herald* estimated that 'the weight in gold is 13 tons, 7 cwt, 3 qtrs, 13 lbs and would require 107 men to carry it, supposing that each of them carried 289 lbs – the equivalent of a sack of flour'. Or, they reckoned, the amount in sovereigns, laid in a line, would stretch for over twenty-four miles.

For the next sixty-four years, as the two heiresses pursued their parallel careers, Victoria watched with interest, affection and sometimes a little jealousy, the quiet woman of whom her people were to shout 'Long Live the Queen of the Poor!'

In the late summer of 1837 there was a remarkable similarity in their situations. Both were young. Victoria was eighteen and Angela twenty-three. Both had charm and grace and particularly musical voices, but neither could be called beautiful. The Queen was small and dumpy and showed her gums when she smiled; Angela was tall, too thin, and her complexion was poor. They accepted the responsibility of their respective inheritances with a serious intensity that would later on affect their health. Angela's calm modest and shy appearance concealed a strong will; and, just as the touchingly innocent young Queen would quickly astonish her ministers, so the Burdetts and the partners at Coutts Bank were soon to be made aware of Angela's quiet determination.

Determined to be independent, Victoria and Angela both removed themselves from parental control. The Queen left her mother's bedroom and set up her own establishment. And Angela Burdett, in the autumn of 1837, stood at the window of her father's grave old-fashioned house in St James's Place, looked through the great trees of Green Park to the house in Piccadilly that now was hers, and resolutely determined to leave home.

In the inevitable isolation of their new lives each had an ally in an influential ex-governess. Victoria had Louise Lehzen and Angela had the vivacious intelligent little Hannah Meredith who had been her constant companion and friend since the time when, eleven years before, she had been appointed as governess to the youngest Burdetts. The influence of Lehzen and Hannah in the lives of the two heiresses was great, and both women used their power skilfully.

Both Victoria and Angela had been brought up in a feminine world – the Duke of Kent had died when Victoria was eight months old, and Sir Francis Burdett, the people's champion and so caught up in politics, had rarely been at home in Angela's early childhood. So each was to seek a father figure, the Queen finding Lord Melbourne and Angela the Duke of Wellington; and each determined to understand the masculine world they had inherited. From the beginning Angela, with no particular aptitude or liking for figures, was obstinately determined to understand the working of the Bank, just as Victoria, with no particular liking for politics, laboured doggedly to master the business of government. Both needed advisers.

Angela's Cabinet, the partners at the bank, were impressive: handsome Sir Edmund Antrobus, the second Baronet; Mr Coulthurst, calm and benign with rosy cheeks and a country air; and probably the most influential of all, Mr Edward Marjoribanks. Over six feet tall, stooping with a vague manner that belied his firm mind and enduring physical strength, he lived to the age of ninety-six. Later, younger members of the Antrobus and Marjoribanks families brought new life and new problems to the bank, but in 1837 the bankers at Coutts, grave, dignified and immensely experienced, inspired the trust and confidence of the Royal family and distinguished clients all over the world. Miss Burdett inherited friends,

18

Sir Francis Chantrey's full-length statue of Thomas Coutts, which now dominates the entrance hall of Coutts & Co. Chantrey considered it 'the best thing I've ever done'.

business connections and clients overseas that she made into an empire of her own.

In 1837, when the two serious young women took up their separate burdens, there was one important difference. Victoria's succession had been automatic and expected. Angela's was unexpected and she had been chosen. Hers was an inheritance of more than wealth. To understand the nature of that inheritance and how and why she, the youngest child of the youngest daughter of Thomas Coutts, was chosen, it is necessary to look back to the years before her birth. For Angela Burdett-Coutts was unusually influenced by those early years and conscious of the roots from which she sprang. Her father Sir Francis Burdett and her grandfather Thomas Coutts were two of the most interesting characters in England at the turn of the nineteenth century.

Thomas Coutts was born in Edinburgh in 1735, the fourth son of John Coutts, Lord Provost of Edinburgh and successful Scottish banker. John Coutts & Co. was concerned primarily in importing and exporting corn between European ports from Ireland to the Baltic, and in dealing in salt, beans and timber. Their banking activities developed from this mercantile business.

From his earliest years, Thomas Coutts understood the importance of the world outside his comfortable Edinburgh home. While he was still at the High School, his older brothers Patrick and John were travelling and working on the Continent. Patrick, the eldest and most intellectual of the brothers, was engaged in mysterious activities in France, for which he was for a time jailed as a spy. John, attractive and intelligent, was sent to Rotterdam as a partner in the firm of Robertson, Coutts and Stephens. Here he too became involved in somewhat dubious activities, helping to supply Scottish smugglers, trading in tea and whisky. Both brothers, when they returned to Scotland, brought with them an understanding of Europe and international contacts of great value to the firm. The third son, James, was the most difficult and choleric of the brothers. He became MP for Edinburgh but his Parliamentary career was cut short by the mental illness which was to dog his last years. Thomas shared his brother John's charm and intelligence, but early showed a combination of precision, tenacity, and energy surprising in one apparently so delicate.

On the death of their father in 1750 the four brothers carried on the Edinburgh business for a time until Thomas and Patrick came south to found a London branch. James visited them, married a niece of the Whig banker George Campbell and became his partner at 59 Strand. When

Campbell died, James took over the bank and asked his brother Thomas to join him. By the terms of the partnership, January 1761, Thomas brought £4,000 capital and was entitled to one-third of the future profits of the Bank. By 1772, the Edinburgh business had passed into other hands.

Thomas Coutts's financial success was not due to any particular talent for speculation. He was cautious to a degree; missing, for example, the chance to be the first banker to introduce the circular letter of credit that was to be such a boon to late eighteenth-century travellers on the Grand Tour. But he was highly intelligent, had a knowledge of the world, a talent for organization and above all could handle people of power as skilfully as the money they entrusted to him.

The partnership with his brother was never a happy one, for James was ill and quarrelsome, and it was finally dissolved in 1775. James spent his last years travelling abroad and died at Gibraltar in 1778. John had died in 1761 and Patrick too had become mentally ill.

After James's departure Thomas's first task was to find new partners, and he chose them well. Two of his earliest appointments, Edmund Antrobus in 1777, and Edward Marjoribanks in 1798, were to remain with him for the rest of his life and their families were to provide partners for Coutts Bank for over a hundred years. Edmund Antrobus (later to become the first Baronet) was 'an efficient young man with his fortune to make',[1] and Edward Marjoribanks similarly brought more intelligence than money. But from the beginning, Thomas Coutts was the directing genius and undoubted master. He insisted that he and his heirs should retain 'the supremacy . . . of the House as well as the half share in the Bank'.[2] The other half was to be divided according to seniority between the other working partners.

This 'supremacy', he explained, was 'the disposal, which is to rest with me while I live and with my family at my death, on the share or shares of my partners who may die or retire. And that everything, on any partner quitting business, shall be left in the hands of the person holding the supremacy.' So the control of Thomas Coutts and his heirs over the bank and the appointment of partners was firmly established. These conditions were later to affect the relations between the partners and Angela Burdett-Coutts.

The partners were undoubtedly influential but it was Thomas Coutts's own shrewd intelligence which kept the bank steady through the years from 1798 when, as he wrote, 'A banker's bed is not a bed of roses, . . . when the whole world is in a very alarming state of confusion and England beset with foreign and domestic enemies.'

His greatest asset in those years was the bank's image of quiet gravity which he had created and which inspired confidence in an age of unrest. The clockwork efficiency with which it ticked reassuringly on during the next century was of his devising. He himself planned every hour of the daily routine of every clerk, from the juniors, who were expected to work on Sundays, up to the intelligent, kindly and utterly trustworthy chief clerk, Andrew Dickie. And though, as he made clear in his long memorandum of 1801, in framing the rules he had 'consulted individual convenience as far as Regard for the Business would admit' in return he expected it to be 'rigidly and punctually attended to'.

He set the example. His punctuality was proverbial. On the stroke of nine, every working day, the slight figure in the simple but formal dress would arrive at the door of 59 Strand. This building, influenced by the style of the Adam brothers, was the perfect classical setting for a bank whose first principles were dignity and harmony. The Adam brothers, those other distinguished exiles from Scotland, had built the Adelphi Terrace between the Strand and the River Thames. The bridge built across William Street in 1799 to link Number 59 with the property on the other side also showed the influence of the brothers' work. Thomas Coutts's Bank was expanding fast.

No customer visiting his apartments could fail to be impressed by the richness and elegance of the magnificent Chinese wallpaper, brought for him from China by Lord Macartney, the first British Ambassador there. Here Thomas Coutts lived comfortably but simply. He was proud of his exotic wallpaper, but the vista through his windows, over the Thames to the Kent and Surrey hills gave him the deepest pleasure. He bought no great estates. His success as a banker, he explained, depended upon his ability to have large sums of money always available. And against this background of order, simplicity and solidity in business life he could allow himself, indeed cultivate, a reputation for eccentricity in private life. His appearance was undistinguished, even shabby. One of his favourite stories, told against himself, was of the kindly person who gave a guinea to a poor frail old man on the sea-front at Brighton, only to discover later, at a reception at the Prince Regent's, that the pauper was the wealthy banker Mr Coutts. On 18 May 1763, to the amazement of his friends, he married one of his brother James's servants. He would never have jeopardized the reputation of his *bank* by such a departure from convention, but in his private life he went his own way with a fine disregard for public opinion.

Susannah Starkie was a spirited Lancashire farmer's daughter who came to work for James Coutts as a housemaid at a salary of £8 a year. At that time Thomas Coutts was living on his own in St Martin's Lane and was immediately attracted to the fresh and blooming country girl who cared with such kindness for his brother's child. Susannah, or Betty as she was often called, had the qualities he most admired: simplicity, common sense and competence. The marriage was accepted surprisingly quickly – it was a time when eccentricity was enjoyed rather than condemned. Susannah seems to have impressed everyone with her good sense and modesty. But in the early years of her marriage she had little time for making impressions. In quick succession she bore seven children. According to Thomas's own account, there were four sons who died in infancy, and three daughters, Susan, Frances and Sophia, who were all born in the house in St Martin's Lane.

After his brother's death, Thomas moved to the apartments over the bank in the Strand and Susannah returned as mistress of the house where, more than ten years earlier, she had scrubbed the stairs. No one could have been better qualified to run his house with the 'oeconomy' he so admired or better care for his three pretty daughters. It was a warm, affectionate and close family life, and the girls were devoted to each other and to their parents. Since Thomas had been disappointed in a son, he gave his daughters the best education available, for, as he once said, since women have the care of their sons they must be well educated. The girls were sent to a good school in Queen Square and later Susan and Sophia were sent to the Penthémont, an exclusive convent in Paris. Fanny was delicate and stayed at home, but from the age of twelve Sophia spent most of her adolescence with her sister Susan on the Continent.

If Thomas Coutts attempted to give his wife some polish he seems to have had little success. Mrs Coutts retained her Lancashire directness. Sir Herbert Taylor, writing of the Coutts' visit to Bologna, recorded with some amusement that Mrs Coutts 'being asked her opinion of the amphitheatre of Rome . . . replied that when furnished and whitewashed it would be a very *pretty* building'.[3] But no one minded. The Duchess of Gordon, herself given to straight talking, enjoyed the moment when Mrs Coutts stunned an elegant assembly, waiting for the delayed Prince Regent, with advice on how to keep the fish hot without spoiling.

Thomas Coutts was kind to his aristocratic clients and they in turn were attentive to his daughters. The Duchess of Gordon was hospitable, while the Duchess of Devonshire took them to the theatre in Paris and introduced them to the ladies of the French Court. The Duchess of Buccleuch presented them to George III when they returned to England. It says

23

much for Susannah that though her daughters were to move in distinguished circles and each made a brilliant marriage – Susan marrying the Earl of Guilford, and Fanny, the Marquis of Bute – yet they were never ashamed of their simple mother. To them she was always 'dearest Mamma', whose death was mourned in the most extravagant terms.

Certainly this surprising marriage made no difference to Thomas Coutts's relationship with his famous clients. His discretion, efficiency and kindness continued to attract them. Some brought him great accounts, some brought him debts but a prestige which outweighed their liabilities. At an early date he earned the friendship and trust of George III. In 1787 he was made a Gentleman of the King's Privy Chamber with the right of direct access to the monarch. Coutts certainly felt confident enough of the King's friendship to ask favours for his wife and daughters – the right, for instance, to drive in their carriages through the Royal parks.

The confidence of the Prince Regent was harder to win. To gain this Coutts used all his influential Whig friends, including the Duchess of Devonshire, the dramatist Sheridan, and Charles James Fox. When necessary he could play the courtier, could even be obsequious, for 'his honour', he wrote, 'was so much interested in being continued banker to the King's Privy Purse'.[4] Although an earlier partner had supplied plate to the Prince of Wales in 1716, George III was the first King to bank with Coutts. Thomas was determined that the Royal patronage should be maintained. He succeeded; and to this day the Royal family bank with Coutts.

Not only was he the Royal banker, the King also employed him on confidential missions abroad. In the years leading up to the French Revolution, when his daughters Susan and Sophia were being educated in Paris, he spent some months there himself, discreetly watching the situation, making friends. It was not surprising that during and after the Revolution French aristocrats exiled in Britain brought their treasures to him for sale or safe-keeping.

When Paris became dangerous, instead of returning home he spent almost a year wandering with his wife and three daughters on a tour of Europe. During his period in Paris, with the help of friends like the Duchess of Devonshire, he was presented to Louis XVI and Marie Antoinette. It was then that he established a friendship with Philippe Égalité, the Duke of Orléans, and his family which lasted all his life. The link held firm for more than a hundred years. Among the archives, carefully preserved by Angela Burdett-Coutts, were letters to Thomas from Philippe Égalité. One, dated 6 January 1793, asked him to send from Mr Josiah Wedgwood medallions of Hope and Justice and bears the pen-

Sir Francis Burdett: a portrait by Thomas Lawrence, painted in 1793.

cilled note in Thomas's hand, 'Égalité was guillotined *Nov. 6* of the year this letter was written'.[5] It was a grim commentary on his letter of 1792 asking the banker to send 'two black seals of Wedgewood representing one *hope* and the other *justice*'. Thomas, the optimist, sent the seals in the 'prettier blue'.

Revolutionary France brought Thomas Coutts some rich accounts from exiled aristocrats; it also roused political passion in the disturbing young man who was to become his son-in-law.

The handsome young Francis Burdett might well have been among the English guests at the banquets and balls given, with unaccustomed lavishness, by Thomas Coutts and his wife during their stay in Paris. He was certainly in the French capital at the time, doing the Grand Tour like other wealthy young gentlemen of the period. While Thomas Coutts was quietly watching over the uneasy coroneted heads of Europe, Francis Burdett was observing that 'mixture of pomp and beggary, filth and magnificence, as may be truely [*sic*] said to beggar all description'.[6] It was in these years that he absorbed those ideas of liberty, justice and equality which were to direct his political career.

When the Coutts family returned to London, Francis Burdett and his brothers Sedley and Jones were soon visiting them in their apartments over the bank in the Strand, welcomed with warmth by Mrs Coutts and her daughters but with suspicion by Thomas.

Burdett was immediately drawn to the homely Mrs Coutts. 'I loved your mother,' he later wrote to Sophia, 'and if ever one mortal was attracted warmly to another, I am persuaded she was to me – in spite of many errors and sometimes being dissatisfied with my conduct . . .'[7] His regard for her was genuine and sprang partly from a Radical's respect for her plebeian background. But there was another element. The warm affectionate home was especially attractive since his own mother had died when he was thirteen.

Born in 1770, Francis Burdett spent most of his adolescence either at Ramsbury Manor, his aunt's house in Wiltshire, or at Foremarke, the Derbyshire seat of his fierce and autocratic old grandfather, Sir Robert Burdett. His father Francis, a shadowy figure, had little influence. His boyhood was spent mostly with this grandfather at Foremarke, a Palladian house set among 'long, green meadows', which he remembered all his life with extravagant delight. During his holidays from Westminster School he was coached by the Reverend Bagshaw Stevens, chaplain to his grandfather and Headmaster of Repton School. It is to Stevens's journal that we owe the record of these years. The Burdett boys were wild and unruly.

The three daughters of Thomas and Susannah Coutts, depicted as the
Three Graces by Angelica Kauffmann. Sophia, the mother of
Angela Burdett-Coutts, is the central figure.

'Who hath got Miss Pyott's maid with child?' the Reverend Bagshaw Stevens asks in his journal and discovers with some relief that it was Sedley, not his favourite Francis.

Francis had a keen mind – he was hungry for knowledge but his was an impatient and tempestuous nature. Rebellious, he was expelled from Westminster for his part in a riot; impatient, he left Oxford before taking his degree. And when he travelled abroad he discovered, like Wordsworth, the excitement of French Revolutionary politics; 'bliss was it in that dawn to be alive'.

It was when the Burdett brothers returned from their Continental tour that they renewed their friendship with the Coutts family. Francis, stimulating, gay and intelligent, was specially popular with the three daughters. He was particularly handsome: 'the handsomest man I ever saw', sighed Miss Seward, the poetess.[8] The girls themselves were much sought after; they were known in London as 'the three Graces' and Angelica Kauffmann painted them as such. Susan, the eldest, was in love with Lord Montague of Cowdray. Fanny was the liveliest, and both Sedley and Francis Burdett fell in love with her. Fanny, however, found Francis too disturbing; he was, she later wrote, 'an uncomfortable man'.[9] She settled for Sedley and so Francis turned to the younger and gentler Sophia and Sophia was always to have the uneasy feeling that she was second best.

Sophia and Francis were quietly married on 5 August 1793, at St Martin-in-the-Fields. If wealth could buy happiness, then the Burdett-Coutts alliance should have been idyllic, for Sophia brought a dowry of more than £25,000. Her father now looked for a larger house so that Sophia could continue to live with them. He leased 1 Stratton Street, a mansion on the corner of Stratton Street and Piccadilly, as his new home. Later, he acquired the lease on two adjoining houses in Piccadilly. One of these he gave to Sophia and Francis, breaking through the inter-connecting wall so that the two first floors communicated. For his part, Francis Burdett brought considerable wealth and ancient lineage – the first Burdett, Hugo, had come over with the Conqueror. But from the beginning the marriage was ill-starred. Their honeymoon was marred by news of a family tragedy. Sedley Burdett and Lord Montague were drowned in a foolhardy attempt to shoot the Schaffhausen falls in Switzerland. Francis shut himself up in his room and the Reverend Stevens genuinely thought that he would die of grief. It was an unhappy prelude to the visit of the Coutts family to the head of the family, Sir Robert Burdett. The old man in any case disliked the connection: he considered the family was unsuit-

Ramsbury Manor, Wiltshire, one of the country seats of
Sir Francis Burdett.

able, in spite of their wealth. He had discovered the history of madness in
the line, and, proud of his ancestry, he feared that the Burdett blood
might be contaminated. It needed all Francis's charm to win him over.

The first encounter with the old man at Foremarke was unpropitious.
The Reverend Bagshaw Stevens, gently malicious, recorded the meeting
and the 'Bart's hurt and alarm at the uncourtly figure of his guests.'[10] It is
not surprising that Mrs Coutts was more than usually gauche. She had to
encounter in turn the great gates, the long sweeping drive, the lake and
terraces, the unnerving flight of steps up to the pillars and portico – and
finally Sir Robert, standing looking down on them with undisguised dis-
approval. Feudal memory stirred and Mrs Coutts remembered what she
had almost forgotten. She was a maid from Lancashire and she was arriving in state at the front door of the big house. The visit was uncomfortable
and Sophia never afterwards liked Foremarke; she went there most reluctantly, even when it became her own.

Sedley's death had already brought Francis estates in Leicestershire; he
inherited more wealth and property when his father died in 1794. Three
years later, in February 1797, his grandfather died, leaving him the

29

baronetcy, the estate at Foremarke and yet more wealth. And as though this were not enough, in the spring of 1800 his mother's sister, Lady Jones, died, bequeathing Ramsbury Manor in Wiltshire to the new Sir Francis. So, by the beginning of the nineteenth century, Sir Francis Burdett was a man of considerable property and he was married to the daughter of one of the richest men in the kingdom.

Sophia, gentle, pretty, young and indulged, thus found herself mistress of vast estates and great echoing houses that she could never hope to manage. The birth of her children, Sophia and Robert and later, Susan, Joanna and Clara, sapped what little vitality she had. She soon discovered that she had married a passionate firebrand whose intellectual and political pursuits she could never hope to share and whose driving energy she could never accommodate.

Burdett, ambitious to play a part in the political struggles he saw as inevitable, and conscious of his inadequate education, shut himself away with his tutor M. Chevalier. In an intellectual frenzy he steeped himself in Shakespeare and philosophy, science and political theory. While he was, as Sophia plaintively reported to her father, 'poring over books', she retreated into the lethargy and loneliness that were in time to turn her into a chronic invalid. From the beginning Sophia made no attempt to make a home. She avoided as much as possible the great houses, preferring to rent temporary furnished quarters in Buxton or Bath rather than Foremarke and Ramsbury. She was happiest travelling with her parents or staying with them in the Piccadilly house, even though Sir Francis had taken a pleasant house in Wimbledon.

In Wimbledon, Burdett was quickly absorbed into the remarkable circle that met regularly at the house of the brilliant lawyer, Horne Tooke, a man who is now almost forgotten but who, at that period, had a great influence on the rising young Radicals.

When Sir Francis moved into the dangerous world of Radical politics his marriage was doomed. Sophia might have shared this intellectual life – she was, after all, cultured and exceptionally well educated – but, to her, revolution was real. She had been in Paris in 1789. Her friends and acquaintances had gone to the guillotine. She had no illusions about the dangerous nature of her husband's political activity.

Thomas Coutts too was alarmed at his son-in-law's passion for revolutionary France. There was even some danger, he believed, that Francis would take his beloved daughter and go to live there. It was to prevent this and not because he sympathized with his politics, that he encouraged Burdett to enter Parliament. He was prepared to pay £4,000 to buy him the Boroughbridge seat. It was ironic that Burdett, like Horne Tooke, who was MP for the notorious rotten borough of Old Sarum, found his way into Parliament through the very system to which they were both so opposed. Parliamentary Reform was to be the most important single issue in Burdett's early political career.

In 1802 Francis Burdett became MP for Middlesex but three years later his election was declared void and in 1806 he was excluded from the House. It was as MP for Westminster, the seat he seized for the Radicals in 1807 and held for thirty years, that his name was made. To the people, he was an idol, to his enemies he was the 'frantic disturber' – a play on 'Francis Burdett'. He was 'Westminster's pride' and 'England's glory'. His eloquence was unmatched. At the beginning of his career his oratory mesmerized his friend Byron, as it did Disraeli at the end. His maiden speech in 1796 was on Ireland, it was an attack on 'the oppression of an enslaved and impoverished people by a profligate Government'. In these years Sir Francis conceived a romantic passion for Ireland which coloured his political life and which he was to pass on to his daughter Angela.

While Burdett was plunging into the dangerous sea of Irish politics, Sophia was left with the children, lonely and apprehensive, hearing, in her imagination, the rattle of the tumbrils. Like the Reverend Stevens, she trembled 'at the connexion of a Warm, Enthusiastic Character with Rash, Ruined, Irish Politicians'.[11] His friendship with the turbulent Irish brothers Roger and Arthur O'Connor would lead him, she was convinced, to the gallows.

He was at the height of his political fame in the first decade of the nineteenth century. It was his campaigns in 1798 and 1800 on behalf of mutinous sailors imprisoned in Cold Bath Fields Prison and his fierce attack on the conditions there that won him popular support. During his election campaigns his appearance on the hustings, elegant and long-limbed, brought cheering crowds. 'He was our idol,' the Radical weaver Samuel Bamford wrote in 1818. The cartoonists of the period drew him borne like a hero in triumph, the words Liberty, Justice, 'Burdett and no Bastille', ballooning around him. A passion for freedom, justice and humanity inspired his political career. 'The best part of my character', he wrote to Thomas Coutts, 'is a strong feeling of indignation at injustice and oppression and a lively sympathy with the sufferings of my fellows.'[12] The memory of the wretched poor in Paris, the swollen legs of the chained men in Cold Bath Fields Prison, the cries of flogged soldiers, all the sights and smells of poverty – these were the mainsprings of his politics.

With the French Revolution raging across the Channel, such ideas were explosive and in such a world of intrigue and riotous elections, Sophia was lost. Canvassing and 'kissing the butcher' were not for her. But besides politics there was another cause for the failure of their marriage.

The shadow of Lady Oxford, that generous but scandalous beauty, darkened Sophia's marriage and even in later years disturbed her daughter Angela. If Sophia was not concerned with Sir Francis's career, Lady Oxford was. The cartoonist Gillray portrayed them together. By 1798 all the world knew that Sir Francis was Lady Oxford's lover. From the early days he had found marriage stifling and, as he put in a surprisingly frank letter to Thomas Coutts, the 'grave of love'. Sophia was gentle and virtuous but she was also plaintive, hypochondriac and demanding. Lady Oxford was warm, vital and uninhibited. Burdett was the first of her loves, and his friend Byron was her last. She was ravishing when Burdett first knew her and even in later years her autumnal beauty was, in Byron's description, like a landscape by Claude Lorraine.[13]

From time to time Sir Francis returned to Sophia, penitent and ashamed. In 1803, on the tenth anniversary of their marriage, he wrote to her, lamenting, in extravagant terms, the change he had wrought in her. For by now she had taken shelter in a mysterious illness that crippled her for the rest of her life. She cosseted herself with nurses and a resident doctor at £400 a year. The companionship she had failed to find in marriage, she now sought among gentle invalids in watering places.

The full story of the Lady Oxford affair will perhaps never be known. It was rumoured that Sir Francis was the father of one of her sons. Certainly a young man, reputed to be the son of Lady Oxford, was brought up at Foremarke, bearing Sir Francis's name. He was packed off to Australia. No one could be quite sure of the children's parentage – least of all Lady Oxford, whose family was known as 'the Harleian miscellany'. Lord Oxford seemed happy enough to accept the situation, but Sir Francis's enemies never let the story rest.

Burdett's tempestuous private life was matched by his public life. As the first Radical MP for Westminster, he was a constant thorn in the side of the Government. They were delighted to find an excuse to remove him. In 1810 a Radical, John Gale Jones, was imprisoned by order of the House of Commons for alleged sedition. When Sir Francis challenged the legality of the proceeding, Cobbett published his speech in the *Political Register* and Burdett, accused of breach of privilege, was condemned to the Tower by the Speaker. Maintaining that such action was against the law, Burdett refused to accept the Speaker's order and for four days he held out in his Piccadilly house defying Mr Speaker and the House. This

The arrest of Sir Francis Burdett in May 1810, a cartoon by Cruikshank. Francis Burdett is shown with his brother Jones on the left and Roger O'Connor on the right, listening to the sergeant-at-arms. A weeping Sophia stands with her son Robert, while in the background can be seen Susan, Lady Guilford and Susannah Coutts.

time Sophia was at his side. After her husband's arrest, Mr Coutts was to write that he had not seen Sophia look so well for years!

Throughout that April weekend she watched the tumultuous scene. Piccadilly was a tossing sea of blue – the Burdett electioneering colours. Workmen and gentry alike filled the air with deafening shouts, 'Burdett for Ever!' Panic-stricken, the magistrates called up the troops in a hundred-mile radius. The Life Guards charged through the milling crowds with sabres drawn, 'prancing their horses on the pavement', as *The Times* reported. Burdett's supporters retaliated by seizing workmen's ladders and barricading the street. Burdett himself, with studied nonchalance, continued to take his afternoon ride in Hyde Park. When at last on Monday morning the troops broke in, they found an embarrassingly calm domestic scene. Jones Burdett and Roger O'Connor were there, ready to defend Sir Francis. Sophia and her sister Lady Guilford were sitting quietly at breakfast. Mr Coutts had discreetly withdrawn, but Mrs Coutts, her Lancashire spirit roused, loyally sat through the distressing scene.

Burdett had arranged a telling tableau. When the Sergeant seized his shoulder he was giving his son Robert a lesson on the Magna Carta.

With a forethought born of his experience of prisons, Sir Francis had sent O'Connor to the Tower to make sure that his quarters were well aired. The Constable of the Tower assured him, with deference, that he would be lodged in a comfortable, dry house next to his own. But as Sir Francis set out he was anything but comfortable. There were riots along the route to the Tower. Leaning forward in his coach, pale and strained, he listened as, above the sound of the jingling cavalry escort and the cheers of his supporters, came the screams of the injured.

The story of the Piccadilly siege was to prove the most stirring legend of Angela Burdett-Coutts's childhood. Its effect on her father was no less profound. The man who hated violence now saw where he was leading his followers. It was then, and during the weeks of quiet reflection in the Tower, that he decided to take the road that led away from revolution. When he was released, knowing that a turbulent mob was waiting to lead him back in triumph to Piccadilly, he quietly slipped home across the water to Wimbledon. The chariot which had been prepared for his triumphal march was dragged, empty, through the streets by his deflated and disappointed followers. Some of them would never trust him again. Although for more than twenty-seven years he remained one of the leading Radicals, and in 1820 was once again imprisoned for his scathing attack on the massacre of Peterloo, much of his magic had gone.

He became increasingly irritated during the years when Radical politics degenerated into squabbling factions and by the late 1830s was moving slowly into the arms of the Tory party, whose candidate in 1837 he was to be. He became Tory Member of Parliament, first for Westminster then North Wiltshire, and brought to his conversion the same passionate enthusiasm that had inspired his Radical youth.

With the fading of political fire came some quietening of the turbulent energy that had so disturbed the Burdett marriage. In 1813 the Oxfords left England. In the same year Angela was conceived. Born on 21 April 1814, she was the child of the reconciliation between Sir Francis and Sophia. But Sophia still had to endure the strain of conflict between husband and father. Thomas Coutts's attitude to his son-in-law can be imagined. During the years before and after Angela's birth even his tolerance was strained. But there was no moralizing on the subject of infidelity. For in the years when Sir Francis was finding release in the arms of Lady Oxford, Coutts was himself finding marriage a 'grave of love'.

Harriot Mellon playing the role of Mrs Page in *The Merry Wives of Windsor*: an engraving after Masquerier.

Raymond Mander and Joe Mitchenson
Theatre Collection/Mansell Collection

Mrs Coutts, becoming senile, suffered attacks of the mental illness that finally destroyed her. She had never been her husband's intellectual equal and though he kept a deep affection for her, loyally tending her during the worst of her madness, she was now no companion. He was fond of the theatre and frequently joined his distinguished clients on their visits to the Green Room of Drury Lane Theatre. There he met an enchanting young actress called Harriot Mellon, who captivated him. Through all the pain and horror of nursing his mad wife, Harriot's image was always before his eyes. 'I see you,' he wrote to her, in 1811, 'dashing among the waves, so fresh and so beautiful.'[14]

The truth about Harriot Mellon's childhood will always remain something of a mystery. Her birth-date is uncertain, her parentage obscure. It is probable that she was illegitimate, it is certain that she was brought up among travelling players by a tough, irascible Irish mother, who took as her second husband a Mr Entwhisle, an itinerant musician.

She was an attractive and lively child who served her apprenticeship in a hard and hungry world. In October 1787 she appeared at the Ulverston Theatre as 'Little Pickle' in *The Spoilt Child*. She was a good mimic and early in her career found a great model. At the Harrogate Theatre she watched Mrs Jordan, mistress of the Duke of Clarence, later William IV, take the North by storm. Harriot had a vision of a soft and luxurious

London world of stage and society and she made up her mind to follow Mrs Jordan into it. Her chance came at Stafford, where for four years she worked with Stanton's Theatrical Company. Here Mr Wright, a banker, and his family, took an interest in her and sent her to school. When Sheridan came up for the Stafford Races, Wright persuaded the actor-manager to offer her a chance in his theatre at Drury Lane.

In 1795 Sheridan cast her as Lydia Languish in *The Rivals*. She was not a particular success. She had neither the elegance of Miss Farren, later to be Countess of Derby, nor the personality of Mrs Jordan; but she shared with these ladies an Irish ancestry and a certain toughness tempered in the hurly-burly of the Regency provincial theatre. The actor Macklin remembered her at this time as 'a countrified girl, blooming in complexion, with a very tall, fine figure, raven locks, ivory teeth, a cheek like a peach and coral lips. All she put you in mind of was a country road and a pillion.'[15] It was this country quality that had first drawn Thomas Coutts to the servant girl, Susannah Starkie.

Thomas and Harriot had first met in the Green Room of the Drury Lane Theatre. The next meeting was in Cheltenham where the old man, ill and depressed, had gone for the cure. But it was Harriot, not the waters of Cheltenham, who rejuvenated him. He gave her five golden guineas as a subscription to the benefit performance there, and took her under his protection for the rest of his life. She kept the guineas, as she kept his love, to the end of her life.

There was nothing unusual in such a relationship. His Royal clients had set the example. Thomas and Harriot always insisted on the purity of their pre-marital friendship. It might well have been true. What Thomas Coutts needed at this stage in his life was affection rather than passion. As the relationship developed, Harriot's interest in the stage waned. With her new wealth she became exceedingly plump, and cartoonists maliciously exaggerated her curves and even depicted her with a moustache. It was the beginning of years of slander and vicious lampoons.

In 1808 she bought, or Thomas had bought for her, a villa on the sunny slopes below Highgate. Here at Holly Lodge, she lived in increasing comfort and style, driving down to the theatre in her own carriage to the envy of her friends. No one believed that the villa was bought with her own money, nor that she had, as she claimed, won £5,000 in a lottery. But reliable witnesses of the time always wrote of her unsullied reputation. The painter Haydon, visiting Holly Lodge, described her 'romps in the Fun Room' but insisted that she lived there 'under the protection of Mr Coutts but certainly not in vice'.[16]

In January 1815 Mrs Coutts, left for a moment unattended by her nurses, scalded herself with boiling water from an egg-saucepan on her fire. She died in agony. On 18 January, four days after his wife's funeral, Thomas Coutts removed Harriot from her invidious position. He secretly married her at St Pancras Church.[17] Thomas Coutts never regretted the marriage even though for the next five years it destroyed the close harmony in which he had always lived with his daughters. Their shock and anger at the sudden acquisition of so astonishing a stepmother was the more intense because of the extraordinary secrecy and subterfuge of the ceremony.

The daughters' anger was predictable. Fanny, Lady Bute, was the least disturbed. The most intelligent of the 'three Graces' and Thomas's favourite daughter, she was the one most likely to understand, as her own love-life had been tempestuous but, now settled comfortably as the widow of the Marquess of Bute, she was nursing a conveniently delicate health in Italy. Susan, Lady Guilford, also a widow, had been living at Stratton Street with her father. With a lack of sensitivity not uncommon in otherwise intelligent men, Coutts had imagined that his daughter would be glad to share her family home with his new wife. He soon realized his mistake. There followed months of bitter feuds. Thomas listened in horror as Lady Guilford and Harriot shrieked at each other like fish-wives.

Harriot won. The girl who had coped with a Liverpool gallery on a drunken Saturday night was more than a match for the delicately nurtured Lady Guilford who, in the autumn of 1815, retreated to a house Thomas provided for her in Putney. Harriot was generous, but neither Lady Guilford nor her family were mentioned in her will.[18]

The Burdetts too quitted the Piccadilly house. Sophia, still weak from Angela's birth, was genuinely distressed at the death of her mother, while Sir Francis was furious about the clandestine marriage. He 'owed nothing to Coutts and wanted nothing'. He took a house in St James's Place, where Angela and her sisters were brought up.

The daughters removed, Harriot's life became easier. Though there were still to be stormy passages, by the end of Thomas Coutts's life she had subdued her violent temper and by her warm-hearted affectionate nature, had won some peace in the family.

*   *   *

It was many years before Angela heard the full story of the storms that raged before her birth and during her early years. She was only four when the Burdetts left their Piccadilly house, but the observant and sensitive child remembered something of the thunder in the air, her four older sisters whispering wide-eyed of the monumental rows next door. All her life Angela Burdett was unusually disturbed at what she came to call 'excitement'. In these early years, she lived with her mother and sisters in an almost exclusively feminine world. Lady Burdett was frequently prostrated with grief or illness, lying on her 'soft sopha', murmuring of pains and cures – hay tea for Susan, . . . leeches for a niece's eyes . . . sea-bathing, so good for Angie and Clara. Around her the women fluttered, maids and nurses always in attendance. Except for her resident doctor, little old Sigmund who hardly left her side, the house was always full of women.

From this soft world of self-indulgence Sir Francis was often absent. And the only other male in the family, Angela's brother Robert, who, after the trauma of the Piccadilly siege, had to be taken away from Eton and placed under a tutor, was a shadowy figure. At Oxford he took to heavy drinking and when he joined the army virtually cut himself off from his family. In fact, it took an order from the Duke of Clarence to get him home. When he descended, as Sir Francis wrote, 'like a bolt from the blue', even the languid Lady Burdett, was put 'in a bit of a bustle' and the effect on Angela was profound. She never forgot the sudden and unexpected appearance of the grave young soldier in the splendid uniform – the brother she hardly knew existed. Throughout her life she searched among her friends for the missing men of her childhood – the absent father, the missing brother.

It was a restless and rootless childhood. Lady Burdett's long procession of carriages and baggage wagons was constantly on the move. They rarely stayed long in their London home, but when they were there in the dark old house, shadowed by great trees, their garden was Green Park. Their neighbour in his house of treasures, the banker-poet, Samuel Rogers, remembered how Angela would run in to see him after her morning walk in the Park. Lady Burdett often took the girls across the river to stay with the Guilfords at their house on Putney Hill where the eccentric old painter Fuseli was a frequent visitor.[19]

Sir Francis took a house on the edge of Richmond Park, where the family could enjoy country air and he could ride over with his friends from Parliament. Sometimes the carriages would be loaded up for the long drive to Ramsbury Manor. From 1814 onwards Sir Francis spent some time every year there. Lady Burdett never liked Ramsbury, she

Angela Burdett-
Coutts: a portrait by
Samuel John Stump,
painted in 1828
when Angela was
fourteen.

Unknown source.

found life in the country excessively dull. But the children adored it –
Joanna wandered round the lake collecting butterflies and Angela was led
down the long avenues on her first pony. In the evening, music rose with
the river mist to the nursery – Clara's voice singing Spanish songs, the
rippling sound of the piano as the poet, Tom Moore played his own sad,
sweet Irish airs. Moore never forgot the pretty girls who sang his 'Meeting
of the Waters' so touchingly that he wept as he played and for the rest of
his life had a special place in his heart for Angela.[20]

Sometimes they spent summer months by the sea, Bognor or Brighton,
Ramsgate or Chichester. Sometimes they drifted to spa towns, Clifton,
Cheltenham, Leamington, or Norwood. But Lady Burdett was happiest in
Bath, in the Royal Crescent, where she always took Number 12 if possible.
Here Angela trotted on her pony, guarded by a faithful servant, and
watched their dashing young neighbour, James Brooke, cantering by.
Many years later when this young man was Rajah Brooke of Sarawak she
reminded him that they had been neighbours, but Brooke had no memory
of the quiet little girl on her pony.

But however restless the life or cheerless the grand furnished houses,

Angela was cocooned in her parents' warm affection. Lady Burdett was especially indulgent to this last, late child. Sir Francis wished she was prettier, but she was intelligent and, as he often told his friends, she had an exceptionally sweet disposition. Even as a little girl she was good with the political friends he sometimes brought home. Men like John Cam Hobhouse were attracted to the solemn little girl who seemed to enjoy the company of adults and who listened so intelligently. But she saw too little of her brilliant and stimulating father in these years. Some echoes of his turbulent political life must have penetrated her sheltered world; the Peterloo Massacre, her father's imprisonment,[21] his triumphant election of 1820. But mostly he was a legend absent and longed for. The child waiting in the quiet Bath crescent would never forget the excitement of his homecomings, the clamour of the dogs, the clatter of the horses signalling the arrival of the father who, present or absent, dominated her life. At the London window she watched him brought home in triumph and remembered him forever as heroic and larger than life.

There was always in the background the fairy godmother to spoil her. Harriot enjoyed the rôle. Nothing pleased her more than dressing up the little girls. She sent them pink gowns for the theatre, bonnets decked with primroses for Angela and Clara. A length of lace, peppermint drops, silks, chintzes and ribbons – parcels from Harriot were always arriving at the Burdetts'. Studious little Angela, however, was far more excited by the box of books than by the black and rose pelisse Harriot sent. And her delight was unbounded when the wagon brought to the house in Bath a piano from Harriot. When the Burdetts were in London, Harriot often sent her coach for the two youngest girls and they would jog off to Holly Lodge where she loved romping with them on the lawns or opening up her old theatrical boxes. There were long evenings by the flickering fire when Harriot told them the romantic story of her life. To a child who lived so much in the hushed, antiseptic air of her mother's sickroom, Harriot, in her soft, scented velvet dresses, opened a door on to a different world, full of warmth, gaiety and life.

In 1822 Thomas Coutts died. Angela had seen little of her grandfather in the last years of his life. Sometimes, in the great drawing room at Stratton Street she had been aware of the old man watching her intently with shrewd and kindly eyes, but often, towards the end, the eyes were hooded, the mind withdrawn and she was glad to get away. Lady Burdett sat with Harriot on the Sunday evening after her father's death and heard the contents of the will. Thomas Coutts had left his whole estate to Harriot for 'her sole use and benefit'. No other person was mentioned and no other legacy left. Lady Burdett's chagrin can be imagined. Harriot's legal position was, however, impregnable. The Burdetts soon gave up any idea of opposing the will.

Thomas Coutts had given final proof of his complete trust in Harriot. His will was concerned not merely with a family fortune but with the future of one of the great banks of Europe. Not only did he trust Harriot to be just and generous to his daughters and their children, he trusted her to safeguard the interests of his bank. On his death Harriot became a partner. But perhaps the most extraordinary aspect of this most extraordinary will was that it was left to Harriot's judgement alone to decide who should succeed *her*.

The bank, the family, the succession – these were the three responsibilities Thomas Coutts bequeathed to Harriot. All three she took seriously and in her handling of them fully justified the unprecedented confidence he had placed in her.

As far as the bank was concerned, she wisely left its management in the hands of the other partners and rarely interfered. Only once did she offend their sense of propriety, when she insisted that her 'dear Andrew Dickie', the trusted Chief Clerk, should be made a partner. To the family she was as generous as old Thomas could have wished. They had already received something like £100,000 each in the years before his death and, except when the bank profits were low, she allowed his daughters about £10,000 a year each. In addition to the annual allowance, they frequently received extra sums which Harriot meticulously recorded in a little book she always kept by her. Towards the end of her life, she noted that she had given Lady Burdett exactly £118,602 15s and Lady Guilford £108,500. Lady Bute presumably received similar sums.

As to the succession, Harriot kept her intentions a close secret. For the next fifteen years she observed Thomas Coutts's grandchildren with the shrewd eye of one who had made her own way in the world and had learnt to judge people in a hard school.

Her first choice was Dudley Coutts Stuart, the son of Fanny, Lady Bute and Angela's cousin. Serious, idealistic and hard-working, Dudley seemed the perfect heir to his 'blessed matchless grandfather'. Harriot wrote enthusiastic birthday letters to him in Italy on 4 January 1824 and 1825 urging him to pack up and come home. But instead he dismayed her by marrying Napoleon Bonaparte's niece Christine, the daughter of Lucien Bonaparte. Sir Walter Scott, an old friend and distant relative of Thomas Coutts, dined with her on 19 October 1826, and found her in a state of 'tragi-comic distress on the marriage of her presumptive heir with a daughter of Lucien Bonaparte'.[22] Christine was not only a pathological spendthrift, she was the niece of the dread Corsican Napoleon. No 'foreign adventurer', Harriot determined, should get his hands on Tom's money. When she came to make her will, she included a clause which barred any successor from marrying an alien. Harriot also realized that Dudley was too quixotic to be a banker. In 1831 he began the work for Polish refugees to which he dedicated the rest of his life. His sister Frances was already an heiress, married to Lord Sandon, the future Earl of Harrowby. Neither Dudley nor Frances ever appeared much disappointed that the golden cup had slipped from their lips.

Harriot firmly ruled out the children of the Countess of Guilford, visiting on them the wrath that their mother had incurred. This must have seemed unjust since they had been Tom Coutts's favourites; he had specifically suggested, at one time, that they should inherit, and he had been heartbroken when his grandson, Lord North, had died in infancy.

So it was to Lady Burdett's family that she turned. Sophia, the eldest, had obviously hoped that Harriot who 'seems very warmly interested and disposed to do all she can for me' would leave her at least part of the fortune. But an unhappy love affair made her difficult and for reasons which are not clear Harriot passed her over when she married the Irish MP Otway Cave. At no stage was Robert considered suitable. The other daughters, Susan, Joanna and Clara, were pretty and talented. But Susan had married a Cornish gentleman, Mr Trevanion, who was always in financial difficulties, and the other two were agreeable girls but clearly had not the qualities that Harriot sought.

Angela was only eight when Thomas Coutts died and four years later, in 1826, Lady Burdett decided to take her younger girls on a three-year tour of the Continent. So once again the cavalcade was assembled, carriage, travelling coaches, and baggage wagons, the couriers were sent in advance. Lady Burdett, who normally complained that she was such an invalid, was perfectly happy planning the tour.

Angela, at twelve, was intelligent, equable in temperament but plain and lanky and needed a good governess. Before setting off, the Burdetts had appointed a bright little woman called Hannah Meredith to accompany them. Bubbling, vital, intelligent and shrewd, Hannah was the perfect companion and teacher for the serious girl, bringing much needed zest into the querulous world of spas and watering places. As they drifted through Europe, Lady Burdett brought in other tutors, drawing masters, singing and music teachers and the girls were coached in Italian, French and German. Their movements were unpredictable. 'Lady Burdett', wrote her husband, 'is a summer bird and loves the sun.' Genoa, Nice, Montpelier, Pau, Baden, Spa, the addresses read like a Baedeker's Guide to good health.

In Paris Angela learned her excellent French, and was presented to Lady Burdett's friends at Court. Madame Adelaide, the highly intelligent sister of Louis Philippe, was particularly kind to the quiet girl who shared her dislike of ceremony and the Orléans family, eternally grateful to Thomas Coutts, welcomed warmly his granddaughters. Angela's early love of Paris lasted all her life.

They returned to London in the autumn. Angela had become tall and graceful, but she was still plain, still with an oversensitive skin that broke out in a rash when she was under strain. The tour had sharpened her intelligence, had taught her much. She spoke three languages well and the roads of Europe were now as familiar to her as those of her native land.

The Burdett family returned to England to find Harriot transformed into the Duchess of St Albans. Half her age, something of 'a fool and a booby' the ninth Duke had finally persuaded her to marry him after two years' assiduous wooing. The Duke wanted Harriot's money and Harriot liked the idea of being a Duchess.

The marriage took place on 16 June 1827 quietly in Stratton Street. Harriot had asked the advice of Sir Walter Scott. He wrote in his journal: 'If the Duke marries her, she has the first rank. If he marries a woman older than himself by twenty years, she marries a man younger in wit by twenty degrees. . . . The disparity of ages concerns no-one but themselves so they have my consent to marry if they can get each other's.'[23]

Sir Walter may have approved but the Burdetts did not. Sir Francis sat up all night before the wedding in a vain attempt to persuade her not to go through with it. So for the next ten years Lady Burdett had to watch Harriot playing her last great rôle – the Duchess – and spending her father's wealth in extravagant festivities.

After their return from the Continent Lady Burdett spent more time in London, for the sake of her daughters. For the first time in her life Angela had a comparatively stable home-life. When her eldest sister Sophia married in 1833, Angela began to take over the rôle of companion to her father. She became his 'pen', as he described it, writing his letters for him when his hands were crippled with gout. Even at that stage of her life her handwriting was virtually illegible and Sir Francis might have chosen Joanna or Clara, but by now he was becoming more and more aware of the intellectual quality of his quiet and thoughtful youngest daughter.

So was Harriot, Duchess of St Albans. A letter from the Duchess to

St Albans House and the Steyne at Brighton in 1825, a cartoon by Cruikshank for *The English Spy*. Harriot Coutts, still in her widow's cap, is shown on the left, holding a parasol. According to the accompanying text, behind her stand 'two liveried emblems of her deceased husband's bounty, clad in the sad habiliments of woe and looking as merry as mutes at a rich man's funeral'.

Angela indicates their growing relationship. Harriot very rarely wrote letters to anybody.

My dear Angela,

I knew you would all be famished when I left therefore I have ordered a *Pie* for you which with *Mulligatawny* what a long word and some Grapes . . . all of which I hope will arrive good *Carriage Paid* . . . Mind you all behave properly till I return, Mama and all, she really is too frolicksome. I beg you consider my writing to you as a great favour; what a beautiful day we had yesterday Arrived at half past two [at Holly Lodge] and ah such primroses and daffodils Love to all Your affectionate
Harriot St Albans[24]

It says much for Harriot's infectious gaiety that she could make the languid Lady Burdett 'frolicksome'.

In the years 1833 to 1837, Angela was often with the Duchess. They were strange companions – Harriot in her vast purple velvet cloak, lined with ermine, beaming and nodding her white plumes at the crowds that always thronged outside her door; Angela, slender and serious, shrinking into the elegant silk-lined ducal carriage. Yet it was no more strange a friendship than that which had bound Harriot and Thomas Coutts. Angela was a constant reminder of him – the same quiet composure, the same goodness, the same dry humour. Even Angela's long slim hands were exactly like those of 'dear Tom'. She was a serious, solemn girl and Harriot did her best to cheer her up. She invited her to the balls and dinners at St Albans House in Brighton. There were the hawking parties on the Downs, for the Duke was the Hereditary Grand Falconer – the one rôle he played with style. Every June fêtes were held at Holly Lodge on the anniversary of her marriage to the Duke, with Morris dancers on the lawn and jugglers in the dell. Famous musicians and singers performed in tents lined with mirrors and pink silk. On the crest of the hill, the Duke and his retinue, splendid in green and gold, sent their flights of hawks to the sound of the horn. After dinner, gardeners dressed as Swiss peasants led out a garlanded white cow and Alpine singers yodelled as she was milked. The astonished guests were served freshly made syllabub in splendid crystal glasses.

Angela watched it all, noting the smiles that turned to sneers when the Duchess had passed by, watching the toadies and hangers-on, catching the scandalous gossip. She must have seen the vulgar cartoons – Harriot ridiculous, moustachioed and bulging. She could not have missed the vicious gossip writers who wrote of Harriot as Creevey did in his journal – 'a more disgusting frowsy hairy old B could not have been found in the Seven Dials'.

Angela also observed Harriot's kind of charity. There were gifts to the starving people of Ireland which ended up in the pockets of unscrupulous agents. Harriot's philanthropy was too often attended by publicity and it was usually undiscriminating. If Angela was later excessively anxious to be the 'lady unknown' in the charity lists it was because she never forgot the dangers of Harriot's kind of giving.

There were months when she travelled with the Duchess in the great cavalcade of coaches, wagons, couriers, liveried servants and armed out-riders. Harriot always travelled like a princess. There was a long tour of the north in 1835 – with a pilgrimage to Thomas Coutts's birthplace in Edinburgh. Harriot was presenting her successor at Tom's shrine – though of this the heiress-to-be was oblivious.

Wherever the Duchess went, the casket of Tom's love-letters accom-panied her and she showed them to Angela. They were proof of the per-

46

Coutts & Co

Harriot Mellon, Duchess of St Albans: a portrait by
George Clint.

fect purity of Tom's love. The story of her grandfather's passion in old
age for a beautiful young woman left an indelible impression on the girl
in whose life strange alliances were a recurring theme.

In 1836 Angela went with the Duchess to Southampton for the summer.
In the following spring Harriot's health began to break down. She
ordered a careful inventory to be made of the contents of Stratton Street

47

and Holly Lodge, and she made her will. In June, the annual fête at Holly Lodge was cancelled. Now, near to death, she was taken for a final tour of the grounds – up the sweeping drive to the house for a last look down the sloping lawns to the fountains and the cedars, to the crest of the hill and the spectacular view of the city. Much as she loved Holly Lodge she wanted to be in the room in Stratton Street where 'her dear Tom' had breathed his last. On Sunday, 6 August 1837 the player-girl Sir Walter Scott had called his 'Dame of Diamonds' died.

$$*\qquad*\qquad*$$

Neither Angela nor her parents knew in advance of the contents of Harriot's will. 'Heaven knows what she has done,' Sir Francis wrote when he heard of her last illness.

The will was read on the morning of Wednesday, 9 August in the presence of the Bute, Guilford and Burdett families. Lady Bute was now dead, Lady Guilford was dying, but Sir Francis was present with his wife and daughters to hear the lawyer's astonishing words. There was a bequest of £20,000 to Lady Burdett. Then came the thunderbolt. To Angela Georgina Burdett were left the profits from half the shares of the banking house in the Strand, the house in Stratton Street and all its movables. All Harriot's 'watches, jewels, trinkets and ornaments of the person' went to Angela and although Holly Lodge and the Piccadilly House were left to the Duke of St Albans for his lifetime, on his death they too were to revert to Angela Burdett. In a codicil to her will the Duchess allowed the Duke to choose silver plate to the value of £2,000 for his use during his lifetime. In addition he had an annuity of £10,000.

The succession was clearly marked. After Angela, 'Joanna Burdett and her son, then Clara Burdett and her son, failing these upon like trusts in favour of Dudley Coutts Marjoribanks and son, then Coutts Lindsay and son, failing these to the partners in the banking house'. But the heirs were not allowed a free hand. They were not to be allowed to interfere in the management of the bank; they were not automatically to become partners as she had been. Neither were they to marry foreigners. They were not to be allowed to forget the name of their benefactor and must take the surname Coutts and Harriot hoped that if they were male, they would be 'brought up with habits of business and industry which were the foundation of the prospects that I am able to hold out to them'.

48

CHAPTER TWO

The Learning Years

1837–46

WHEN ANGELA inherited, the balance in her bank account stood at £948 16s o1d. When the will had been proved, duties and legacies paid, that balance was multiplied sixty times. She was now one of the richest women in Europe, with a fortune which, in modern terms, was roughly equivalent to between thirty and forty million pounds.[1]

The provisions of the will placed certain restrictions. The half-share in the bank stood at £100,000. She could not touch this capital, nor could she anticipate the income from it which she received annually. But that annual income was in itself enormous. This was by no means all. Most of Harriot's possessions came to her; the silver plate and jewellery were valued at £37,277, the jewellery alone being worth £10,905.

The girl who had been noted for her shyness now showed an unexpected firmness and competence. The Duke of St Albans had to prove his right to his family jewels before they were released to him. With Miss Meredith at her side, she carefully checked her possessions against the detailed inventory. They drove up to Holly Lodge. The house still seemed to echo with Harriot's laugh, her lucky horseshoe was still in front of the porch. Thomas Coutts's maps of the world, of South America, Africa, Asia, Europe, hung in the hall – a reminder of the far-flung connections of the empire Angela had inherited. In the dining room the looking-glass with its carved eagle reflected the crystal chandeliers, its convex glass diminishing the long mahogany table where she had so often sat with Harriot's brilliant friends. The grand piano in the drawing-room next door was covered and silent. Harriot would never again encourage her to sing in her soft sweet voice, or persuade her to follow her talented older sisters as they played and sang their Italian songs with enviable ease. Through the glass doors Harriot's exotic flowers still bloomed in the conservatory. And upstairs, her bedroom was still heavy with scent. Angela took away with her the huge cut-glass scent bottles, the trinket boxes with watches and thirty mourning rings. But she left, in the exotic bathroom, the seven cases of stuffed birds, the collection of sea shells. Red velvet curtains, bath and shower, all would remain unchanged until after the Duke's death in 1849 when she came back again.

She was glad to let the Duke keep the vast collection in the wine-cellar. There were over a thousand bottles of madeira and the same number of port; and forty-seven bottles of champagne marked 'very bad'. And she was happy to leave Harriot's old horses to end their days on the farm.

1 Stratton Street was a treasure house, magnificently furnished in Harriot's dramatic style. The bow windows of the downstairs drawing-room were curtained with gold damask, the walls lined with blue, fluted silk. There was a superb India-Japanned screen, display tables with yet more scent bottles; up the scarlet carpeted stairs, the great drawing-room was even more splendid. The chairs were black and gold, there were swagged golden curtains, rich cut-glass chandeliers and, reflected in the mirrors, and dominating the room, Chantrey's huge marble statue of Thomas Coutts. In the library on the second floor, was an astonishing range of books, reflecting Thomas Coutts's wide-ranging taste. There were sermons, Oliver Goldsmith, Gibbon, chemistry, theatre history, travel – and Malthus on Population next to *The Magic of Wealth*.

But for the young heiress, wandering with Miss Meredith through corridors lined with books, rooms hung with famous paintings and filled with display cases of priceless china, with marble busts and gilded mirrors, the magic of wealth was overwhelming. It was a relief to turn from the magnificence to the trifles – the spinning wheels in the attic, the grey parrot in the hall. And there were the great wardrobes in the bedroom, filled with Harriot's clothes – shoes and muffs and bonnets and gloves; yards of fine Brussels lace; and twenty 'flannel drawers'. There were seventeen Indian shawls, dresses in black velvet and white satin and the white feathered headdress in which Harriot had been so cruelly cari-catured.[2] In the darkened bedroom the huge glasses reflected the two figures of Angela and Hannah among the finery. On the shoulders of the tall slim girl, the vast purple, ermine-lined cloak sat heavy and incon-gruous.

In accordance with the terms of the Duchess's will, the heiress added the name of Coutts to that of Burdett. Gradually dropping the 'Burdett',

Angela Burdett-Coutts: a portrait by Masquerier painted in the mid-1840s.

Harrowby Mss Trust, Sandon Hall

Half-length portrait of Queen Victoria, painted in 1843 by Winterhalter. This became Prince Albert's favourite portrait of her.

By gracious permission of H.M. the Queen

she became simply Miss Coutts. In all her long life few people outside her closest family ever called her by her Christian name. Only to her parents was she 'dearest Angie' and to their friends 'Miss Angela'. This was partly Victorian formality, but even more it was the outward mark of the isolation that was the heavier part of her inheritance.

Miss Coutts once wrote that her wealth had brought her little real happiness. Certainly in the first years after Harriot's death her inheritance bred discord. There was trouble in the family. Miss Coutts and Miss Meredith set up their own establishment in Stratton Street. It is unlikely that Sir Francis 'turned her out of doors' as was sometimes said, but he was certainly reluctant to allow his twenty-three-year-old daughter an independent life. Racked with gout, worn out with political work, he may well have shown his famous hot temper. But if there was an estrangement, it was short-lived. Certainly, by the spring of 1838 they were writing to each other with the old affection.

Her sisters, however, were not so easily appeased. Sophia might with justice have been jealous. She might have expected a larger inheritance, since she had been particularly close to the Duchess. But it was Susan, now Mrs Trevanion, who was most difficult. She was, as Sir Francis said, in 'a peck of trouble'; her husband was a 'sad man, reckless and un-principled . . . twice before he had ruined himself'. For a whole year Angela was subjected to Trevanion's 'unfair and improper applications', she had given her sister Susan large sums but refused to bail out her hopeless husband.[3] In the autumn of 1838 Angela settled a handsome allowance of £2,000 a year on each of the other sisters and peace was restored for a while. Robert, as his father's heir, received his allowance from Sir Francis. To Lady Burdett, she gave £8,000 a year.

It had taken some courage to establish her independence so firmly. But she had the constant support of the shrewd little Miss Meredith, an in-creasingly important influence in her life. This relationship was so vital that although Hannah was unofficially engaged to Dr William Brown, she was prepared to postpone her marriage in order to support Miss Coutts during this difficult period. Happily, Dr Brown was a patient, kindly man who was prepared to wait.

Begging letters poured in, many distressingly genuine, others trans-parently false. She could never forget Harriot's hordes of besieging beg-gars or the perils of undiscriminating charity. The memory of the un-pleasant publicity that had always accompanied Harriot's bounty made her excessively sensitive. But to investigate each claim properly would have needed a secretariat and in those early days there was only Hannah.

Nor was she much protected from the swarms of suitors who suddenly surrounded her. In an age of bankruptcy when many a young man gambled away a family fortune in a night, an heiress of twenty-three was the answer to a prayer. Lord Houghton told the writer, Augustus Hare:

> . . . Miss Coutts likes me because I never proposed to her. Almost all the young men of good family did: those who did their duty by their family *always* did. Mrs Browne (Miss Coutts' companion) used to see it coming, and took herself out of the way for ten minutes, but she only went into the next room and left the door open, and then the proposal took place, and immediately it was done Miss Coutts coughed, and Mrs Browne came in again.[4]

She learned to dread the long envelopes with unfamiliar writing, bulging with the prolix life-stories of hopeful young bloods. 'This is not a proposal', her father's old friend Sir George Sinclair wrote. Gossip flourished, as *Punch* reported:

> . . . the world set to work, match-making, determined to unite the splendid heiress to somebody. Now, she was to marry her physician; and now, she was to become a Scotch countess. The last husband up in the papers is Louis-Napoleon. How Miss Coutts escaped Ibrahim Pacha when he was here, is somewhat extraordinary. For if the Emperor of China were to vouchsafe to let fall his shadow upon the British Court, in the shape of an Ambassador, it would very soon appear in the papers that 'His Excellency Ching-Chow-Cherry-Chow – having cut his pigtail and conformed to the Christian religion – was about to lead Miss Burdett Coutts to the Hymeneal altar'.[5]

To a shy and sensitive girl this sudden popularity was deeply distasteful, even more so when the suitors were obviously acting under instructions, like the young Lord Fitzalan whose ambitious mother pushed him into proposing. Queen Victoria observed with amused interest the failure of his suit. She recorded in her journal: 'Spoke to Lord Melbourne, Lord F's marriage to Miss Coutts being off.'[6]

Lord Melbourne said she was clever, for that she had behaved very well about the money for Ma's debts; when they came to her (as she is the principal person in the House) she made no difficulty about it; they told her she must not speak of it; she said she never told her father these things as he was engaged in politics, but that she would not mention this even to her mother.[7]

One suitor was to cause her real distress for many years. Richard Dunn, the wild-eyed and bankrupt Irish barrister, pursued her with insane persistence for eighteen years.

In the summer of 1838, hounded by beggars and suitors, she fled to the fashionable spa, Harrogate. It was an ideal retreat for the over-strained young heiress. With Hannah she drove over the moors to Bolton Abbey. They jumped the stepping-stones in the clear Wharfe and took long walks in the Dales; the brisk northern air restored her. She drank Harrogate's sulphurous springs and declared that they cured the 'irruption' on her face. But Dunn followed her north, even breaking into the house she had rented. Though he was arrested, the magistrate let him off lightly and he was free to continue his persecution. Two years later the *Spectator* described her 'martyrdom' at the hands of this terrible Irishman:

> Dunn had blockaded Miss Coutts for two mortal years. If she went to Harrogate he followed her; if she returned to Stratton Street he entrenched himself in the Gloucester Hotel; if she walked in the Parks, he was at her heels; if she took a walk in a private garden, he was waving handkerchiefs over the wall, or creeping through below the hedge. With his own hands he deposited his card in her sitting-room; he drove her from church, and intruded himself into the private chapel in which she took refuge. In vain her precaution to have policemen constantly in her hall, and a bodyguard of servants when she moved abroad. Denied the use of his tongue, he *bombarded* her with letters, smuggling them into her hands under all sorts of disguises. He is unparalleled in history.

To Lady Burdett's relief, Angela sent for Mr Marjoribanks, her grandfather's wise old partner at the Bank and he came with his daughter to join her in Harrogate. 'To be without a protector I see cannot be, nor did I *ever* think it right.'[8] Sir Francis was appalled: a dastardly assailant, his daughter the damsel in distress, a fight for justice and he not called to battle!

> Why did you not send for me? [he wrote from Foremarke]. I could have put an end to your annoyance better than anybody but you mentioned it so slightly I had no idea of its having been so tormenting and distressing. I should like to know the names of the magistrates you say behaved so odd and how. I am really mortified at not having been sent for and think moreover it must wear a strange and unaccountable appearance and cause unpleasant and unfavourable animadversions in the not-over good natured.[9]

Dunn's persecution haunted her for years. All her life she was afraid to be alone.

It is not surprising that in the years following her 'accession' she was often ill. Masquerier's portrait of her shows a drawn and tense young face. Her parents were concerned – she was so excessively thin. Sir Francis sent half a dozen bottles of port and a pound of Epping butter, and some tactless fatherly advice: 'Pray do not let your hair be plaited to look like Miss Alway – so hard and unnatural.' But Angela kept that sleek, tight hair all her life. It was perhaps a rejection of femininity, a protection against unwanted suitors.

Although she was not at her best in these years and although she was no beauty, she had at this time a quiet charm. As Lord Broughton later noted, her complexion was not good. She suffered from a recurrent rash. But Broughton admitted she had, nevertheless, a pleasing face. 'Her figure, though not full, is good. Her voice is melodious, her expression sweet and engaging.'[10] Disraeli, meeting her in 1838 at a brilliant assembly at Lord Salisbury's found her 'a quiet, unpretending person'.

In the autumn of 1838 she returned from Harrogate to London, too ill to join her parents at Foremarke. They rushed to London to take care of her and slowly through the winter of 1838 and spring of 1839 she adjusted herself physically and mentally to the burden of her inheritance.

What was she to do with what Sir Francis called 'her great means'? What alternatives were open to her? The most obvious was, of course, marriage; but the idea of 'buying' a husband repelled her. She might have bought a great estate, but, like her mother, she had no interest in setting up a home. Or she could spend in the way that Harriot had spent, on extravagant entertainments. She might have bought jewels but she preferred to wear simple flowers rather than the precious stones she owned. She could emulate her grandfather and patronize artists – Thomas Coutts had supported men like Fuseli, Nollekens, Lawrence, Haydon and Chantrey – and this she later did. But her great means, her father told her, demanded a great cause.

Miss Coutts was, at this period, deeply religious, partly as a result of Hannah Meredith's influence, partly because the prevailing mood of the time was one of intense theological interest. She believed that her fortune was divinely bestowed and she set about training herself to administer it. By far the greatest influence in this learning process was her father. It was through his unobtrusive guidance and through the talented and stimulating circle of friends she met in his house that she found her cause – the relief of poverty.

William Ross' watercolour portrait of Sir Francis Burdett. In the background stands the bust of the Radical politician, John Horne Tooke.

National Portrait Gallery, London

She was only a few minutes walk across St James's Park from her father's house and she was often there. At last she learned to understand, admire, even worship the father she had so seldom seen in her childhood. Among his friends she found both intellectual stimulus and relief from the acute unease that overcame her in the presence of younger men. At St James's Place or at Brighton where the Burdetts spent much of their last years, she met politicians of the old school like Brougham and John Cam Hobhouse, the Radical MP for Westminster. Her father introduced her to judges like Lyndhurst, Abinger and Denman, men of letters like Crabb Robinson and Samuel Rogers. Little Tom Moore came to sing his Irish songs in the Burdetts' drawing-room, reducing himself and his audience to tears. These were men who had lived through stirring times, the French Revolution, the war in Ireland, the years of struggle for Parliamentary Reform. No university could have better taught Miss Coutts the history of the last fifty years.

An interest in public affairs, she wrote to a friend after her father's

Prince Louis Napoleon: an engraving with allusions to his disastrous
invasion attempt of 1840.

death, had been one of his most valued legacies to her. She learned to share the distaste he felt, in his last years, for party politics, and she watched with mistrust the alternate excitement and exhaustion that accompanied election fever. But she absorbed his values, which, in spite of his change of party (he was now a Tory MP) remained humanitarian and progressive. His roots were in the eighteenth century, in the world of Charles James Fox, but he also had an eye for the men of the future. He was particularly attracted by three young men, whose stars were as yet low on the horizon; Louis Napoleon, William Gladstone and Benjamin Disraeli. All three became his daughter's friends for life.

The Burdetts took more than a neighbourly interest in the grave young Prince Louis Napoleon, when he was living with his mother in a hotel in St James's Street, since he was related to them through Dudley Coutts Stuart's marriage to Christine Bonaparte. In 1838 when Louis Napoleon returned to London, he found the quiet Miss Burdett transformed into an heiress. Their friendship was renewed. Angela appealed to the serious side of his nature but, although there was some gossip later, their relationship was always friendly but platonic. The rumour that they were to be married, one of many such, was quickly scotched by a denial in *The Sunday Times*.

William Ewart Gladstone, handsome, serious and brilliantly clever, was already a rising star in the Tory Party. He was attracted to the earnest girl who genuinely shared his interests in theology and anxiously asked his advice about reading. And she was such a good listener.

But of all the younger men in her father's circle, none was more dazzling than Benjamin Disraeli. She had known him for some years. Harriot had been much taken by the exotic young man. She invited him to her fêtes and routs and Disraeli practised on her that potent art of flattery that he was to exercise with such effect on Queen Victoria. In his novel *Vivian Grey* he transformed Harriot into Mrs Millions. Angela could hardly have failed to notice the outrageously dressed young man that Henry Layard describes so vividly. 'He wore waistcoats of the most gorgeous colours and the most fantastic patterns with much gold embroidery, velvet pantaloons and shoes adorned with red rosettes . . . his black hair pomatumed and elaborately curled and his person redolent with perfume.'[11] She must have often seen him shaking those curls under the chandeliers in Stratton Street or settling on the green lawns of Holly Lodge like some strange bird of paradise.

In June 1832 Sir Francis supported Disraeli as the Radical candidate for High Wycombe. Disraeli wrote to his sister in January 1836, 'at Lady

Benjamin Disraeli:
a portrait by
A. E. Chalon, 1840.
The National Trust, Hughenden

Blessington's last night I passed two or three hours with Burdett who was very engaging'. In May 1837 he was on Burdett's committee during the Westminster election and canvassed on his behalf. Night after night he joined the excited throng in Sir Francis's dining-room where the old Baronet, gout and age forgotten, shone again. Disraeli portrayed him in *Endymion* as Sir Fraunceys Scrope:

> . . . He was the father of the House, though it was difficult to believe that from his appearance. He was tall, and had kept his distinguished figure; a handsome man, with a musical voice, and a countenance now benignant, though very bright, and once haughty. He still retained the same fashion of costume in which he had ridden up to Westminster more than half a century ago, from his seat in Derbyshire, to support his dear friend Charles Fox; real top-boots, and a blue coat and buff waistcoat. (*Endymion*, p. 79)

In September 1837 Disraeli turned a lustrous and speculative eye on the youngest Burdett daughter. A young lady of such means would have been very convenient to one who was at this moment both bankrupt and ambitious. To be son-in-law to Sir Francis, to graft his exotic bloom on that ancient stock, was a doubly attractive idea. Certainly he made his hero in *Endymion* seriously consider marrying Adriana 'the greatest heiress in England' the 'angelic being' who was so closely modelled on Angela. He was often at her father's house in 1838; Sir Francis with his easy hospitality would invite him to 'take his mutton'; and they would slip away together from the House of Commons for a relaxed meal 'in boots'.

Disraeli's Adriana was a perfect portrait of Angela at this time. Like Adriana, she had 'an interesting appearance' a 'melodious voice' 'choice accomplishments and agreeable conversation and the sweetest temper in the world'. Unfortunately she 'wanted a little self-conceit' and was too often remarkable in the London salons for a 'doleful look' and 'air of pensive resignation'. And if Disraeli had approached Angela with matrimonial intent as Endymion did Adriana he soon realized that 'alas! this favoured maiden wished for nothing. Her books interested her, and a beautiful nature; but she liked to be alone, or with her mother'.

So Disraeli, who had a liking for older women, found another heiress and not until many years later was their friendship renewed.

*   *   *

It was in her father's house too that Angela met some of the greatest English scientists of her day – men like Faraday, Babbage and Wheatstone. Quietly, she began to provide funds for research in physics, geology, archaeology and the natural sciences, and to follow, with an informed mind, the new discoveries in these fields. In those days, science was still an uncertain study, part magic, part philosophy and, as some thought, part dangerous heresy. Faraday and his friends always called themselves 'natural philosophers'. Child of her age, Miss Coutts was there, on the frontiers of knowledge, probing into the unknown with that particular Victorian mixture of courage and curiosity.

In Michael Faraday she found a brilliant, searching mind combined with a simple child-like faith that matched her own. The greatest experimental genius of his time, the man who discovered the laws of electrolysis, of light and magnetism, he was at ease in her company. The blacksmith's son who hated the social scene, made exceptions for her. Faraday's earliest letters to her, from 1839 to 1845, were formal and mostly requests for her proxy votes for his protégés at the Orphan Asylum of which they were

Michael Faraday, the scientist: a portrait by Phillips, 1841–2.
National Portrait Gallery, London

both patrons. As their friendship grew, he would call on her after the Friday lectures at the Royal Institution, eventually persuading her to apply for membership of the Royal Society. He could offer no greater proof of his confidence in her as a serious student of science.

> For twenty years [he wrote to her] I have devoted all my exertions and powers to the advancement of science in this Institution; and for the last ten years or more I have given up all professional business and a large income with it for the same purpose . . . you will not wonder therefore, that I am earnest, enthusiastic and perhaps too forward in such a concern. . . . Although I earnestly desire to see lady members received amongst us, as in former times, do not let anything I have said induce you to do what may be not quite agreeable to your own inclinations.[12]

A few other ladies were persuaded to apply for admission to keep her company and in February 1847 she became a full member. On 29 May 1856

Faraday was even induced to join her other guests in celebrating the end of the Crimean War. The Rev. Young remembered him climbing to the roof of the house, watching the fireworks, when he 'halloaed out with wonderful vivacity, "there goes magnesium, There's potassium" '.[13] No one but Miss Coutts could have so brought out the child in Faraday. In 1859 he wrote to her at Torquay to help her with an experiment with an ozonometer – an instrument to measure the ozone content of the air there. He had great respect and affection for Miss Coutts. Neither her fame nor her fortune impressed him and his friendship was certainly disinterested.

Whether that of his friend Charles Babbage was equally so is perhaps open to question. The brilliant mathematician could not have been more different. Gregarious and out-going, he brought a brilliance and radiance to every gathering. Even his writing-paper was cheering – illuminated like medieval manuscripts or bordered with pink and yellow and blue. When he first met Miss Coutts he was desperately anxious to get financial backing for his 'calculating engine', the forerunner of the modern computer. In July 1839 he invited her to see it though he feared 'he had intruded upon her an uninteresting subject'. But he wanted the engine to be seen by 'sympathetic English eyes'.[14]

In August Miss Coutts, after seeing the famous calculator, was obviously impressed and judging by Babbage's grateful letter she must have given him more than verbal support.[15]

In 1851, he had considered dedicating to her his book on 'the views of the industry, the science and the Government of England. The diatribe of a disappointed man,' but decided against it; so disgruntled a book was not worthy of her. But he never forgot her kindness in considering it. Miss Coutts was dazzled by him from the time he invited her to take tea with his own 'silver lady'. This little mechanical toy had the place of honour in his drawing-room; a tiny silver lady revolving on a silver base while on its slender arm a bird soundlessly opened and shut its beak. Miss Coutts sitting beside the silver lady quietly listened as around her the talk of the 'philosophers' spun off into new worlds of electricity, magnetism, light and sound. Silent she may have been; but she absorbed it all and from it sprang a lifelong interest in and patronage of science. She was, for instance, one of the first to encourage the development of photography.[16]

Her Friday soirées, after the lectures at the Royal Institution, attracted famous men of science, among them Charles Wheatstone, who remained a friend until his death in 1873. The son of a Gloucester music-seller, Wheatstone had first been interested in sound. He had invented a kaleido-

Charles Babbage, the father of the computer: a portrait by Laurence, 1845.
National Portrait Gallery, London

phone – and the concertina! Later he invented the stereoscope and made an important contribution to the development of the electric telegraph.

At this period Miss Coutts was also absorbed in the study of astronomy and Sir James South was delighted to be her tutor. From his observatory at Campden Hill, Kensington, came florid, courtly letters inviting her to see the 'occultation of stars and planets' and even, in 1845, the passage of a comet. Sir James was one of the founding members of the Astronomical Society and for many years its President. Miss Coutts could not have had a better guide to the heavens. With Babbage as escort she spent many an evening at Campden Hill. Here she sometimes met another young woman who became her friend, and whose career paralleled her own throughout the century – Florence Nightingale also had an interest in the stars.

She may have owed her introduction to the men of science originally to her father, but it was her own intelligence and genuine interest that won their respect. Science, particularly in its practical application, was certainly her subject. But it was also the magic of science that enthralled and disturbed her. Like many intelligent Victorians she saw science almost as a 'black art', a challenge to religious faith.

*   *   *

It is not known at what date Miss Coutts first met Charles Dickens. Probably it was in 1839 that her grandfather's partner, old Marjoribanks, asked her to dinner to meet the brilliant young writer. Dickens remem-bered it as being on a Friday. Much later he wrote to her, 'I have never begun a book or begun anything of interest to me or done anything of importance to me, but it was a Friday . . . it must have been on a Friday that I first dined with you at Mr Marjoribanks's'.[17] But by 1839 Dickens knew her well enough to refer to their 'intimate' friendship.

Certainly his biographer Forster remembered that, although Dickens was disinclined 'to the dinner invitations that reached him from every quarter . . . the marked attentions shown him by Miss Coutts which began with the very beginning of his career were invariably welcome'. In fact, Forster exaggerated. There were more rejections than acceptances among the early formal letters of 1839 and 1840.

The Burdetts had been among Dickens's earliest admirers. Miss Mere-dith had read *Pickwick Papers* aloud in her careful governess voice, always, as she was later to urge the author himself, with 'the proper emphasis'. Lady Burdett invited him to dine and preserved his letter of refusal among her papers. (The envelope bears her pencilled 'from the author of Pick-wick'.) But it was *Oliver Twist* that most impressed and disturbed Sir Francis.

On 27 November 1838 he wrote to Angela, 'I have finished the first volume of *Oliver Twist*, it is very interesting, very painful, very disgusting, and as the old woman at Edinburgh, on hearing a preacher on the suffer-ings of Jesus Christ, said, "Oh dear! I hope it isn't true . . .". Whether anything like it exists or not, I mean to make enquiries for it is quite dreadful and, to society in this county most disgraceful. I will however go through it now though it is anything but entertaining.'[18]

In December, speaking at a Conservative dinner in Birmingham, Sir Francis referred to *Oliver Twist*. Dickens was flattered. Like other pro-gressive young men of his time, he had little sympathy with Sir Francis in his reactionary old age. Like *Punch*, he saw Sir Francis as a sad renegade. But he was sufficiently impressed to ask Forster to send the newspaper report. The editor thought that Sir Francis, like Oliver, was 'so jolly green' and Dickens thought the comment 'exceedingly happy'.[19]

Charles Dickens: a photograph taken by Claudet in 1852. This is probably the photograph referred to in a letter from Dickens to Angela Burdett-Coutts of 23 December 1852, when he describes his visit to the studio as 'the little piece of business between the sun and myself'.

From the first Angela was enchanted by Dickens. In the first glow of his sudden fame he was remarkably attractive. From his luxuriant hair, lustrous eyes and fresh glowing complexion to the brilliant buckles of his shoes there was such a shine about him. There was also a frankness of expression, a look of goodness that Miss Coutts, like other ladies of the day, found irresistible. If there was a little too much of the dandy in his dress she could forgive him. She had, after all seen Disraeli in full bloom.

In 1839 Miss Coutts sent repeated invitations, but Mr Charles Dickens 'regretted' more often than he 'had pleasure in accepting', though he did dine with her on 25 July 1839. But an evening on the 15 August 1840 in the great drawing-room with the bay windows overlooking Green Park was not a success. From the start he had been 'filled with a shadowy dread'. He wrote to Marjoribanks 'Miss Coutts's card for the fifteenth has solemn mention of a Royal Duke and Duchess – *are* gentlemen expected to wear Court dresses in consequence? . . . I have already appeared in that very extraordinary costume and am prepared for the worst; but I have no confidence in my legs, and should be glad to hear that the etiquette went in favor of Trowsers.'[20] He sat all evening in a draught between a door and open window and the next day raged with toothache.

At the turn of the year he accepted an invitation but cried off at the last moment; perhaps his courage failed at the prospect of more dukes and draughts. It was not until January 1841 that he began to get the measure of the shy heiress with the diffident manner. By the end of the month, he was sufficiently impressed to include her among the six special friends to whom he sent advanced news of the death of little Nell, the tragedy that was to set the nation weeping. He sent her two numbers of *Master Humphrey's Clock* in which the Old Curiosity Shop made its first appearance, thinking that 'you might possibly desire to know what the next [number] contained, without waiting seven days . . . Beseeching you to withhold this might revelation from all the world – except Miss Meredith who is free to share it to the utmost'.[21] In April Dickens dined with Sir Francis at the house in St James's Place. Given in honour of Thomas Moore, the dinner-party was enlivened by political argument. Dickens 'greatly enjoyed a quiet setting down of Moore by [Samuel] Rogers at Sir Francis Burdett's table, for talking exaggerated Toryism'.[22] In May Dickens sent her a presentation copy of *The Old Curiosity Shop*, as a 'slight but very sincere tribute of my respect and esteem', which she returned so that he might add an inscription. Now he knew her well enough to write amusingly of his dead raven whose 'body was removed with every regard for my feelings in a covered basket'.[23] It was the first of many such letters. They shared a love of animals and a delight in those individual quirks which distinguish one creature from another.

During the summer Dickens was away in Scotland, and in August and September he retreated to his favourite Broadstairs. Miss Coutts's invitations pursued him. Dickens was particularly anxious that she should not suppose him

'careless of your kind Invitations – regardless of your notes – insensible to your friendship – and a species of moral monster . . .' He was driven to tell 'you how notes and cards of Invitation from you have reached me in Scotland, in Yorkshire, in Kent – in every place but London, and how I have reason to suppose that some others are still taking sportive flights among the Post Offices, and getting very brown from change of air, in various parts of the United Kingdom.'[24]

'Notes and cards', replied Miss Coutts, 'were not the only means employed to find you. These failing, a body of cavalry, headed by Mr Marjoribanks and myself last Thursday week, made an attempt on your house but with no other result than the ascertaining that the house belonged to an individual of your name who was just gone out of town.'[25]

Dickens had hoped to call on her on his return to London in October, but in that month a painful operation for fistula laid him low and though he was grateful for the present of game she sent, he refused her invitation to stay a few days at a house she had taken in Roehampton. But he did visit her briefly in Stratton Street on 26 December in the rushed days before he set off for his tour of America.

Dickens was away for four and a half months, and wrote almost at once on his return on 2 July 1842, reporting his safe arrival, and sending her his present of a rocking chair. For Miss Meredith there was an eagle's feather, 'whose owner fell over the great fall at Niagara', for Lady Burdett a piece of Virginia marble for her geological collection.[26] It was not until the spring of 1843 that the friendship deepened into that mutual understanding which Dickens later writing to Hannah called 'the freemasonry that is between us'. In April he knew her well enough to ask her help for his brother Alfred. (While he was in America his father, John Dickens, had caused him acute embarrassment. The original of Mr Micawber had sent a letter to 'Miss Coutts & Co' asking for a loan of £25 since 'contemporaneous events . . place me in a difficulty from which without some anticipatory pecuniary effort I cannot extricate myself'.[27] Coutts & Co. firmly refused.) She was established as a family friend, enchanted by his children – especially the eldest, Charley, the bright six-year-old whose face 'shone like burnished copper' at the sound of her name.

By the summer of 1843 Dickens was confident enough of his in-fluence with her to write to Forster that Miss Coutts would 'do whatever he asked' in the matter of the Ragged Schools.[28] He had seen her name down for £200 in the Clergy Education Subscription List and had decided to re-direct her charitable hand towards the Ragged Schools. Started, as Forster said, 'by a shoemaker of Southampton and a chimney sweep of Windsor' these early Ragged Schools provided almost the only secular education for the very poor. This was too wretched a project to attract fashionable philanthropists but Miss Coutts was different. She was, thought Dickens, 'very, very far removed from all the Givers in all the Court Guides between this, and China'.[29] He paid a visit on her behalf to a Ragged School which stood on the very ground where he had set Fagin's den in *Oliver Twist*, and sent her a 'sledge-hammer account'. Miss Coutts was amused and moved by his letter. In his white trousers and bright boots he had aroused immense interest among the Ragged boys. One boy expressed his opinion 'that I wasn't a barber or I should have cut my hair'. But although he had been amused by their lively cheek, it had been a depressing visit. The masters, 'quiet, honest, good men', were wrestling with an impossible task. The boys were unbelievably wretched; a little match boy, 'not much older than Charley, clad in a bit of a sack', haunted him.

Miss Coutts offered to provide public baths for them, and a larger school room. To the end of her life she continued to give help to the Ragged Schools and took an interest in her friend Lord Shaftesbury's work. But she and Dickens quickly realized that the Ragged Schools scratched at a problem which could be solved only by large-scale Govern-ment help. The teachers were well intentioned but untrained and often inadequate. They had wretched premises and little equipment. And the children themselves were too poor, too exhausted after their day's work to make much of their education.

The summer and autumn of 1843 were dogged by illness. First, Hannah Meredith succumbed and Dickens wrote with concern and came to visit. He listened with amusement to her account of the tipsy nurse Miss Coutts had hired. And in Miss Meredith's sick room 'Sairey Gamp' was born. 'Pray tell Miss Meredith', he wrote, 'I have written the second chapter [in the next number] with an eye to her experiences.'[30] Three years later, he wrote that though he did not wish her ill again he wished she would do something 'which would lead to her suggesting another character to me

68

as serviceable as Mrs Gamp'.[31] Their friendship was sealed when, on 27 December, he asked her permission to dedicate *Martin Chuzzlewit* to her. It appeared with the words 'To Miss Burdett Coutts this tale is dedicated with the True and Earnest regard of the author'.

Miss Meredith recovered, in spite of Mrs Gamp, under the tender care of her old admirer, Dr William Brown. They planned to marry in the autumn but the wedding had to be postponed when first Miss Coutts and then Lady Burdett fell seriously ill.

Their old friend Sir James Morier the diplomat, traveller and author of *Hadji Baba of Isapahan*, now retired in Brighton, urged them to join him there. 'Pray do not delay,' he wrote. 'Our air is bark quinine and port wine all in one and makes anybody live whether they will or not. . . . Let Miss Meredith rejoice in the prospect . . . such is the pungency of the air that with her natural spirits it will be as much as we can do to keep her well in her skin without corking.'[32]

They took his advice and spent the rest of the autumn in a house in Eastern Terrace overlooking the sea. But neither the dry air of Brighton nor the most expensive medical care could save Lady Burdett. Dickens sent his cheery Christmas message to a sad house. 'If every Christmas that comes to you, only makes you . . . one half as happy and merry as I wish you to be, you will be the happiest and merriest person in all the world.'[33]

In fact 1844 was to bring double tragedy and Dickens's next note to Miss Meredith on 13 January was one of condolence. Lady Burdett died on 12 January. Dickens had, he wrote to Miss Meredith,

> often thought of Miss Coutts in her long and arduous attendance upon her poor mother; and but that I know how such hearts as hers are sustained in such duties, should have feared for her health. For her peace of mind in this and every trial and for her gentle fortitude always, no one who knows her truly, can be anxious in the least. If she has not the material of comfort and consolation within herself there are no such things in any creatures nature.[34]

Miss Coutts needed all her inner resources in the coming days. In the last years Sir Francis Burdett had become deeply devoted to his gentle and indolent wife. He had written brokenly to his old friend Sir George Sinclair 'Lady Burdett, alas, alas'. On 12 January there were few words, 'My dear Sinclair. All is over.' Almost fifty years earlier, the Reverend Bagshaw Stevens, watching his distress at the death of his brother, had written with prescience that Frank was the only man he ever knew who could die of grief. Eleven days after Sophia's death, Sir Francis followed her. 'They were lovely in their lives and in their deaths they were not divided,' Angela wrote to Sir George Sinclair.[35]

On his father's death, Robert, the long-absent and unsatisfactory son, took charge. Now Colonel Burdett, he ran the funeral arrangements like a military operation, to the infinite distress of his sisters. Sir Francis and Lady Burdett were to have a joint funeral at Ramsbury and Robert counted the available beds and curtly refused invitations to some of Sir Francis's dearest friends. To Sir George Sinclair he wrote a graceless letter countermanding his sister's invitation to the funeral. Nevertheless the funeral cortège was accompanied to Ramsbury Church by a huge crowd of mourners.

The months after the funeral were painful and disturbed. Angela had bought a small house near 1 Stratton Street where she lived while her own house was under repair, but she came across the Park almost daily to her father's desolate house.

There was much unpleasantness in these months. She and her sisters were convinced that hydrotherapy, not grief, had killed their father. They may well have been right. At the end of his life, having tried homeo-pathology, Sir Francis had become a passionate devotee of the water cure. It is not surprising his daughters were aghast. There was a bitter exchange of letters in *The Times* between the family and the doctors who were promoting the system.[36]

An old shadow from the past darkened the days after her father's funeral. Her brother, now Sir Robert Burdett, received letters on behalf of a Lady Charlotte Bacon asking that the allowance which Sir Francis had paid her annually should be continued. Lady Charlotte, it was believed, was Sir Francis's natural daughter by Lady Oxford and he had certainly in the years before his death made her an allowance of £50 a year. He had always been scrupulously generous in providing for the natural children of other members of his family, his brother Sedley's child and that of his grandfather old Sir Robert. Now whether or not Lady Charlotte was his daughter was, as far as he was concerned, irrelevant. He had had a love affair with Lady Oxford and this story might well have been true. To a man of honour of Sir Francis's generation, this was a debt that no gentle-man would refuse to pay. Certainly all his older friends expected the allowance to be continued. But the new Sir Robert washed his hands of the affair – he was not prepared to take on his father's responsibilities and had had no knowledge of his father's affairs. Lady Charlotte's husband was on the verge of bankruptcy. Her friends, in a final effort on her behalf, approached Miss Coutts through her cousin, Dudley Coutts Stuart. The

The cold water cure, depicted by George Cruikshank. Angela Burdett-Coutts was convinced that such a cure had 'destroyed one of the noblest constitutions ever given to man' and hastened her father's death.

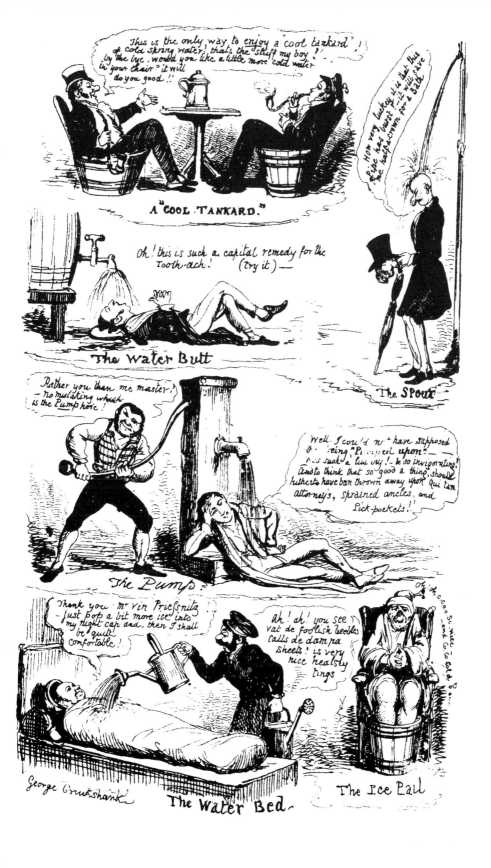

story shattered Miss Coutts. Deeply distressed, she refused to continue the allowance. Such help, she believed, would have confirmed a story she could not believe to be true. Dudley appealed to her again in vain, and not even Lord Brougham's intervention moved her. 'I would not have her conscience for all her gold,'[37] the old man wrote in fury. In his eyes and in the light of Regency morals it was dishonourable not to support a natural child. To Miss Coutts and the new Victorians the dishonour was in having one.

*   *   *

The sudden death of both parents, coupled with the revelations about Lady Oxford, deeply wounded Miss Coutts. She had idolized her father. She refused to believe that he had been an adulterer. Bruised and shaken she took refuge in the world that had always sheltered her mother, the twilight world of spas and elderly invalids. She retreated to Clifton where she deliberately avoided the social life that at that time distinguished the town. Never had she been so grateful for the cheerful correspondence from her elderly friends at Brighton. Sir James Morier urged her to go into society and sent amusing letters.

However, Miss Coutts did not stay long in Clifton. In June, she abruptly decided to leave England, again following a pattern set by her mother, who invariably sought solace in travel. Her elderly admirers followed her in their thoughts as she moved from spa to spa. The little coterie in Brighton read her long letters to each other with great pleasure.

Sir James Morier was amused by her sudden departure. But he was glad that 'considering what sad scenes you have lately gone through, how they must have acted upon your health and the incessant worry of which you complain,' she should have decided on a total change of life. He sent her gossip about Disraeli and the stir that his new novel of *Coningsby* had created in England. When she settled in Frankfurt, he warned her about the mineral waters and curious treatments.

> Notwithstanding your aversions I have a presentiment that you will this very summer be found in a bath with a snake; one hears such extraordinary accounts of the efficacy of that sort of companionship and that you will not be able to resist making a trial: but pray contain your ambition of becoming Madame Laocoon and take an attendant with you lest the snakes should make a rush. . . .[38]

Her description of the woods at Wildebad filled him with envy, 'what with your running streams, your verdant valleys, your frowning forests crowning the heights which surround you'.

Miss Coutts and her party returned home in the autumn of 1844, bronzed and restored. Now at last Hannah Meredith could marry her patient admirer Dr William Brown. They had been long engaged and he had stood aside in 1837 so that Hannah could give Miss Coutts the support she needed in her new life in Stratton Street. He had waited throughout 1844 for Miss Coutts to recover from the loss of her parents but on 19 December they were finally married at St George's, Hanover Square.

Now Miss Coutts was more alone than she had ever been, though Hannah was as devoted as ever and Dr Brown was a welcome addition to her aides. A plain, simple man, he had risen from humble origins by his own efforts and in the years following he was to be an invaluable adviser in her work for education among the poor. Miss Coutts lent them the adjoining house in Piccadilly where she was born and, since their drawing-room doors opened directly into her own house, she was not entirely deserted. Nevertheless it was a sharp break with the woman who had been her constant companion for eighteen years.

Mrs Brown, who was so important a part of Miss Coutts's life, deserves some attention. For some years past she had suffered from a succession of mysterious maladies which Dr Brown had never been able completely to cure. From the earliest days, until her death, Hannah's ill-health provided the postscript to hundreds of letters. Dukes, generals, bishops, writers, even the Queen herself, all were to send their 'compts to Mrs Brown', 'greetings to Mrs Brown', 'love to Mrs Brown' and mostly they added a kind enquiry after her health.

Hannah's chronic illness appears to date from the early summer of 1843, although there are earlier references to her colds. Thereafter, she was rarely in good health. Dickens had great difficulty in persuading his children that 'that lady did not spend all her time in bed'. Her complaints were mysterious; sometimes a cold, sometimes rheumatism, sometimes fever. Like Lady Burdett, she puzzled the doctors; and like Lady Burdett she almost certainly suffered from psychological rather than physical illness. Her social position was a difficult one.

When Angela Burdett had lived at home with her parents Hannah Meredith had no difficulty in exchanging the part of governess with that of companion and friend. The Burdett family was easy and democratic. At Stratton Street her position was very different. Was she a lady's companion? Was she to be considered a secretary, engaged to undertake Miss Coutts's voluminous correspondence? The haughty servants in a Victorian great house had their own hierarchy in which it was difficult to place Miss Meredith. Neither did Miss Coutts's friends always feel totally at ease with Hannah in the early days. All her life Miss Coutts insisted that Hannah should be treated as an equal. The social embarrassment is reflected in the fact that Hannah accumulated nicknames – 'Tiny', 'Trip', 'O' – which were more affectionate than a surname and easier than a Christian name.

Subconsciously or consciously, Hannah found her solution in the sickroom. As an invalid she could be waited on, could receive her visitors in state. As an invalid she could sit comfortably at her little side-table at Miss Coutts's dinner parties, with no embarrassment about precedence, as an invalid she could always have an excuse to retire when she wished.

Like Lady Burdett, she had a devoted doctor and Hannah conveniently married hers. Miss Coutts, so it was said, was never so happy as when she had someone to look after. Hannah gave her that happiness for many years. Gradually Hannah found herself accepted – letters were addressed to her as one of 'the ladies'. But she never lost the convenient habit of ill-health.

No one understood the shrewd taut mind behind the merry, often gushing manner, better than Dickens; he relished watching her flash out in contradiction and argument. He baited her cheerfully. She was his 'perpetual contradictor'.[39] 'Tell O', he once wrote, 'I am collecting materials for a pitched battle with her.' 'O' stood not only for 'the great objector', but also for 'obstinate'. When Miss Coutts proved unusually obstinate, Dickens was moved to write 'you are in your way as obstinate as – Mrs Brown, I can't say more!'[40]

When he had penned a particularly fierce onslaught on the Government for its behaviour in India, he finished with 'my love to Mrs Brown with these sentiments'. It was many years before he could write to or of her without a certain wariness, even irritation. In a revealing letter to his sister-in-law he described how Mrs Brown's foolish remarks had provoked him into a passionate defence of the French. In England, Dickens insisted, people dismiss the mention of social evils and vices, but in France they 'habitually recognize their existence. After crying several times "don't say that! don't say that! It gives me such pain to hear you say anything that I can't agree with" (to which I, as many times, replied, "oh, but I must say it, you know, when according to our great national vanity and prejudice, you disparage an unquestionably great nation"), she pulled out her pocket handkerchief and burst into shower upon shower of tears.'[41]

Writing of *David Copperfield* Forster recognized traits in Rosa Dartle's

74

Angela Burdett-
Coutts with
Mrs Brown, 1864.
Mansell Collection

character taken from Mrs Brown, and there were many times when she was, like Rosa, 'all edge'. Dickens was in no doubt about her intelligence. He even suggested that she should write 'Passages in the life of a General Objector' or 'Scraps of my daily observation By a shrewd Woman' for *Household Words*.[42] Perhaps, too, he detected, with his novelist's insight, an element in the close attachment between Hannah and Miss Coutts that a post-Freudian observer would see as sexual. Such unconscious leanings have been attributed to Queen Victoria and many other women of the period. The pursuit of this theme, however, is best left to the psychoanalysts. Of such ideas Miss Coutts and Mrs Brown, like Queen Victoria, were happily unaware.

*   *   *

In the loneliness of her new life Miss Coutts turned with relief to the company of the elderly gallants who were so devoted to her. She was such a good listener. For the hundredth time she listened patiently to Crabb Robinson's memories of Goethe and Schiller, and sent him kind notes and presents of game. Her Brighton friends rallied round her. Morier was devoted and amused her with long tales of Persia, of djinns and fairies. Masquerier interested her in his art collection, much of which he would later bequeath her. The old actor Charles Mayne Young revived her interest in the theatre. The acid old banker-poet, Samuel Rogers, 'one of the whitest bare scalps . . . the eyes, shrewd, sad and cruel . . . his slow croaking sarcastic insight',[43] became positively warm and mellow in her company. She had known him from her childhood, often dropped in on him on her morning walk through the park, wandered into his magical house to admire the priceless collection of pictures and objets d'art. He was particularly fond of Miss Coutts. He called himself her uncle, accepted her invitations with enthusiasm and unaccustomed gallantry. 'Cara carissima, I was writing to accept an invitation from elsewhere but I will come and meet you at the Somnambular tomorrow. Yours ever. SR.'[44] He escorted her to the Palace, to the Opera, and on her country house visits. The man of whom all London was afraid, who could 'work on you with those large blue eyes cruel, sorrowful, and that sardonic shelf chin'[45] and whose acid tongue could wither the grandest lady, became gentle in her company. 'Pray forgive me my many infirmities. I am duller than a superannuated parrot.'[46]

At Miss Coutts' assemblies, Lady St Helier noted, 'elderly gentlemen were certainly too numerous'. It was also noted that there was a preponderance of bishops. For at this time of great loneliness Miss Coutts found great comfort in religion. Even as early as 1836 she had been impressed by Henry Phillpotts, the robust and eccentric Bishop of Exeter. Throughout his long life he remained a close friend and a strong influence, stimulating her enquiries into the theological arguments which racked Britain at this time. Although she did not share his High-Church Tory attitudes, she liked his passionate belief in simplicity. Like him she would always oppose elaborate church ritual; but her sympathies were with the Evangelists.

Miss Coutts and her sisters had been early enthusiasts of the religious revival of the 1830s. In the forming of their religious beliefs Miss Meredith played some part – certainly Sir Francis had not been conspicuously devout and there is little hint of deeply religious conviction in Lady Burdett's letters. Harriot was superstitious rather than religious. But the Burdett girls were profoundly influenced by and interested in the tracts and sermons of the day, and their letters, especially Clara's, were written in that contemporary pious, even sanctimonious style that makes a modern reader uncomfortable.

Angela's own religious beliefs were then, as always, simple, even childlike. She had a deep conviction that she was directed by the hand of God to 'feed my sheep' and the parable of the Good Shepherd is a recurring theme in her letters. So was her belief that 'all life is sacred whether in man or beast'. 'The earth' as she was constantly to repeat, 'is the Lord's', and it was her mission to care for God's earth and beasts and people. Her wealth had been bestowed on her so that she might use it in God's service.

Her first duty, as she saw it in the early years, was to the Church. Lord John Russell's speech in Parliament in October 1839 and the appeals of the Bishop of London and the Dean of Westminster in 1841 directed her attention to what Russell described as the 'appalling condition of the Metropolis where there were for a population of 1,700,000 only 34 parishes with church accommodation for 101,000 and with practically no financial assistance for social work'. Until 1837 there were only two churches in Westminster – St Margaret's and St John's, Smith Square. The area around, which was owned by the Dean and Chapter of Westminster Abbey, was notorious. It was known as 'The Devil's Acre'. The streets were rightly named – 'Rogue's Acre', 'Dirty Lane', 'Long Ditch', 'Pickpocket Alley', 'Bandy-leg Walk'. After her father's death she could conceive of no more fitting memorial than a church in the middle of this, the poorest part of the constituency he had represented for thirty years. But she determined to build a church which would care for more than souls. It was to be a centre for education and social work, a practical demonstration of working Christianity. Her church, St Stephen's, must have a sense of social responsibility to the people in its parish.

In 1847 there were many who saw no hope in the crowded slums of Britain, however regenerated, and who emigrated to the colonies overseas. Miss Coutts was one of the earliest to assist families from the slums to emigrate and it was for the sake of isolated and lonely emigrants that she founded the bishoprics of Adelaide, South Australia and Capetown, South Africa. To each she gave £50,000. Bishop Short sailed for Adelaide in 1847 and Bishop Gray for South Africa in the same year. In Canada, too, her interest was that particular Victorian mixture of philanthropy, imperialism and trade. She established the bishopric of Victoria on Vancouver Island, British Columbia. As she had done to Adelaide and Cape Town, she gave £50,000, of which £25,000 was for church endowment, £15,000 for the bishopric and £10,000 for the clergy. She paid for families to emigrate, invested in Canadian railways, took an interest in the Hudson's Bay Company and provided the emigrants with churches. Two towns in Canada still bear her name, a reminder of her assistance to emigrants, and in Victoria she helped to found Angela College, and despatched a prefabricated 'iron church' which lasted for years. According to the social historian William Howitt, no one beneath the rank of Queen did so much for the Church as Miss Coutts. In 1864–5 she built a second church dedicated to St Stephen in Carlisle. As in Westminster she provided beautiful stained glass and a peal of eight bells.

Absorbing though this work was, it was not enough. At thirty-one, it was becoming increasingly unlikely that she would marry, and the prospect of a childless and lonely future stretched before her. Just as she sought a substitute father and mother, she now looked for a substitute son and found him in Dickens's enchanting little boy, Charley. In January 1845 she sent Charley a magnificent Twelfth Night cake on his eighth birthday, 'which you made a proud night for Charley in Genoa' wrote Dickens, in a belated letter of thanks in March 'and a happy night to me in the more secret quarter of my own breast'.[47]

Miss Coutts did more than send birthday cakes. She decided to pay for Charley's education. Perhaps this was a delicate way of reimbursing Dickens, who was gradually becoming the unpaid almoner in her charitable work, tirelessly and conscientiously investigating, administering and advising. He was 'argus-eyed', watchful on her behalf, never allowing her to be cheated or imposed upon. Or was it perhaps something more? At this time, she was much concerned over the succession to her partnership at the bank. After her death, her share of the capital would go to the next heir, Clara, or her son. Clara, however, was not to marry until late in life. Her eldest sister Sophia was childless, Joanna unmarried; so who would inherit her fortune? Did she turn a speculative eye in the direction of the son of England's greatest novelist? Certainly for the next fifteen years she was Charley's unofficial godmother. She and Dickens worried over his career like a couple of anxious parents. Catherine, Dickens's wife, seems to have played little or no part; Miss Coutts made the decisions even if sometimes they were against Dickens's own wishes. Charley was, for example, sent to Eton though Dickens would have preferred Harrow.

St Stephen's Carlisle in
1864. (The church has
since been demolished.)
Below: Angela Burdett-
Coutts laying the
foundation stone of St
Stephen's Carlisle in
1864.

Mansell Collection

Poor Charley! England's richest woman and her greatest novelist directed their joint powers to his upbringing with a terrifying good will and intensity. It is not surprising that the boy who was never allowed to forget the name he bore never quite fulfilled his bright promise. 'The kind of fading' that came over him in his childhood developed as he grew older. Gentle, affectionate but lacking in energy he was something of a disappointment to his father, 'though an excellent boy, good to his brother and sisters – but he wanted that habit of perseverance. He merely takes short rides on his Pegasus and jumps off again when he ought to be putting him at great leaps.'[48] He was remarkably similar to Richard in *Bleak House*, and like Esther Summerson Miss Coutts did her best tactfully to guide him.

In the spring of 1846 Miss Coutts asked Dickens's advice concerning a Home she proposed to set up for women of the streets. The sight of the nightly parade beneath her window in Piccadilly had of late deeply disturbed her. It was perhaps the discovery of her father's affair with Lady Oxford that had shaken her into an awareness of another world. Certainly among the begging letters that had engulfed her since her 'accession' there were many heartbreaking stories from the victims of rape and seduction. It was another ten years before Dr Acton produced his massive report on prostitution in London and other large cities, and it was not until 1862 that the fourth volume of Mayhew's *London Labour and the London Poor*, turned the spotlight on what the Victorians called the 'social evil'. At that time, Mayhew estimated the number of prostitutes to be probably well above 80,000 in London alone. His descriptions brought philanthropists and social reformers bustling into the work of salvation.

In 1846 a thick curtain still divided the two worlds of Victorian society. Miss Coutts, however, had only to look from her window to see where the two worlds met, feeding on each other's pleasure and misery. The successful ladies of pleasure cantered by to dazzle young gallants in Hyde Park, but, as she knew from her postbag, many of them would finish up across the road hiding their ravaged faces in the shadows of Green Park. Visitors to London at this period found the Haymarket and Piccadilly offensive even in the daytime, and at night 'there were flashing satins, and sporting gents and painted cheeks and brandy-sparkling eyes and bad tobacco and horse-laughs and loud indecency'.[49]

It was the sight of the young ones on her own steps that kept Miss Coutts awake at night. Much later W. Stead forced Victorian respectability to face up to the 'maiden tribute'. Miss Coutts needed no journa-

'The Great Social Evil': The romanticized prostitute of *La Traviata* contrasts with the reality of the young prostitutes outside the theatre. Angela Burdett-Coutts would never allow her box at Covent Garden to be filled for *La Traviata*.

Mansell Collection

THE GREAT SOCIAL EVIL.

Time:—Midnight. A Sketch not a Hundred Miles from the Haymarket.

Bella. "Ah ! Fanny ! How long have you been *Gay* ?"

list's report. The children were there, soliciting under her own window. In the light spring evenings of 1846 the sight became intolerable. In May she talked to Dickens and discussed with him the foundation of some sort of Home. At first Dickens was cautious. He was still anxious to keep her involved in the Ragged Schools and he knew she had enough in hand already with the church and school she was building in Westminster. He saw the difficulties and dangers of the scheme and was concerned for her good name.

Later on Miss Coutts accused Dickens of being impetuous, but at this stage it was Miss Coutts who, seeing the problem, wanted to leap headlong at a solution. Dickens's advice was sound. She should try to interest the Government. Not that he had much faith in Parliaments.

> . . . I have (with reason) a doubt of all Governments in England considering such a question in the light, in which men undertaking that immense responsibility, are bound, before God, to consider it. And therefore I would suggest this appeal to you, merely as something which you owe to yourself and to the experiment: the failure of which,

81

does not at all affect the immeasurable goodness and hopefulness of the project itself.[50]

Then, he suggested, 'study the reports of all the similar kinds of institutions – nothing much of this kind had been done hitherto in England', but France had some interesting experiments to study. 'Give', he advised, 'the partial schemes that exist a chance and learn from their success or failure.' Finally, 'If you cannot improve on their performance then help existing ones rather than establish new ones.' It was good advice which set the pattern for all her later work.

Dickens now felt such a

deep sense, dear Miss Coutts, of the value of your confidence in such a matter, and of the pure, exalted, and generous motives by which you are impelled, that I feel a most earnest anxiety that such an effort as you contemplate on behalf of your Sex, should have every advantage in the outset it can possibly receive, and should, if undertaken at all, be undertaken to the lasting honor of your name and country. (In this feeling I make the suggestion I think best calculated to promote that end. Trust me, if you agree in it, I will not lose sight of the subject, or grow cold to it, or fail to bestow upon it my best exertions and reflection.)[51]

From the beginning their Home was to be different. It was not to be merely a refuge, like the Magdalen, where girls were kept for a year and then thrown back on the streets, or an asylum, or nunnery as some of the religious houses were, where girls were expected to remain for life. They intended to restore the girls to health and then prepare them for a life in the only places where they could be certain to be able to make a fresh start, in the Colonies. The group must be small like a family for, above all, both determined from the beginning it was to be a Home run with compassion and without cant or condescension.

For all his caution, Dickens's imagination was caught. During the spring and summer he sent Miss Coutts long letters from his house looking over the blue waters of the lake of Lausanne. He dreamed of a bright and cheerful Home, with a flower-filled garden, where clean and regenerated young women could sing and work and prepare themselves for a new life beyond the seas. For both of them, organizing other people's lives was an immense pleasure and they warmed to the idea. But both had other things on their minds. Dickens was writing *Dombey and Son* and his *Christmas Book*. And Miss Coutts? Miss Coutts was falling in love with the Duke of Wellington.

CHAPTER THREE

The Pen and the Sword

1846-52

IN JULY 1846 Miss Coutts and the Duke of Wellington were both facing a lonely summer. Hannah was married and Dickens had taken his family to Switzerland for a year.

The Duke was out of power, the Tory Government had been defeated on 25 June. To the dismay of friends and the chagrin of enemies, he had helped Peel to bring about the repeal of the Corn Laws, a measure the Opposition had been pledged to bring in and the Tories to resist. Peel had steered the Bill through the Commons and the Duke through the Lords. The people were delighted – the Duke had never been so popular. But the outraged Tories, led by a brilliant and bitter Disraeli, brought about the defeat of their own party. Wellington was seventy-seven. It was unlikely that he would get office again.

It was exactly the sort of situation in which the affection and reassurance which Mrs Arbuthnot had given him would have been invaluable. But Mrs Arbuthnot had died twelve years before. When the young heiress from the neighbouring house in Piccadilly came to ask his advice, he had time and the inclination to consider her affairs. He had known Sir Francis Burdett and his daughters for many years and, although for most of their lives they had been political poles apart, Sir Francis, as a Tory MP, had latterly become more acceptable and in the 1840s they were writing of each other with some respect.

From Apsley House, 1 Piccadilly, Wellington had watched the career of his neighbour the Duchess of St Albans with amused tolerance. After Miss Coutts took over 1 Stratton Street in 1837 he was courteous and helpful. His early letters were kindly but formal. He sent her tickets for the House of Lords, she sent him a turtle. He asked her to a concert at Apsley House, she invited him for dinner. It was not until two years after the death of her father that their acquaintance ripened into friendship.

Miss Coutts was having trouble with her partners and it was natural that she should turn to one of the bank's most distinguished customers for assistance. Two problems worried her. She wanted to settle an annuity on Mrs Brown and she needed a Trustee. She wanted to raise the salaries of the clerks in the bank. Old Mr Marjoribanks was being difficult on both counts and Wellington was called in as an independent adviser.

There was nothing Wellington liked better than receiving the trusting confidences of young women. During his long life, he had had in his own words 'plenty of that, plenty of that!' So throughout August there were courteous notes and formal visits. Sitting with her in the August afternoons in the shaded drawing-room at Stratton Street, he learned to respect the calm and competent young woman who was tackling her duties as head of a great bank with courage and tenacity. By 19 August the Duke was writing with some warmth, 'I hope you will always write to me whenever you wish to communicate with a friend.' On 2 September he allowed himself to be persuaded to sit for a portrait by her friend Richmond – 'Chalk or water colour say what you choose I have.'

Early in September when the Duke moved to Walmer Castle near Deal in Kent, his official residence as Lord Warden of the Cinque Ports, Miss Coutts looked for a house nearby, and on 3 September he rode over to 'the heights of Ramsgate' to dine with her at her hotel. 'No lunch,' he wrote. 'I thank you but I never eat anything between breakfast and dinner.' Four days later, he decided that he need not go back to London as he had planned. Instead, he thought it would be agreeable if Miss Coutts would come over and stay a night at Walmer Castle: on Wednesday, 9 September Miss Coutts and Mrs Brown arrived.

The Duke was all gentle solicitude. Her apartment was carefully prepared, she should have 'a sleep before dinner'. Miss Coutts was enchanted. From the time of that visit until his death almost exactly six years later, she was his most devoted and loving friend. When they were apart he wrote to her daily, sometimes twice a day, and Miss Coutts treasured every letter in that bold, illegible hand. After his death she carefully bundled them together, tied them with strips of paper and sealed them with her own ring. The instructions were clear. In case of her death they were to be forwarded either to Mrs Brown or the Duke.

At the end of September he was still helping her with her banking problems and by 14 October Mrs Brown's annuity was arranged. The

The Duke of Wellington reading his letters to his grandchildren. This portrait by Thorburn was specially commissioned by Angela Burdett-Coutts, and painted after the Duke's death, in 1853.

Duke was doubtful about Mrs Brown. In his opinion an ex-governess turned companion should remain, discreet and anonymous, on the twilit edge of the servants' world. Mrs Brown was certainly uneasy with him. The 'great objector' met her match in the great Duke. Always courteous, he nevertheless kept Mrs Brown firmly in her place. 'I will mention your companion since you desire it,' he once wrote to Miss Coutts and did so in the next letter. But he frequently spelled her name wrongly and in the next year was to suggest that Miss Coutts came without 'Mrs Browne'. Occasionally he wrote an unusually formal little note to Miss Coutts in which he thanked Mrs Brown for her 'recollection of him'. These were clearly intended to be shown to Mrs Brown.

At the end of September they were again at Walmer Castle. Miss Coutts's favourite apartment was prepared: 'You shall have the same apartment as before though I flatter myself I could lodge you better.' By October they had established that mutual understanding that was always to mark their friendship. He was happy he wrote, 'to find your mind and mine were travelling the same road . . . I hope you will always communicate with me freely upon any subject which interests you and which you feel a wish to write confidentially with a friend.' Later in October he was 'glad of the intercourse between two people who feel a respect for each other'.[1]

In November Miss Coutts and Mr Marjoribanks were still at logger-heads over the bank clerks' salaries. She sent him a letter, which the Duke drafted:

> You must recollect [he wrote for her] that there are points connected with the management of my House upon which I cannot alter my opinions, founded as they are upon the invariable practice of my grandfather and of the Duchess of St Albans. I am anxious to know whether you will consent to have prepared by next week our arrange-ment for a general rise in public salaries of the clerks of the House; which contrary to the practice of my grandfather and of the late Duchess has not taken place for some years.

Marjoribanks dug his heels in and the argument continued until the Duke intervened, counselling patience: 'You did right in telling Mr Marjoribanks that I would converse with him if such conversation were likely to conciliate him.' But he was clearly not sure that she was right. 'I am fully sensible of your . . . understanding, of your justice, rectitude and moderation and when I urge patience it is only because of my ignorance.' He was, he felt, 'not sufficiently informed of the characters and reputations of the men belonging to your House'.

The Duke always used, in his letters to her, that tone of gentle modesty when he knew he was right. Later he arranged a meeting with Marjori-banks and effected a reconciliation. It was Miss Coutts's *right* to intervene that he was supporting, rather than the cause of the clerks. The Iron Duke most likely had some sympathy for Marjoribanks and he had not in the beginning clearly understood her particular position in the bank. She had, in fact, been specifically denied the right to intervene in the running of the bank. On 9 September 1848, when the partners proposed following general banking practice and shortening working hours, he wrote a crusty letter. 'I hope', he growled, 'that you have reduced the pay of those whom you have relieved from Work at an earlier Hour in the Afternoon.' They would obviously have to follow the practice of other banks,

> But there never was anything so absurd: not one Clerk will seek In-struction at that Hour of the afternoon. He will go [to] the Publick House, the Coffee House, the Play House or other place of resort of

vice or Idleness, and the Hour lost to himself, His employers and the Publick Interests will be passed in Dissipation and only lead to renewed Idleness and Mischief. This concession is like many others advocated and applauded by the Newspapers, such as Feasts and Shews for the people which occasion only idleness and vice, loss of time, increase of Want.

The Duke directed her to 'go through the stationery accounts it will have a good effect to show your partners that you can and will go thoroughly, and what is more it is your duty to attend as head of the House'.

In November they exchanged presents. Miss Coutts sent a purse she had netted. It was most acceptable – he always carried them – so many old soldiers he met wanted something and he liked to gratify them. And then, in the phrase he used so often 'your mind and mine were again heading the same road, when you were occupied about the purse I was at the same time thinking about a present for you; which I have got and which I hope you will wear as constantly as I do your present'. This was probably the Breguet watch that she treasured all her life.

But by the end of November he was not only helping to direct her affairs, he was showing a delicate interest in her health. 'Don't forget', he wrote, 'you are to leave a pair of your shoes for me that I may have some galoshes made for you. I am in earnest with this; you like walking and appear not to mind much in which state of streets or roads you go out in.'[2] And the next day he repeated, 'let me have a pair of those shoes, all that I care about is that you must be kept dry when you go out into the wet streets'. The Duke's own neat brown gutta-percha galoshes are still preserved at Stratfield Saye, his country house near Reading.

In turn Miss Coutts gave him advice. He should take no part, she gravely counselled, in the controversy over his statue. Benjamin Wyatt's colossal work had hardly been placed on its arch at the top of Constitution Hill before an outraged public wanted it removed, so absurd and ill-proportioned did it appear. The Duke, who privately was considerably offended, took her advice. 'Upon that subject I am dead,' he wrote. He had enjoyed, however, being advised so solemnly by a young woman and wrote: 'It is very kind of you to think of my position, and to occupy your Mind with reflecting upon circumstances likely to occur which may affect it. I am very much obliged to you for your excellent advice. I shall always be delighted to receive it; and will certainly act accordingly in this case.'[3]

By the end of the year, the Duke had become deeply attached and Miss

Coutts was in love. It had been, she wrote, the happiest year of her life. 'Nothing', he replied on 1 January 1847, 'shall be omitted on my part as your friend to make this year as happy as the last.' The intensity of her love was hardly surprising. The Duke, in spite of his age, was still a remarkably charismatic figure. Haydon, who painted his portrait, thought he 'looked like an eagle of the Gods who had put on human shape, and had got silvery with age and service'.[4] Women found the combination of power, glory and simplicity irresistible. Even that wise and canny Scot, Jane Welsh Carlyle, had secretly kissed his shoulder in a crowded assembly.

For Miss Coutts there was more than a touch of idolatry. She was shy and sensitive; the flattery of the great man's attention bowled her over. Into her worship for the Duke flowed all the love for her lost father, and all the affection of a lonely woman. And at last she had found an admirer who could not possibly be thought to be courting her for her wealth.

He gave her confidence. He persuaded her to take up 'skaiting'.

> . . . Don't repine! My Dear! that you are a Woman! There is nothing to prevent your skaiting; excepting the difficulty and the want of opportunity now, possibly, of learning. But Women skait habitually in the Countries in which the Ice is certain annually, and in England I have seen Ladies skait beautifully. The best that I have seen, I think, is Lady Catherine Cavendish, and Her skaiting was admirable! But I have seen many who skait very well; as well at least as most Men . . .[5]

He gave her advice. She was beginning to take stock, to plan her philanthropic work more systematically. She had a long list of charities which she discussed with him and he was all attention. 'I have been occupied by you and Your Affairs and your Charities ever since I received your letter of Sunday night; as you would have found me in your musing of last night! Indeed you would seldom find me otherwise employed.'

There was a brief nod of approval for St Stephen's Church. 'I don't exactly know where your Church or Chapel is. But wherever it may be, I entertain no doubt that it will do good. I don't think that the sort of congregation signifies much.'

There was approval for her kind of philanthropy. 'It appears to me that in administering Charities as well as in most other matters, your Mind and mine very naturally travel on the same Road. You as well as I like and endeavour to do good effectually. I cannot bear to be called upon and to be used [as a] stop Gap to provide the Means for going on in the same vicious course, and there to leave the matter. You appear to have the same

88

feeling, and you are quite right.' As for the proposed 'Home for Fallen Women' – he was less than enthusiastic.

> There are certainly no such objects for Commiseration as those to whom you have referred. Whenever I can hear of the Means of saving one, I make the endeavour. But, alas, I am much afraid that experience, as well as the Information to be derived from Statistical Works, have taught us that there is but little if any hope of saving in this World that particular Class of Unfortunates to whom you have referred: such as those very young whom you saw on the Steps. I am afraid that it has been found that there are irreclaimables of that particular class who earn their Bread by the commission of the Offence. Others misled by bad example, deceived, influenced by their feelings, may be reclaimed; but the others never! The only chance for them is that which it is your object if possible to attain: the removal of them to another scene in which they may be placed each in a situation in [which] she will not know want, and will not be exposed and tempted by its feelings to Her former Practices for Relief.[6]

Dickens had no illusions about the 'tarnished and battered images of God' either, but his faith in human nature was never daunted. The Duke, on the other hand, was profoundly sceptical.

In 1846 the Irish potato crop failed, creating widespread distress, and Coutts Bank had been invited with other banks to contribute to an Irish Relief Fund. The Duke had even less faith in the Irish than in fallen women. 'Best to wait', he advised cautiously, 'to see what the Bank of England does and what the great and ancient houses do.' He was afraid that a subscription of large sums by merchants and bankers of London would be injurious. 'Not an Irishman would work anywhere! All would flock to the spot at which he could receive His share of the Eleemosynary Gift without working for it! So much is not known of the Highlands of Scotland, as is of Ireland.'[7]

The Duke enjoyed his rôle as counsellor, and Miss Coutts loved to listen to him. But in fact she rarely took his advice. Her Home for fallen women occupied a great deal of her time for the next ten years; her concern for the clerks in Coutts Bank lasted until her death; not only did she use her influence to raise their salaries, shorten their day and improve their working conditions, she also introduced and paid for free lunches and set up a library and reading room for them at the top of the bank. As for the hopeless Irish – fifty years later the hillsides round Baltimore were thronged with enthusiastic crowds welcoming her as 'Queen of Ireland'.

The Duke fondly believed that their minds were 'leading the same road'; in fact all Miss Coutts's philanthropic work was to be directed by the Radical principles that had guided her father's early life, and along that road, for the next ten years, Dickens was her chief guide. But wherever her mind was leading, her heart was with the Duke until the day of his death.

In the bitter January of 1847, the Duke was alone with his grandson at Stratfield Saye, feeling 'the want of your society'. Only a heavy cold prevented her from driving down to join him. The Duke was persuasive. 'I hope this house is catching-cold proof; every part of it is as warm as possible.' He was proud of his central heating. The system he installed still works today.

Back in London in February, he basked in the warmth of the affection that he had needed all through his life. Miss Coutts's calm repose, her sympathetic, quiet attention, enchanted him. 'You have', he wrote, 'a clear correct judgement: which with an excellent heart will always keep you right.'[8] It was exactly Dickens's assessment – he called it her gift of 'seeing clearly with kind eyes'.[9] But there were times when that clear judgement clouded. When, on 7 February, Wellington called on her, quietly and gravely she proposed marriage.

The idea was startling but not preposterous. Wellington was seventy-eight and she only thirty-three, but had not that wise old banker, Thomas Coutts, married again at eighty when Harriot was half his age? Angela had read Thomas's love letters and she knew what genuine and deep happiness such a marriage could bring. And Harriot had married the Duke of St Albans although he was half her age – and the marriage had not been unsuccessful. But the Duke, after careful thought, gently refused.

My dearest Angela, [he wrote] I have passed every Moment of the Evening and Night since I quitted you in reflecting upon our conversation of yesterday, Every Word of which I have considered repeatedly. My first Duty towards you is that of Friend, Guardian, Protector. You are Young, My Dearest! You have before you the prospect of at least twenty years of enjoyment of Happiness in Life. I entreat you again in this way, not to throw yourself away upon a Man old enough to be your Grandfather, who, however strong, Hearty and Healthy at present, must and will certainly in time feel the consequences and Infirmities of Age. You cannot know, but I do, the dismal consequences to you of this certainty. Hopeless for years! during which you will still be in the prime of your Life!

I cannot too often and too urgently entreat you to consider this well. I urge it as your friend, Guardian, Protector. But I must add, as I have frequently, that my own happiness depends upon it. My last days would be embittered by the reflection that your Life was uncomfortable and hopeless. God Bless you My Dearest! Believe me Ever Yours Wn.[10]

The Duke's rejection strengthened rather than weakened their friendship. She had paid a visit to him at Stratfield Saye and he longed for her to come again. On 26 February he had been 'looking out and measuring walls with a view to break out doors and make passages, with a view to make fresh communication with my Apartment. In recollection of what you said to me some time ago as to your wishes.' The Duke, who liked to sleep on the ground floor, had a cosy wing at Stratfield Saye; a small study, a tiny bedroom with just enough room for his narrow army bed and a bathroom and water closet. Miss Coutts's apartment was above the study; she had obviously wished to come privately down to his room beneath; so the Duke broke open a wall and built in the little winding staircase which still exists.

In April the Duke longed for her return. They would walk in the spring evening to his new summer house, or stroll arm-in-arm down the terraces to the river. Pacing the long avenues, they might outstep the ever-present Mrs Brown. Wellington could never quite place her, never accept her as a friend and equal. What he had to accept, as all Miss Coutts's friends did, was the importance of Mrs Brown in her life.

During the summer of 1847, the Duke was always at her side. Gallant and upright, he escorted her to balls and assemblies – and the gossip began.[11] In July Greville noted that the Duke was

. . . astonishing the world by a strange intimacy he has struck up with Miss Coutts with whom he passes his life, and all sorts of reports have been rife of his intention to marry her. Such are the lamentable appearances of decay in his vigorous mind, which are the more to be regretted because he is in most enviable circumstances, without any political responsibility, yet associated with public affairs, and surrounded with every sort of respect and consideration on every side – at Court, in Parliament, in society, and in the country.

By September, the rumours had spread to France. Princess Lieven, who had seen in her old lover Metternich a similarly unaccountable taste for young ladies, observed with resignation, 'Tell me if it is true that the Duke of Wellington is marrying Miss Coutts. I can hardly believe it, yet such extraordinary things happen in this world that I should never say anything was impossible.'[12]

In April 1847, Dickens was back in England. If he had not done so before, he certainly picked up the astonishing rumour now. Miss Coutts to marry the Duke of Wellington? It seemed incredible, but his friend Samuel Rogers had no doubt about the state of Miss Angela's affections. He had, much to the Duke's envy, squired her on a country-house visit to Nuneham Courtenay, in Oxfordshire.

A year ago, Dickens had left Miss Coutts bubbling with ideas for their Home, full of affectionate interest in Charley and the family. Now, when he called, she was often 'not at home'. For the Duke she always was. Is it possible that Dickens in those months sometimes paused at the sight of the Duke's carriage at her door? Did they cross on the steps of Number 1 Stratton Street? Certainly there were days, like 23 May, when her discreet old porter was roused from his black leather chair to take in letters, one addressed to 'Miss Angela' in the Duke's bold eighteenth-century hand and impressively sealed, the other to 'Miss Coutts' in Dickens's clear modern script.

The Duke was as attentive as any young gallant. There were gifts of gloves, bouquets from Stratfield Saye. In turn she sent him 'the produce of her garden'. At Nuneham she had, to his delight, 'worn his favourite colours round her head'. Among the packets of letters at Stratfield Saye in an envelope marked 'the Duke's favourite poplins', lies a swatch of patterns – splendid purples, shot or striped with gold, plaids of lavender and grey, gold moiré and cinnamon brown taffeta. Trim, elegant and upright he escorted her to the Palace and lost her in the crowd. 'I looked for you in the Drawing Room but in vain: but the truth is that the rooms had been darkened to keep them cool, so nobody could be seen. My carriage having been called ... I came away in despair.'[13]

Queen Victoria kept silent, though she must have observed with concern her beloved Duke's new attachment. It was not for the first or last time that there was rivalry between the Queen and Miss Coutts.

In these circumstances it was not surprising that Dickens found her so elusive. In April he had 'appointed a certain day for calling on you. I called on that day . . . heard you were out of town . . . have not heard anything more.' On 16 May, he was still despairingly pursuing. He had found a house at Shepherds Bush suitable for the Home. He longed to discuss it with her. Was she in Brighton or where? A week later he wrote asking for a new appointment and sending details of the house, Urania Cottage. 'Less than two miles I should say . . . from Hyde Park in Oxford

Street. . . . It may be got I think for £60 or £65 a year on lease for seven, fourteen, or twenty-one years. It is retired, but cheerful. There is a garden, and a little lawn. The taxes are very low. A stable would have to be changed into a washhouse, and I would decidedly fence the garden all round.'

On 27 June, even the tolerant Dickens was offended. He was invited to dinner. 'Mrs Dickens and I (in great state) repaired to Stratton Street in accordance with an invitation still producable in any court in Christendom, and not being able to get in, withdrew in melancholy splendor.'[14] His pride was hurt. He let more than a week go by before he drew the snub to her attention. 'He had been so extremely busy.' Miss Coutts did apologize, but his letter of 30 June was unusually chilly. 'Pray don't think there was the least occasion for writing one grave syllable or semi-syllable of explanation about the party that did *not* take place. I mentioned it as a droll occurrence.' Nevertheless he took care to keep his children and their whooping cough in her recollection. 'They never cry, but go into corners to be convulsed and come out cheerful.'[15] Dickens knew exactly how to touch Miss Coutts's heart.

His letters became increasingly urgent. The builders ought to make a start; Cubitts were to turn a stable into a washhouse; he wished to impress upon her 'that it would be an immense thing for the Institution to begin before it is winter weather and while the garden is green and sunny'.[16] He was incurring expense. By August the builders' estimates were ready and he was anxious to show them to her, but on 26 August when he called, – 'I have missed you as usual'.

Rumours of an impending marriage grew louder. If Miss Coutts married the Duke, Dickens had every cause for concern. Miss Coutts and Mr Dickens might run a 'Home for Fallen Women' with success; add the Duke of Wellington and the idea became preposterous.

It is possible that Miss Coutts's interest had flagged, probable that she had been a little influenced by the Duke's scepticism. But it was not in her character to take her hand from the plough and, though she saw little of Dickens, she encouraged him in her letters to go ahead. There had been a time when Dickens had been her chief adviser. He had shown her how to spend money wisely. Now the Duke was in control and he counselled 'Oeconomy'. Urania Cottage looked like being an expensive folly; Miss Angela needed guidance.

In August the Duke moved to Walmer Castle as usual and Miss Angela settled in nearby Ramsgate. Daily the Duke's letters came, directing her charities, her reading, her devotions. He had heard, he wrote, of the Manner in which you dispose of your Money; and indeed, judging from the expense of the Demands upon myself, I am astonished that you should have any left! You, like me, are supposed to be made of Gold, and everybody supposes that it is only necessary to touch you to partake of the Prize. I find that the Parent of generosity is Oeconomy. Indeed it is difficult to be just, impossible to be generous without it. You are right. Form no large establishments or engagements; in the position in which you are placed they will only embarrass you and prevent the generous use of what would otherwise be in your Power. I see that the Duchess has in Her will taken the utmost care to prevent your anticipating anything, which circumstance you should never lose sight of.[17]

As he paced the ramparts of Walmer Castle, the Duke found that his mind was

strangely occupied by things past, present and future, in contemplation of the present and in expectation of the Future, and in endeavouring to ascertain the last by referring back to my experience of the Past I must add that the result is gloomy . . . I know everything! all our danger! I am sensible of my old age! Of the Possibility that I may live to see it realized, and the probability that if I do I may no longer have the power of Mind or body to contend with it! . . .[18]

With this vision of the 'reality of the future' before him, the old Duke turned to this last, autumnal love with an especial tenderness and longing. In September he and Miss Angela wrote daily, sending each other the 'product of their walks', a flower, a delicate leaf, a fragrant herb. Almost every letter bears the brown stain of their pressed leaves. Though the Duke might feel the chill breath of approaching winter, for Miss Coutts it was high summer.

Meanwhile, Dickens was still vainly trying to catch her attention. In July he was 'fated to miss you', in August 'I have missed you of course'. His spirits had been raised by 'the rumour that someone on your behalf was looking at a house in Broadstairs'. Dickens was settled there for the summer.

On 30 August Dickens at last managed to catch her with an irresistible bait. Hans Andersen, one of his most enthusiastic admirers, was in Britain on his first visit. He had met Dickens in London and wanted to see him once more before he left. Dickens invited him to supper at Broadstairs and immediately sent a note to Miss Coutts asking her to join them. Andersen recorded: 'To coffee came a young lady as guest, one of my admirers said

94

Dickens to me; she had been promised that she would be invited if I could come.' After supper they both drove back to Ramsgate, she to the Pavilion, he to the Royal Oak. This was probably the last Dickens saw of her until the end of November. In September, 'Where can I see you?' he appealed, but Miss Coutts remained elusive.

At the beginning of October Miss Coutts set off for France and he lost track for two months. He wrote long letters directed to her at Stratton Street, each one calculated to keep her interest engaged. Although he was, at the same time, in 'transports of Dombey' he had been excessively busy for months with the affairs of the Home.

If Dickens did not know where Miss Coutts was, Wellington did. Whether at Walmer or at Windsor he was following her every inch of the way. He was 'happy in her recollections – you make me see all you see'. Striding the beach at Walmer he was

> enjoying the fine weather all day yesterday, reflecting upon your en-
> joyment of it in the walks of Paris! I know Tours and the road along
> the Valley of the Loire, which is beautiful, and its fine bridge over the
> River. You could not choose a more beautiful Mile! . . . I am delighted
> that you are amused because it is good for you! but don't imagine that
> I doubt for a moment where your Mind, your Heart and Soul are
> during all these amusements. As mine are from morning till night and
> during the whole night. We have both much to occupy our attention!
> But I believe we both of us give as much of our thoughts to the other
> as is possible.[19]

The Queen summoned him to Windsor. Isolated by his deafness he would sit apparently dozing but, in reality, dreaming, dreaming that he was with Miss Angela in the sun-warmed valleys of the Loire. She was '. . . ever in mind yesterday at Windsor Castle, this day in London, and the first thing upon my arrival here. I leave you to decide whether you was so during the whole period of my stay at Windsor day and night and during my whole journey down! I am become like you. I have you with me constantly! God bless you ever yours with the most sincere affection. Wn.'[20]

Suddenly he became apprehensive. His letters were becoming so inti-mate; what if they should go astray?

> When you quit Paris [he directed] take care to leave directions that all
> your letters may be sent to you in London. [He had] written with the
> utmost freedom and really as if I were talking instead of writing – still
> I should not like to see any of them published, which would be the

wretched consequence of any of them falling into any hands but yours. One of them would make the fortune of the faithless postman or gentleman of the Press who should employ him! It would be sought for more eagerly and perused with more satisfaction than newly discovered poems by Lord Byron or even tragedies of Shakespeare.[21]

By the end of October, he longed for the return of his 'companion . . . whom I look at and caress, who is happy and delighted and smiles on me in return!' Although she was not due to leave Paris until 11 November, already he was worrying about her crossing. She must, he wrote anxiously, keep herself warm, 'lay down and endeavour to compose yourself to sleep between Antwerp and Flushing! You will then . . . sleep till you reach the Nore in the Thames! The way to avoid sea-sickness is warmth! a recumbent Posture! and Fasting!'[22]

He was as careful of her health, the warmth of her feet, the circulation of her blood, as he was of his own. She was concerned about her 'over-sensitive skin'. 'I am convinced' [he wrote] 'that the most important thing of all for health is to keep up the circulation on the surface of the person which is in fact keeping the skin in order. Above all keep your feet dry and warm. If mine are very cold I rub them against each other at night as I have entreated you to do! I think of you when I am in the act of doing so and whether you have adopted that practice and it succeeds in making you as comfortable as it does me and that immediately.' He was convinced of the good effect 'upon the extremities of exercise without fatigue. It aids all the powers of the human frame. It would warm you throughout and would relief you of the tenderness of skin of which you complain! Then you might think again of your companion who has given you this advice! Do this My dearest and tell me how you feel. Let me know and feel that you have enjoyed it God Bless you ever yours with sincere affection. Wn.'[23]

From the walls of Walmer Castle he looked out across the Channel and waited for her return. But Mrs Brown was taken ill and they were delayed. On 20 November he was still waiting, calculating the distances, the time of her arrival at Boulogne . . . at Dover . . . at London.

He sent notes greeting her at Boulogne and Dover and London. He liked her to get 'his nonsense' every day. Back in London at Apsley House, 'on a windless day, remarkably cold with hoar frost and fog', he was depressed to get her message. They were snowbound in Paris.

On the same day, Dickens, too, was waiting impatiently for her return. 'If you don't come home . . . I shall think the spell impossible to be broken until I can find a Hermit sitting on the road to a mountain, unable to speak in consequence of the length of his white beard; having cut off which, with a pair of scissors, I shall receive his instructions where to find the talisman that will do it.'[24]

On 24 November both Dickens and Wellington were waiting. The Duke was up at six in the morning, watching the moon; an eager note was sent to Stratton Street – should he come that night or wait until tomorrow? On the next day Dickens called on his way to Shepherds Bush: Miss Coutts was 'not at home'. 'The spell', he wrote, 'was in perfect vigour.'

Never again would the Duke write with quite the intense longing of those autumn letters. Indeed when in December he retired as usual to Stratfield Saye for Christmas, she must have written that his letters were 'not as they had been before'. The Duke had not sufficiently complained of their separation, he had written in a matter-of-fact manner about his concern for the nation's defences; and he had also mentioned that Mr Arbuthnot was spending Christmas with him: the ghost of Harriet Arbuthnot, the Duke's old love, cast her shade. To her rather hurt letter, he sent a gentle, reassuring reply, and he finished the year with a letter of great tenderness. 'I know and feel, God Bless You! that I have only to say the word and that I shall have you at my side at all Times! Is that reflection very presumptuous? No. It is the truth, you delight in it as I do.' It had been Wellington's year. It needed all Dickens's delicate skill to win her back.

*   *   *

So far almost all the work for Urania Cottage had been done by Dickens himself; now it was important that Miss Coutts become involved. Ever since they had first discussed the project in the spring of 1846, he had become increasingly obsessed. He had an 'unspeakable interest . . . in a design fraught with such great consequences'.[25] It was an experiment of immense interest to him as a social reformer, as an author and as a man.

She had not entirely neglected him during her autumn absence. At his suggestion she had inspected the Colonie de Mettray – the orphanage in France. (Wellington thought she would have done better to have visited his favourite institutions, the Orphan Asylum in London and a Boys' Reformatory on the Isle of Wight.)

In October, she had written to Dickens at length; she wanted to have a hand in choosing the chaplain of the Home and in planning the religious instruction. In July he was 'holding himself ready for a summons from her', so that he might bring the proposed matron. At the end of August he had interviewed the prospective inmates at the Middlesex House of Correction and was anxious Miss Coutts should visit them there: 'You can sit in the room perfectly unnoticed and unknown – to see . . . the young women . . . in their prison dresses. You will feel so much more, afterwards, the change that, with God's leave, will be worked in them.'[26]

He had written an Appeal to be read in the cells. It was a remarkably touching invitation to an institution totally unlike any other reformatory of the day. It was addressed 'to a woman – a very young woman still – who was born to be happy and has lived miserably'. 'There is a lady', he continued, 'in this town who from the window of her house has seen such as you going past at night, and has felt her heart bleed at the sight. She is what is called a great lady, but she has looked after you with compassion as being of her own sex and nature, and the thought of such fallen women has troubled her in her bed.'

By 28 October the Home was almost ready. Dickens had planned every detail himself, visited the house almost every day, superintended builders. He had bought the dresses and linen – wholesale, from Shoolbread's in the Tottenham Court Road. He made the dresses 'as cheerful in appearance as they reasonably could be – at the same time very neat and modest'.

He had searched 'high and low' for a piano to stand in the housekeeper's room, and later found a second-hand one for £9. Pianos? For prison girls? His friends were aghast. Even progressive reformer Mrs Chisholm was incredulous. Did the girls, she later asked Dickens, really have pianos? 'I shall always regret', Dickens wrote, 'that I didn't answer, "Yes – each girl a grand, downstairs – and a cottage in her bedroom – besides a small guitar in the wash-house!" '[27]

His only worry was that Miss Coutts might appoint the wrong kind of chaplain, he would have preferred to have chosen one before she returned. 'The best man in the world', he insisted, 'could never make his way to the truth of these people, unless he were content to win it very slowly, and with the nicest perception always present to him . . . of what they have gone through. Wrongly addressed they are certain to deceive.'[28] He knew enough about the prospective inmates to realize that one whiff of a Chadband or religious cant and they would be over the fence and off. He had met some of Miss Coutts's clerical friends and had not been impressed.

In November, the Home was opened in Miss Coutts's absence. There were four girls to begin with, two were coming in the following week, and Mrs Holdsworth, the matron, had the assistance of Mrs Fisher as the second lady. 'I wish', he wrote, 'you could have seen them at work on the first night of this lady's engagement – with a pet canary of hers walking about the table, and the two girls deep in my account of the lesson books, and all the knowledge that was to be got out of them as we were putting them away on the shelves.'[29]

But the youthful Mrs Fisher of the 'mild sweet manners', accustomed to teaching young people, and who had known great sorrow, was soon, at Miss Coutts's insistence, to be dismissed. She had concealed the fact that she was a Dissenter. Dickens strongly disagreed with her dismissal. 'I have no sympathy whatever with her private opinions, I have a very strong feeling indeed – which is not yours', he wrote firmly, 'at the same time I have no doubt whatever that she ought to have stated the fact of her being a dissenter to me, before she was engaged . . . With these few words and with the fullest sense of your very kind and considerate manner of making this change, I leave it.'[30] Miss Coutts was no bigot, some of her best friends were Dissenters. It was the dishonesty, not the Dissent, that damned poor Mrs Fisher.

It was probably not until early December that Miss Coutts and Mrs Brown drove up the muddy lane at Lime Grove. When she saw the neat house, freshly painted, in its little garden, Miss Coutts was as delighted as Esther Summerson with her new Bleak House. There were neat bedrooms (the first girl had cried with joy when she saw her bed), there was a laundry with 'ingenious domestic devices', there were framed inscriptions on the sitting room walls, one of them Dickens's own 'referring to the advantages of order, punctuality and good temper'! Dickens had put his heart into the planning of the house and Miss Coutts was completely captivated. For the next ten years, she and Dickens wrestled with the problem girls and difficult matrons, with the gas and the drains and the fences. She visited the home and sometimes attended the monthly committee meetings.

But now Wellington was becoming increasingly unwilling to be her 'cicisbeo', and she was glad to have Dickens at her right hand. When she needed an escort to hear an Oratorio and Wellington failed her, she turned to Dickens. On this occasion he was not prepared to be a stop-gap. 'Sorry', he wrote, 'I can't get to Exeter Hall with you tomorrow.' But usually he was at her service, her most 'devoted and attached friend'.

The truth was that as Wellington got older he increasingly longed for a quiet life. In spite of the temperamental affinity between himself and Miss Coutts, their values and attitudes were totally different. Wellington was rooted in the eighteenth century, in Miss Coutts the seeds of the twentieth century were already ripening. Her enthusiasm for social reform, for popular education, for clearing slums and sewers, all these were outside his comprehension. And he certainly did not share her passion for the new railroads in which she was investing a great deal of money.

Wellington was beginning to discover, as many of Miss Coutts's friends did, that the calm exterior was an illusion. There were many who embarked with her on an apparently quiet stream only to find themselves caught up in powerful currents, through which she would urge them with a terrifying determination.

In these years, the Duke's deafness made him difficult, withdrawn and irritable. He was oppressed by the thought that his powers were failing at a time when he was most needed. He was desperately worried about the state of the nation's defences. Five years later the Crimean War justified his fears. As for Ireland, he was as convinced as he had been in 1841 that 'we were on the brink of a Great War which sooner or later we shall have in Ireland for the dominion thereof'. 'God send', he added gloomily, 'that it may occur in my time! I see nobody else to settle it.'[31]

The Queen had come to rely more and more upon him. He had to hold himself ready for a call to Windsor, 'though really', he growled, 'the Queen might be as well to leave an old gentleman in his comfortable house'. She even consulted him on her approaching accouchement, and whether or not she should use the new chloroform. 'I conclude that care will be taken', he wrote cautiously, 'to ascertain the effect of the use of the medicine before it is administered to the Sovereign.'[32]

In March he was forced to neglect Miss Coutts: he had to be ready for the call to be present at the birth. The Queen, usually so ready to gossip about Miss Coutts's suitors, appears not to have mentioned the remarkable romance her beloved Duke was conducting under her very nose.

Greville noticed that he was 'in wonderful vigour of body, but strangely altered in mind, which is in a fitful uncertain state, and there is no knowing in what mood he may be found; everybody is afraid of him, nobody dares say anything to him; he is sometimes very amiable and good humoured, sometimes very irritable and morose'.

Miss Coutts did not escape the thunder. Sometimes he found her piety excessive. On 8 January he wrote drily to thank her for the 'engraving of the Pope for which I am much obliged to you. . . . But dearest!' he exploded, 'in the Name of God! what am I to do with the Lives of the Saints you sent for the children? The father and mother would think that I was quite mad if I were to proffer them. You forget that one of them is twenty months, the other nine months old!' Nevertheless he remained remarkably gentle, and though sometimes he was 'unable to call upon you for some days' he continued to send her flowers pressed in his letters and 'was delighted to hear from her'.

For six years, the Queen and the Duke, Miss Coutts and Charles Dickens danced this strange quadrille. At times the Queen and Dickens would step aside, silent and observing, waiting for the moment when once more each could claim a partner and lead away to dance to other music.

And the Duke, often oppressed by conflicting claims, became increasingly irritable and moody. But still he took care of her. In March 1848 he planned her five-hour journey to Claremont like a military campaign. Miss Angela was visiting her friends in exile, the deposed French king Louis Philippe and his wife Marie Amélie. As the granddaughter of their loyal banker and friend she was welcome at Claremont. The Duke was always deeply interested in her 'French intelligence'. For Louis Napoleon, her other French hero, he had scant admiration. There was undoubtedly a touch of jealousy allied to suspicion of the man who had usurped the name of his old adversary. Later, in November, when Napoleon was back in France, Wellington wrote to Miss Coutts with some prescience, 'I shall not be surprised if Louis Napoleon was to be elected President. What thirty-six millions of *rabble* can *know* of anything!'

But when, in 1848, Wellington had been in charge of the defence of the capital threatened by the Chartists proposed monster demonstration, he had accepted Louis Napoleon's help as special constable. On 10 April, the day of the demonstration, he had put him on guard in Trafalgar Square. At 6.30 when the expected riot had fizzled out he wrote reassuringly to Miss Coutts, 'The Mobs have dispersed. There are but two or three hundred people about Palace Yard, . . . not a shot has been fired or an individual injured – nor has a single soldier been seen' – he had concealed soldiers in her cellars. There was some historical irony in the situation: Wellington aided by a Napoleon, was calling to tell Burdett's daughter that the people's revolution would not after all take place!

But there were gentler moments. Her trust and kindness he wrote, 'were the delight of his life'. Her devotion 'released that spring of tenderness that, even in old age, kept his heart green'. In 1847 and 1848, as one of the directors of the Concerts of Ancient Music, he was responsible for the programme. His choice was unexpectedly sentimental, especially since the object of the concerts was to preserve old music, but it reflected his delight in his autumnal love. The concert of 21 April 1847 had included 'Where E'er you Walk' and 'Dr Arne's Air':

> *Restore him with that innocence*
> *Which first inspired my love.*

He was upset that a cold kept her away from the 17 May concert in 1848. She would so have enjoyed Matthew Locke's song:

> *One smile of Venus too did more*
> *On Mars than armies put before*
> *Thus love can fiery spirits tame*
> *And when he pleases cold rocks inflame.*

A little envelope, marked 4 June 1848, bears silent testimony to their real devotion. It contains a lock of silver hair looped in a bow and encircled with strands of Miss Coutts's brown hair.

There was May music too in that other world into which Dickens was so skilfully drawing her. Mr Bannister, the music master Hullah had recommended for the Home, had given up in despair. The fallen sparrows could not be persuaded to sing. So Hullah himself, the great singing master, consented to try his skill, and Dickens took Miss Coutts to hear him. They persuaded him finally to give the girls two lessons a week.

While the Duke was reporting with triumph his concert for thirty queens, princes and princesses, Miss Coutts and Charles Dickens sat in the little sitting-room at Shepherds Bush listening to Mr Hullah and the fallen girls singing to the accompaniment of a second-hand piano.

By the summer of 1848, these new interests were gradually drawing her away from the Duke; and he was becoming increasingly difficult. Even Miss Coutts was frequently peppered with grapeshot.

She certainly expected a great deal. Giving unstintingly herself, she always demanded in return a great deal from her friends. Wellington, who had found this amusing in the leisured summer days of 1846, found it increasingly irritating as he got older.

I am afraid [he wrote on 6 August 1848] that I cannot hope to be able to go to see you this day, notwithstanding that I have particularly wished it in order to apologize for having omitted to go with you to Covent Garden Theatre on Thursday, and having so unceremoniously stated my reason for going to the other Theatre. But I am afraid that I shall never be able to prevail upon you to consider me as quite unfit for social purposes: Deaf, eighty years old, and seeking for repose! The truth is that I am superannuated in reference to all that is required from me, publick as well as social, civil, military, political and Private; everything must come to me: I am always on the Gallop, my recollection and thoughts constantly on the Screw; and I am obliged to seek Repose. I admit that it is natural for a Young Lady in High Health not to be readily sensible that it can be possible for a Man in vigorous Health to be so pressed or rather *oppressed* as I am.

Her soft answer, as always, turned his wrath. He wrote the next day, 'I write you one line My Dearest! to tell you how delighted I was by your kindness in writing this afternoon. God love you! I will never hurt you or say you one word that can annoy you. I will call this afternoon. Ever yours with sincerest affection.'

But on 4 September he wrote her a letter of unaccustomed ferocity, his handwriting diagonal with rage. Miss Angela had passed Apsley House on her morning walk and had thought to pay him a visit. This would not have seemed odd to her. For years she had dropped in on Samuel Rogers during her walk through St James's Park. But the Duke was furious.

I must tell you that I don't admire your little Gentillesse of this morning! [he thundered] If we don't respect ourselves, How can we expect that our Servants will respect us?

The Queen's Servants, the Adjutant and Quarter Master General, the Military Secretary, private Secretary, my aides de Camp, acquaintances and relatives are in the Habit of calling at all Hours. Lord John Russell is frequently here before I have done breakfast shortly after ten o'clock. Other Ministers come also at an early Hour. They would be greatly surprized to find me still dressing, and a young Lady in possession of my room!

This Practice is not consistent with our [compact]. If you wish to see my Room and every Article it contains, I have no objection. Fix your Hour regularly. Bring your friends with you. I will attend you. But do not be found here alone, like an ENFANT DE LA MAISON, and this by Official Men, entire Strangers to you. In short I tell you very firmly I will not allow it. I will lock up the Room as I would and as I do a writing desk or Secretaire, and will not allow it to be entered excepting when I am present. I am very sorry if this note should not be agreeable to you, but I cannot help it. I did not think it possible that you would be guilty of such folly!

In fact Miss Coutts had not actually entered the house, as the Duke later realized. If the Duke's outbursts were spectacular, his apologies were endearing.

Matthew Arnold, the poet and educational reformer: a *carte de visite* from the Baroness' collection.
Mansell Collection

On the same day:

I am very much ashamed my Dearest Miss Angela, [he wrote penitently] of having written anything to annoy you; whether you mention it or not. The fact is that when my servant brought me your note, I was naked! And I was ashamed of his seeing me in that state; and requested him to tell you I was dressing. I heard nothing more of you till I returned from the House of Lords and after I received your letter, I concluded that you was not in the House at all!

I was ashamed of the servant having found me naked when you was waiting to see me! And was annoyed that I should have appeared to him to treat you with so little respect; as he must have concluded that I had been appraised of your intention to come. I beg you to excuse me.

Miss Coutts spent the autumn of 1848 in Lancashire and Yorkshire. A year ago, it had been the Hôtel Bristol, Paris, and the châteaux of the Loire. This October it was the Adelphi, Liverpool (recommended by Dickens as one of the finest hotels in the country). Her tour was to the country houses of her friends like Lord Brougham and Dr Kay Shuttleworth, serious men concerned with social problems.

104

Brougham and Shuttleworth were her trusted guides into the flat lands of educational theory that others found so dull. Brougham talked too much, Wellington growled. Even Dickens yawned at Kay Shuttleworth's 'supernatural dreariness'. His educational theorizing made him feel as if he had 'just come out of the Desert of Sahara where my camel died a fortnight ago'.[33] But Miss Coutts was genuinely interested as Shuttleworth talked of poverty in Manchester, inadequate sanitation and infected water supplies, cholera, and the breeding grounds of disease; his ideas on model housing and finally his belief in the desperate need for popular education. She had enough experience to impress on him her own ideas – particularly on the need for practical education for girls, and for technical training. Now she had more confidence, could give Dickens inspiration for *Hard Times*, a novel which, he declared, had grown out of their discussions on education.

But all this was in country beyond the Duke's horizon. He wanted peace. 'Poor deaf old man', he complained from Windsor Castle, 'obliged to pass my days in society.' At Windsor the Queen kept him going at a railroad pace. When Miss Coutts sent him 'a recipe for cholera', 'Not much faith in such recipes,' he growled. 'The only efficient precaution that I know of is to attend to the derangement of the stomach in the usual manner.'[34]

When Miss Coutts wrote a long, illegible letter from the Lake District on damp paper, he replied irritably. And when she suggested bringing Lord Brougham to visit him at Walmer he exploded. 'I shall certainly beg leave to decline to receive any excepting those whom I may myself invite. When a man comes to Eighty Years of Age he may claim the privilege of not receiving to this house those who he has not invited to it. God help me! The only favour I crave from the world is to leave me to repose in Peace!' Nevertheless he ended gently, 'God Bless you Dearest with much affection. Wn '

He needed her patient understanding more than ever. He could not understand the world into which she was moving, nor had he much sympathy with the causes she was supporting; nevertheless, 'God Bless You!' he wrote, 'nothing ever prevents me from thinking of and for you and I cherish and encourage your good disposition.'

Whenever he could manage it, he was still her gallant escort. He was beside her when Jenny Lind, now almost at the end of her career, thrilled the crowded assembly at Exeter Hall in a Haydn oratorio. (A note on her programme records that Mrs Brown was 'outside'.) But such outings were rarer now. In spite of his ingenious hearing aids, he was deafer than

St Stephen's Westminster: an illustration from *The Illustrated London News* for July 1847. The church still stands, but has lost the top of its spire.

ever, and more irritable. His conflicting duties to the Queen and Miss Angela were tearing him apart.

Gradually even Miss Coutts accepted the Duke's increasing infirmity. Once he had dominated her life, now he was quietly in the background. With a new self-confidence, his most enduring gift to her, she was developing her own brand of practical philanthropy and her reputation was growing. Visitors came to inspect the Home; the Sheriff of Midlothian was impressed. Mrs Gaskell wrote to Dickens for a 'prospectus of Miss Coutts's refuge for female prisoners'.[35]

During the spring and summer of 1850, Miss Coutts had little time for Dickens or the Duke: she was busy preparing for the consecration of St Stephen's Church. More than five years had passed since the Dean and Chapter of Westminster donated the site in Rochester Row, Westminster. There had been delays; rotting houses had to be cleared, the owners compensated, and the verminous ground fumigated.

Miss Coutts had concerned herself with every detail. Benjamin Ferrey, the architect, must often have wished she had been less interested. The spire had to be made excessively tall so that it could be seen from her

Piccadilly house. Her taste was Gothic, and she insisted, as always, on solid, lasting workmanship. St Stephen's was built massively in the Curvilinear style of the Decorated period. It was lit by brilliant stained glass windows, the pillars crowned with rich carvings of birds and flowers, the chancel floor laid with Minton tiles, the risers of the sanctuary steps inlaid with delicate brass. It was a worthy but somewhat quixotic memorial to Sir Francis Burdett whose tastes had been simple and modern rather than mediaeval.

Dickens was horrified at the cost, which far exceeded the original estimate of £100,000, and it was not surprising that the Duke anxiously recommended 'Oeconomy'. However he certainly must have approved of Mr Sylvester's 'Warming Apparatus', though the central heating caused trouble for years. Mrs Brown was in her element, organizing ladies to work the sanctuary carpet; even the Duke of Wellington's little granddaughter was roped in to make a square.

The consecration ceremony was impressive, the congregation distinguished. Miss Coutts sat near the altar on which glowed a rich velvet tapestry – the gift of the Duke of Wellington. He had seized it from the tent of Tippo Sahib, Sultan of Mysore, at the storming of Seringapatam in 1789. It was an Old Testament touch: the warrior laying his heathen trophy on the altar of the Lord.

Afterwards the workmen were given a banquet in a tent on the school playground – and later Miss Coutts entertained a splendid assembly in Stratton Street.

Dickens was down in that 'neglected area' too – but souls were not his immediate concern, and his Christianity was strictly New Testament. 'I went to look at the church', he wrote, 'and I cannot tell you how pleased I was with the little gardens. I am confident of the humanizing influence of a few leaves and flowers in that place. They will suggest to the commonest mind that you wish to please the poor, and will make a thousand people think about you, who might not be addressed otherwise.'[36]

In the spring of 1849 he had shared with her all the agonies of creation, from the first restlessness that always preceded his novels, through those times when he was 'rigid with Copperfield from head to toe' until the last breath on 23 October 1850: 'I have just finished Copperfield', he told her, 'and don't know whether to laugh or cry.' As the plot unfolded she must have seen in Agnes Wickfield more and more clearly the image of herself. It was not merely the superficial clues – their initials were the same, there were repeated echoes of her name. Agnes was 'always his good angel', his 'better angel', the 'benignant angel in my life'. Agnes also had those qualities her friends found remarkable in Miss Coutts – the 'beautiful calm manner' and the 'sweet composure', the eyes 'mild but earnest' in the 'serene and listening face'. The likeness is unmistakable. Just as David saw Agnes 'always associated with a stained glass window in a church' so Dickens must have seen Miss Coutts, earnest and absorbed, in the light of the new stained glass windows of St Stephen's.

It was through Miss Coutts, too, that part of *David Copperfield* was set in Highgate. Since boyhood Dickens had been fascinated by Holly Lodge, the rambling, eighteenth-century house set in mysterious glades and gardens which had become Miss Coutts's property after the Duke of St Alban's death in May 1849. Many times, walking or riding to Highgate and Hampstead, he had taken the steep road on the western boundary of the estate, past the home farm on the right, the drive sweeping through high rhododendrons, and up past the house with its painted shutters and its view over long lawns sloping down to the fountains and groves and honeysuckle walks that Harriot had loved so well.

So attached to Highgate and Holly Lodge did he become that in January 1851 he tried to buy a small house nearby. Unfortunately, he was to be outbid; but he was frequently welcomed as a family friend at the comfortable house so little changed from Harriot's day except that the finery was shabbier now. His friendship with Miss Coutts flourished in the informal atmosphere. Standing together at the crowning height of the gardens they could look down at the smoky city and away below to Bethnal Green and the slums that they would strive to transform.

Dickens understood her as Wellington never did. The Duke had never shared her affection for Holly Lodge, though he sometimes walked with her in the gardens there. As for her naïve and touching request that he should send her seeds from his garden at Walmer Castle to be planted at Holly Lodge, the symbolism escaped him. He replied tetchily: 'It is very flattering! But I am apprehensive that, as my manager is a man who was a sergeant in the Guards, I shall have some difficulty in making him understand what it is you want; more particularly as I don't understand it myself, excepting it be to give me a little more occupation!'[37] Dickens would have understood. Did he not himself ask for a tree from her garden to plant beside the grave of his little daughter Dora in the Highgate cemetery over her garden wall?

In *David Copperfield* Steerforth's red-brick house with its terraced garden and the view of London was not Holly Lodge, but in the vibrant relationship between Mrs Steerforth and Rosa Dartle there is an unmistakable reflection of Miss Coutts and Mrs Brown. In fact Forster, in his own copy, firmly pencilled 'Mrs Brown' against Rosa Dartle's first appearance, and repeated 'Mrs Brown (Dartle)' at the end of Volume 1. She was evidently, Forster considered, the lady friend very familiar to Dickens 'from whom he copied her peculiarity of never saying anything outright, but hinting it merely and making more of it that way'. But there was not much other similarity between the two, and from the tone of Mrs Brown's letters of 5 and 6 September 1850, it seems highly unlikely that she saw anything of herself in Rosa Dartle – any more than Dickens's mother recognized her own portrait in Mrs Micawber. 'Thank you dear very much for the Copperfield,' she wrote from Holly Lodge to Miss Angela, who was at Walmer Castle without her, 'lots of amusement', and the next day 'he [Dr Brown] read Copperfield to me last night. How charming some parts of it are, but *so sad*. Dear Dora!'

Whether or not Miss Coutts herself saw the shadow of Mrs Brown in the familiar Highgate landscape of *David Copperfield*, she must have recognized in Agnes's sisterly love for David an aspect of her own friendship with Dickens. In the Duke of Wellington she had found a lost father, in Dickens she met again the absent brother of her childhood. Later, in 1860, Dickens would write of his love: 'I think you know how I love you – how I could do anything in your name and honor but thank you' – but it was always the love of a brother. In a postcript to his letter announcing the end of *Copperfield* he wrote, 'I beg my regards to Mr and Mrs Brown. I hope "she" will like the end of the story – to say nothing of YOU!' His meaning was unmistakable: the book ends with David looking into the 'beautiful serenity' of Agnes's face – and, 'O Agnes, O my soul, so may thy face be by me when I close my life indeed; so may I, when realities are melting from me like the shadows which I now dismiss, still find thee near me pointing upward!' Who else in his life was 'ever pointing upward'?

The pen was proving mightier than the sword.

*   *   *

1851 was a difficult year for the Duke of Wellington, but he still found time for Miss Angela. When, in January, she was ill he was most concerned. On her return she found him as affectionate as ever. 'I am very happy to learn that you are satisfied with the tickets for the House of Lords. To be sure! It does amuse me mightily at times to find a veteran eighty-two years old, deaf with all! turned into a lover!'[38]

Eighty and 'a lover'. Wellington would not have used the word lover

St Stephen's School, Westminster, photographed on an outing to
Holly Lodge in the 1870s.

lightly. Neither would Miss Coutts have easily set aside her high morality.
Was he her lover? Undoubtedly their relationship was very close. The
tone of his letters, the winding staircase to his private rooms, the inter-
twined locks of hair show how close it was.[39] But it is easier to believe
that she secretly married him than that she was his mistress. There is no
proof of such a marriage, only persistent rumours in both their families.
After the Duke's death, she was certainly treated as though she was his
widow. Both were capable of an action so extraordinary and both were
capable of keeping the secret inviolate.

In May he was busy with preparations for the Great Exhibition. As
Ranger of the Parks he was responsible for security and he was full of
foreboding. It seemed a lunatic idea, when Europe was convulsed with
revolution, to build a great glass palace in his Park; it was certain to
attract all the rogues in Europe.

Nevertheless when on 1 May the Exhibition was opened, the Duke was
there, frail but delighted. He paid many visits and each time was mobbed
by enthusiastic crowds: he was the greatest exhibit of them all. That night
Miss Coutts gave a brilliant birthday banquet for him. After dinner, under

110

the chandeliers in the great dining room, each speaker outdid the other in extravagant praise. The Duke's reply was brief – he was tired. It had been a long day for an old man. The old veteran could no longer stand the pace.

By August he was even more tetchy and difficult. He wrote impatiently 'it is absolutely impossible for me to call upon you this day! I wish that it could occasionally occur to your reflections that I am eighty-two not twenty-eight years of age. It would save you a good deal of disappoint-ment and be less trouble for me.' In September further rumours of their impending marriage deeply concerned him. It was perhaps partly to escape the gossip that Miss Coutts left England on 3 September for a four-month tour of Germany and France. Wellington wrote frequently, but now his letters were often merely brief acknowledgements. He was not sure that he approved of the new confidence with which his 'Miss Angela' plunged into the disturbing modern world. 'I had observed and perused the account in the *Morning Post* of Friday of the crisis at Paris. It frequently occurred to me that your journeys and the periods of time at which made, are rather eventful, most particularly this last tour ending by your visit to Paris at the very moment of the coup d'état. However, you know best.'

Miss Coutts might have been forgiven her excitement. It was, after all, her old friend Louis Napoleon who was securing his position as Head of State. The name Napoleon disturbed Wellington. He knew too much of the horror of revolution to enjoy her breathless account.

I should have thought the Ambulances quite sufficient to shock any Person not even a Young Lady, who should have to see them. The dead, the wounded, the dying of loss of Limbs or other severe mortal[?] Wounds, Men killed in the streets all [round] you! Surely this is too much for even any Tour of Pleasure!

Even the Fascination of sleeping in your Cloathes in order to be prepared ready-dressed for a Start, if necessary to escape or even to [word illegible] does not appear very desirable on a Tour of Pleasure![40]

In 1852 the Duke attended his last Waterloo Banquet. Braced in his splendid uniform, he still made a brave show. But too often now Miss Coutts would see him riding through the Park, his head sunk on his chest, lost in thought – or sleep. In August he was back at Walmer Castle, once more an unwilling host. He sat for hours, inaccessible in his deafness, longing for repose, longing for his distinguished guests to go.

When, in August, Mrs Brown became seriously ill, he prescribed for her

Adams' bust of the Duke of Wellington. Dickens was called in, after the Duke's death, to advise on the features.

Duke of Wellington, Stratfield Saye. Photo: Courtauld Institute

the medicine that he most wanted for himself – tranquillity. There was a soothing magic in the repeated word. 'It occurs to an unlearned man with common sense that the best thing for a person in her situation is tranquillity in good air . . . tranquillity above all things.' Mrs Brown improved, Miss Coutts proposed to come to Dover but the Duke wrote that he would not be able to see her until after the 22nd. But he was never to see her again. In the afternoon of 14 September he sank into that final tranquillity for which he had so long waited.

It was a strange chance that took Charles Dickens that afternoon to Walmer. 'I have just heard of what you will have long been prepared for', he wrote, 'but what I fear will cause you, notwithstanding, some natural distress. I was walking at Walmer this afternoon, and little thought that the great old man was dying or dead. He had been a steady friend to an uncle of Mrs Dickens who was Colonel of Engineers here; and his son left word a little while ago, while we were at dinner, that the Duke was dead.'[41]

Wellington, in his last moments, was as unaware as he had always been, of the man walking nearby who had shared the affection of his last and gentlest love.

112

Did they ever meet in her presence? Did Miss Coutts, in some crowded assembly, present Mr Dickens to his Grace? It is probable. Certainly, after the Duke's death, Dickens was called to advise the sculptor, Adams, over his bust of the Duke. 'I found', he wrote, 'according to my eye, the mouth much too tight, and a general want there about of a suggestion of flexibility.' Adams accepted Dickens's suggestions and made alterations accordingly. It is ironical that it was Dickens who softened the features of the Iron Duke.

In the days after the Duke's death, the family was as affectionate and considerate to Miss Coutts as though she were his widow. Lord Douro wrote that he was giving copies of the death mask 'to no other ladies but you; that is votre affaire'. He took care to see that his brother escorted her to the lying-in-state at Chelsea 'at the most convenient and least observed moment'. It was an exhibition, wrote Lord Douro, 'devoid of taste and feeling. State, unashamed state, as Madame Vestris would be ashamed of.' Two days later he wrote even more strongly. 'The lying-in-state is a disgusting affair – seven people were killed by the crowd. Pray burn this disloyal letter!' But Miss Coutts preserved it – she shared the horror felt by many at the vulgarity of this 'trading in death', as Dickens called it, in an article he wrote for *Household Words*.[42]

On the day of the funeral, Miss Coutts took Lord Douro's advice and, accompanied by the faithful Dr Brown, started from and returned to his own house in Upper Belgrave Street. So perhaps she missed the monstrous funeral car trundling through the milling crowds past her house in Piccadilly. 'For form of ugliness, horrible combination of colour, hideous motion, and general failure', reported Dickens, 'there never was such a work achieved as the Car.'[43]

The day after the funeral she went quietly to meet the Dean, her old friend Milman, at St Paul's. In the empty and echoing Cathedral, all glory done, she remembered not the Nation's hero, but the simple kind old man she had so dearly loved.

Letters of sympathy came to her from all over the world. An unsigned poem particularly touched her,

> *While Nations mourn for him*
> *I grieve for Thee.*

Two days after the Duke's death she wrote to the aged Dr Routh, President of Magdalen and her father's old friend, with that earnest piety that had always amused Wellington.

A heavy affliction has fallen on our country and private sorrow is scarcely deeper than the public, so fully and warmly was the great spirit, gone from amongst us, appreciated; but great and good as he was, none but His Master I believe knew how pure and honourable his spirit was – God grant us to follow his inimitable example – and it is possible to do so, for his resignation, fortitude, untiring zeal in his duty, sensitive conscience, humility in respect to these great natural gifts, and earnest desire to use them to the best of his ability were Christian virtues and duties within the endeavour of all men.

CHAPTER FOUR

At Work with Charles Dickens
1852–56

ON THE day of the Duke of Wellington's funeral Miss Coutts's sister Clara, wife of the elderly Reverend Money, gave birth to a son. He was named Francis after his grandfather. His arrival must have seemed almost miraculous, since Clara was forty-six. Here at last was the long wished for heir, the only grandchild of Miss Coutts's adored father, the bright hope of her future. Miss Coutts would have liked to take over the child completely but this Clara would not allow. The late child was too precious.

Miss Coutts was now thirty-eight, full of unbounded energy. The Duke had given her confidence. Dickens gave her a sense of purpose and for the next three years they worked closely together, tirelessly fighting for social reform. Some of their charitable projects were inspired by the memory of the Duke. She offered, for example, financial support to the wives of soldiers fighting in the Crimean War, sent help for the wounded in the Zulu Wars and aided army hospitals in South Africa.

The most unusual and yet most typical of all Miss Coutts's gifts to the army was the drying machine she sent out to the Crimea. Her friend Florence Nightingale had written of the sodden misery in the hospital at Scutari and Miss Coutts's response was prompt and practical. On Dickens's advice, at the end of January 1855, she ordered from Mr Jeakes of Bloomsbury a machine which could be shipped out in parts and re-assembled, like a gun-carriage. By 9 February it was built – at a cost of £150 – and Dickens took her to see it. The machine was 6 feet square and 7 feet high, made of iron with a wooden covering. The practical Mr Jeakes suggested that he should attach a copper to it for washing, the water in the copper being kept hot by the waste heat from the drying closet. According to *The*

Illustrated London News '1000 articles of linen can be thoroughly dried in 25 minutes with the aid of Mr Jeakes "centrifugal machine"' which took 'the wet out of the linen before it is placed in the drying closet'. So a spin-dryer went too! It cost an additional eighteen guineas. The army was enthusiastic. 'The wet clothes', reported Dr Sutherland, 'give in as soon as they have seen it and dry up forthwith. The machine does great credit to Miss Coutts's philanthropy and also to your engineering.' Miss Nightingale wrote a grateful letter to Miss Coutts. Dickens wrote drily that the machine was 'the only solitary "administrative" thing, connected with the war that has been a *success*!'[1]

By now Dickens was alone in inspiring, directing and administering Miss Coutts's public and private charities and charitable works. He dealt with thousands of the begging letters which poured into Stratton Street. 'No human creature can imagine', he wrote to Mrs Gaskell in 1861, 'how impossible it is for that lady to keep pace with her correspondents.'[2] She never travelled without her portable desk, its pigeon-holes stuffed with letters, and whether at home or abroad she regularly sent packets of letters for his consideration. Many letters intended for her eye Dickens threw in the fire, others haunted them both for years. There was Mrs Antonia Matthews, a clergyman's wife, who nagged with a deadly persistence from her damp vicarage in Kendal. Year after year they decided to send her no more – but each time a new tale of woe weakened their resolve. Mrs Matthews was never quite convincing and yet they never had the heart to turn her away.

It is impossible to discover the extent of such private charity. Many entries in Miss Coutts's bank account are marked simply 'Donations'. Often she sent her steward to the bank and many a brief, cryptic note 'sent £500' records the transaction. Dickens was amazed that she should so often send her servants through the streets with such large sums.

No one appreciated the limitations of this kind of giving better than Dickens and Miss Coutts. But Miss Coutts had a horror of publicity, preferring to remain the 'lady unknown'. It took Dickens two years to persuade her to let him describe the Home in Shepherds Bush in *Household Words*. In 1853 he finally won her over by promising that he would conceal her identity. He could, he suggested, 'substitute founder for foundress, or such an artifice might be used as 'two maiden sisters', or 'an old lady'.[3]

The aim of the Home as he described it was twofold: 'replacing young women who had lapsed into guilt in a situation of hope and secondly to save young women who are in danger of falling into the like condition'. Early on they discovered the difficulties involved with the first category,

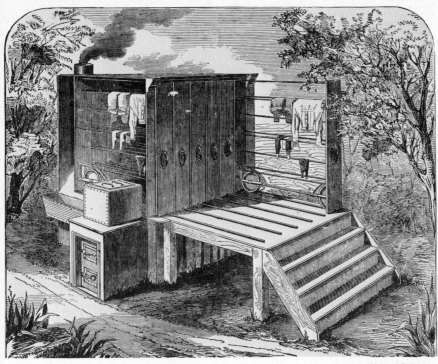

An illustration from *The Illustrated London News* for 1855 showing a drying closet sent by Angela Burdett-Coutts to Florence Nightingale at Scutari for the benefit of casualties from the Crimea. Dickens helped Angela to design it, so that one thousand articles of linen could be thoroughly dried within twenty-five minutes.

some of whom were chronic offenders, thieves and alcoholics. In later years they accepted more of the second type. Of the fifty-six girls who had passed through the Home since November 1847, thirty had been a success. 'Two to one are consolatory odds,' Dickens wrote to Dr Brown. Since many of the girls had been considered hopeless, this had been much as expected. They had 'no romantic visions or extravagant expectations. They were prepared for many failures and disappointments.'

Among the girls were:

starving needlewomen, poor needlewomen who had robbed . . . violent girls imprisoned for committing disturbances in ill-conducted work-houses, poor girls from Ragged Schools, destitute girls who have applied at Police offices for relief, young women from the streets – young women of the same class taken from the prisons after undergoing punishment there as disorderly characters, or for shoplifting, or for thefts from the person: domestic servants who have been seduced, and two young women held to bail for attempting suicide.[4]

In the running of the Home, there was a difference of emphasis between the ideas of Miss Coutts and Dickens. He insisted that it was important to encourage the girls with the prospect of marriage. Miss Coutts saw no reason why one should not be single and saved. It was difficult to find matrons who could both understand and control this motley band. There were failures like the genteel Mrs Groves who couldn't get up in the morning, the thorny Miss Furze who was like a nutmeg grater and thought her function was 'to rasp or file the girls into shape', or Miss Cunliffe who seemed unsure at the beginning, developed an atrocious temper and finally took herself off in a fly. But Mrs Holdsworth, Mrs Morson and Mrs Marchmont, the three who stayed the longest – were kind, wise and competent.

Not surprisingly there were many failures among the girls too. There was Jemima Hiscock, 'that very bad and false subject who forced open the door of the little beer cellar with knives, and drank until she was dead drunk; when she used the most horrible language and made a very repulsive exhibition of herself'.[5] Hannah Myers and Ellen Walsh broke out, taking with them the linen – after it had been washed and ironed. As for the vain little Sesina Bollard that 'draggled piece of fringe on the skirts of all that is bad', she could, Dickens believed, 'corrupt a nunnery in a fortnight'.[6]

But they had their successes. Gentle Louisa Cooper, who sent such a touching letter to Miss Coutts on the eve of her departure for Australia, returned in November 1856 'nicely dressed and looking very well-to-do', bringing Dickens a present. It was 'the most hideous ostrich's egg ever laid, wrought all over with frightful devices, the most tasteful of which represent Queen Victoria (with her crown on) standing on the top of a church receiving professions of affection from a British seaman'.[7]

Miss Coutts and Dickens spent a great deal of time and money in rehabilitating the girls. It was an expensive experiment but one that achieved much good. They created a model for the cottage homes of the future which was run with good sense and compassion, and if the discipline was strict, it was not more so than in many Victorian homes and schools, and the emphasis was always on self-discipline.

Miss Coutts kept an eye on the girls long after they had left the Home. Her friends in the colonies helped them on their arrival and reported on their progress. The Bishops of Adelaide and Cape Town and, later, British Columbia owed their positions to her and were only too willing to undertake commissions of this kind. In South Africa Sir Henry Smith, the Governor of the Cape, owed her a debt of gratitude[8] and his wife took care of some of the earliest girls to be sent out.

Dickens found, in the case-book he so painstakingly kept, life-histories beyond his previous experience. Miss Coutts began to understand a world far remote from her own and she learned to handle the people of this foreign world. Dickens taught her how to be practical, how to deal with gas, sewage and builders. Looking into the faces of their girls, hearing their lives, she was brought to the edge of what later Victorians were to call 'the Abyss'. It was a far cry from the abstract 'poor' of the sermons she had studied so earnestly. In Urania Cottage Miss Coutts learned at first hand of the appalling conditions that bred these girls. Now she saw that she must attempt to deal with the causes, the roots of their distress. Dickens kept her eyes on unromantic reality and applauded the 'moral bravery' of her approach.

In 1851 she began planning the rebuilding of an area in the East End and it was no coincidence that she chose Bethnal Green as the site for her model redevelopment. This was where Nancy, the prostitute in *Oliver Twist*, had lived. Later she attempted to restore the sordid area on the other side of the river where Bill Sykes had met his death. It was characteristic of her to choose one of the most desperately squalid areas of the capital and to design buildings for the poorest. It was a place where few outsiders ventured unless guarded by police and where the Church despaired. A local preacher wrote that he had never seen such complete helplessness as here in Bethnal Green. Engels described how not one father of a family in ten in the whole neighbourhood had other clothing than his working suit, many had 'no other covering for the night than these rags, and no bed, save a sack of straw and shavings'. Here was 'a towering crag of refuse and an enormous ditch or stagnant lake of thickened putrefying matter; in this Pandora's box dead cats and dogs were profusely scattered, exhibiting every stage of disgusting decomposition'. It was this area that Miss Coutts, with Dickens's help, chose to rebuild.

Though Dickens advised and gave practical help, especially in the early stages, the original idea was her own. But Dickens insisted she should visit model buildings already in existence in Calthorpe Street off the Gray's Inn Road. It was he who made the first enquiries, he who urged Miss Coutts to consult Dr Southwood Smith, the authority on Public

Photo: Angelo Hor

Baroness Road, E2, showing modern blocks of flats on the site of Columbia Square. The only memories of that enterprise are now contained in the road names.

Health, who knew the area. Dickens brought in his brother-in-law, Henry Austin, an experienced architect and sanitary engineer to advise in the early stages.

The first architect Miss Coutts employed was Philip Hardwick, the man Wellington had used and whom she had engaged to make improvements in the offices of Coutts Bank. The efficient Dickens had little faith in Mr Hardwick, who arrived at their meeting without plans, and he was later replaced by the architect H. A. Darbishire. In April 1852 Miss Coutts sent

Dickens the draft plans. Left to herself it is possible that she would have built a model village of small houses as she did later in 1865 on the edge of her Highgate estate. An ornate, Gothic development, it was an early prototype of the Garden Suburb.

Dickens however argued in favour of flats. He was acutely aware of the problems of feeding and housing the workmen brought in to construct London's new roads and railways. Appalled at the 'advancing army of bricks and mortar laying waste the country fields', he believed that if 'large buildings had been erected for the working people, instead of the absurd and expensive separate walnut shells in which they live, London would have been about a third of its present size, and every family would have had a country walk, miles nearer to their work and would not have had to dine at public houses'. Besides, the ever-practical Dickens suggested, in flats 'they would have had gas, water, drainage, and a variety of other humanizing things which you *can't* give them so well in little houses'.[9]

Above all, Dickens knew, as Miss Coutts did not, the oppression of a tiny house filled with lodgers. At that time, any workman with a room to spare let it, often to more than one family. Dickens knew all about 'passing strange boots on the way to bed', and the 'smell of strangers' dinners steaming from the kitchen, and the hats of men who despise them hanging in their hall'. It was this experience of lodging letting, 'the black art' of the nineteenth century, practised 'in no less than three out of four of all the houses in London',[10] that made him persuade her to put a clause in the lease forbidding sub-letting. This was done, but in fact it was almost impossible to enforce. 'The black art' continued to cast its spell.

Dickens was a powerful influence in the early stages at Bethnal Green, indeed he set its direction. But although he followed its progress with interest he does not appear to have had much to do with its later development.

In 1862 the buildings were opened. *All the Year Round* devoted an article to its praise entitled 'Hail Columbia Square'. The four blocks, each containing forty-five apartments, were so arranged that light and air could flow through free spaces at the corners on to which the windows of the corridors looked. Into these long corridors the 'different suites of apartments opened'. Ventilation was important too, it was believed that infection bred in the foetid air of the close, confined courts, a deadly miasma. The largest suite was of three rooms. There were some single rooms but most were family sets of two rooms. The living room contained a range, boiler and oven and was twelve feet by ten. The bedroom, in which the whole family slept, was twelve feet by eight.

Modest though they were, these flats were a world away from the slum courts where it was not unusual to find twenty-six inhabitants sharing a four-roomed cottage. In Columbia Square gas and water were laid on and a resident superintendent and two porters kept the corridors and staircases clean. On the top floor there was a vast laundry and drying space where, in little screened booths, eight tenants at a time could do their washing at individual boilers. In the middle stood a huge spin-dryer. One 'ingenious device' was well ahead of its time. There was 'a trap in the floor of each corridor, down which the inhabitants shoot their dust and refuse into a great dust heap underneath'.[11] Some of these refinements were criticized as unnecessary luxuries, but Miss Coutts had insisted on them – and in addition had the exterior attractively adorned with floral mouldings. She also made sure that a reading room was provided – though in practice this was little used.

Later, critics complained that projects like Columbia Square gave philanthropists a false sense of achievement. This Miss Coutts never had. She didn't claim to be the first in the field, nor did she have any illusions about the extent of her influence, though Peabody and Octavia Hill learned much from her. But she set an example, opened up a road to an East End which at that time was a foreign land to the citizens of Mayfair.

Miss Coutts and Dickens next turned their attention to Bermondsey. They were dependent on the local clergyman for advice on conditions in his parish since at this period there were few other educated men prepared to live in such squalid areas. The Reverend Gallaher did not inspire Dickens with much confidence. 'An Irishman, I am sorry to say.'

On 7 January 1853 he went down himself to the St Mark's district of Bermondsey to investigate on Miss Coutts's behalf. He found the area 'the last and hopeless climax of everything poor and filthy'. In a remarkable letter he described for her the odious sheds, the fever-haunted wooden houses and a

wan child looking over at a starved old white horse who was making a meal of oyster shells. The sun was going down and flaring out like an angry fire at the child – and the child, and I, and the pale horse, stared at one another in silence for some five minutes as if we were so many figures in a dismal allegory. I went round to look at the front of the house, but the windows were all broken and the door was shut up as tight as anything so dismantled could be. Lord knows when anybody will go in to the child, but I suppose it's looking over still – with a little wiry head of hair, as pale as the horse, all sticking up on its head – and an old weazen face – and two bony hands holding on the rail of the gallery, with little fingers like convulsed skewers.

One of the scandals of this area, called Hickman's Folly, had been the ditch which Dickens described in *Oliver Twist* and which was both sewer and water supply for the district. The ditch had at last now been filled in, he reported, but the problem of sanitation and water supply in London as a whole occupied them much in these years. Miss Coutts, early in 1852, had hoped to improve the sanitation in an area in Westminster. Two years later 'Death's Doors' in *Household Words* was to describe the 'thick black putrid stream of an open sewer', which flowed only three minutes away from the scented gardens round the Queen's Palace. But long before, Miss Coutts had often made similar journeys from her house in Piccadilly to the 'vile stink' of the 'Devil's Acre' surrounding her church in Westminster. She regularly sat among its poor congregation, and inside and outside the church Miss Coutts was powerfully reminded of the need for sanitary reform. It was no wonder that, like the Elizabethans, she always wore to church at St Stephen's a posy of sweet herbs in her Sunday gown.

In September 1852 once again she consulted Dickens and on 14 September he wrote encouragingly. '. . . If I were to tell you what I foresee from your lending your aid to what is so practically and plainly Christian with no fear of mistake, your modest way of looking at what you do would scarcely believe me. But you will live to see what comes of it, and that will be – here – your great reward.' By December, with the help of Dr Southwood Smith and Henry Austin, a survey and plans for improved sanitation for a block of houses lying between Willow Street and Coburg Row was prepared at her expense. But the eighteen proprietors of the 150 houses, well-off though they were, seemed unwilling to share the £420 the scheme would cost, and Dickens advised Miss Coutts against doing as she proposed, paying one-third of the cost. The Reverend Tennant, Vicar of St Stephen's, seems to have handled the difficult landlords badly. Dickens suggested she should give him a gentle hint 'to be practical and business-like above all things, *and not on any account to talk to them as if they were children*'. But not even Dickens could make the worthy Mr Tennant succeed. The landlords of Westminster were not convinced. The scheme was abandoned.

It is an indication of his devotion to her, that at the same time as writing *Bleak House* and *A Child's History of England*, and editing *Household Words*, Dickens found time to do so much for Miss Coutts.

In May 1853, for example, he was investigating another case for their

One of the four blocks of model housing in
Columbia Square, from an illustration in *The
Illustrated London News* for March 1862. The
laundry ran right across the top floor.

already full Home, chivvying Cubitts, the builders, who were working on a new bedroom and sitting room at the Home, and arranging temporary accommodation for the matron and girls in rented houses in Broadstairs. Not surprisingly, in June he became seriously ill and retreated to Boulogne to recover.

By the summer of 1853 Miss Coutts was exhausted too. Hers had never been mere cheque-book charity; in all those projects she was continuously and actively involved. Besides she had other worries. Richard Dunn was once more harassing her. Back in 1845 he had, with astonishing effrontery, sued her, claiming that while he had been in prison she had written verses offering 'his sweet person to free' and telling him to apply to Coutts Bank for £100,000. The verses were preposterous, manifestly a forgery and it was inconceivable that Dunn should have believed Miss Coutts wrote them.

> *When to Harrogate sweet papa beats a retreat,*
> *To take spa waters supersulphurious,*
> *I could hear your heart thump as we stood near the pump,*
> *While you bolted that stuff so injurious.*
>
> *But at last I'm relenting, my jewel, repenting*
> *Of all that you've suffered for me;*
> *Why, I'm even grown tender, disposed to turn lender*
> *Of cash, your sweet person to free.*
>
> *Send to Coutts's your bill – there are lots in the till –*
> *I'll give the clerk orders to do it;*
> *Then get your discharge, your dear body enlarge,*
> *And in Stratton-street do let me view it.*
>
> *And, by-the bye, love, my affection to prove,*
> *For your long cruel incarceration,*
> *Fill a good round sum in (as I've plenty of tin)*
> *To make you a fair compensation.*

Dunn was convicted of perjury but on his release in 1851 renewed the charge. As a barrister he knew how to use the law with cunning. Even Miss Coutts's legal friends, and she had many, were powerless and Dunn succeeded in forcing her to appear in court. Dickens was concerned for her health and sent advice from Boulogne. Never had the law been so clearly an ass. It was, he wrote, 'a striking illustration of the only intelligible and consistent principle of English law – the principle of making business for itself'.[12] Dunn was finally disposed of in the summer of 1856 when he transferred his affection to Princess Mary, later of Teck, but his persecutions had made Miss Coutts seriously ill. 'Remarkable', wrote Dickens, 'how brisk people were to perceive his madness the moment he begins to trouble the blood royal.'[13] Once more Miss Coutts retreated to the shelter of Continental spas.

As her mother had done, Miss Coutts always travelled on impulse. Her friends found it difficult to keep pace with what Dickens called the 'eccentricity' of her movements. In September she tried Vichy, but found it cold and depressing. Her letter gave Dickens a 'dim oppressive sense of windy discomfort'. In October she was back in London, then off again to Paris, where Dickens dined with her on his way to a tour of Switzerland and Italy. He had 'misty visions' of meeting her somewhere in the Alps and in fact they dined together at the house in Lausanne of their mutual friend, the eccentric Reverend Chauncey Hare, who was devoted to them both.[14]

She spent the last months of the year in the French capital, cheered by long amusing letters from Dickens. There was, at this time, such a family ease between them that he could ask her to look after Charley in Paris, book rooms for him and his friends Wilkie Collins and Augustus Egg.

Their affectionate friendship kept them together through the years 1854 to 1856 when political differences might well have driven them apart. Dickens was at his most Radical, furious over the incompetence and mismanagement of the Crimean War.

Many of Miss Coutts's friends were on the other side. Dickens had little time for Lord Raglan, the devoted friend of the Duke of Wellington, and even Lord Shaftesbury he felt was 'an amiable bull in a china shop of good intentions'. As for the reactionary bishops of London and Exeter, Blomfield and Phillpotts, Dickens abominated them and told her so. Bishop Phillpotts, he believed, had done 'much harm to real Christian brotherhood and goodwill'.[15] Her faithful clerics often irritated him. The Reverend Tennant, vicar of St Stephen's, Archdeacon Sinclair, vicar of Kensington, and Prebendary Barnes of Exeter, were beginning to take his place as her almoners and he sighed over their earnest efforts.

Nevertheless, they still had many friends in common. Samuel Rogers, now old and more crotchety than ever, adored them both. But Miss Coutts must have raised an eyebrow at some of Dickens's friends, too. Layard, the impulsive archaeologist turned Radical MP, was her friend and remained so until the end of his life, but his fierce campaign against the administrative incompetents running the Crimean War worried her. She tried to persuade Dickens to calm him down and warned them both of the dangers of 'setting class against class'. She was radical in the sense that she was determined always to search out the roots of problems but politics as such frightened her and she never allied herself with any political party. Her political ideal was the state in equilibrium and she feared any movement which might disturb this balance.

She was concerned not only at Dickens's fiery politics but also with his frenetic search for youth in the company of Wilkie Collins and she watched with increasing anxiety the driving restlessness which in these years found relief in acting. She believed that it was Dickens's true mission to write and that the theatre would exacerbate his nervous condition. Their relationship was more than ever that of a particularly affectionate brother and sister. He was totally at ease, could discuss his earache, his visits to Cartwright his dentist, 'chipping away like Old Mortality among the tombstones'. She kept a sisterly eye on his health, sent him anti-sea-sickness powders and warned him against his passion for cold showers. She had never forgotten the fatal effect of the water-cure on her father.

Though normally vain about his appearance, he would often drop in at Stratton Street dirty and travel-stained. Unless that is, he saw an impressive carriage at her door, as on the April afternoon in 1855, when the prospect of meeting Louis Napoleon drove him away, 'being dusty and anti-Napoleonic'.[16]

Dickens, the homemaker, gave her some brotherly advice on furnishing her dining-room at Stratton Street although he scarcely believed she would take it. As always, he took immense pains, carefully went over the room with her housekeeper and his instructions were as professional as any interior decorator's. On 1 November 1854, he wrote to her suggesting, 'the fitted couches and writing table are exceedingly good and satisfactory', but he felt that the compactness of this important part of the room was marred by there being nothing in the little piers on either side of the looking glass opposite the door. He insisted that the centre of the room should be kept clear of furniture – nothing must 'destroy the fireside'. He wanted chairs around the hearth, a carpet of a warmer hue – 'dark chocolate or russet, with may be a little green or red', light walls and 'rich coloured damask'. Dickens longed to bring some cosiness into her great house.

In October 1855, when tragedy struck, no brother could have helped Miss Coutts more. On 23 October after a short illness, Dr Brown, who was recuperating with Hannah and Miss Coutts at Montpellier, suddenly died. Dickens's concern was not so much for Mrs Brown but for Miss Coutts. 'She is', he wrote, to his sub-editor W. H. Wills, 'so isolated in the midst of her goodness and wealth. I have that respect and admiration for her that I cannot bear to see her distressed.'[17] He was writing *Little Dorrit* at the time and had anyway an abnormal horror of funerals. Nevertheless he took charge of the funeral arrangements. Miss Coutts and Mrs Brown had journeyed with the embalmed body to Paris. Dickens made sure they were comfortable and then went across to London to arrange the burial. Miss Coutts had long ago decided that she and the Browns should be buried in St Stephen's and had prepared a vault under the altar. In that wet October, with a streaming cold, Dickens crossed the Channel. At 8 a.m. he was in his office in London, at 12 he was at the Home Office checking on the regulations concerning embalmed bodies. A new vault had to be made in the chancel at St Stephen's as the tomb they had prepared was too near the heating. The Reverend William Tennant was ill in the country and Mr Meyrick, the curate-in-charge, was understandably flustered. It took all Dickens's drive and efficiency to make the proper arrangements.

Funerals, red tape and helpless clerics – it could not have been a more distasteful task for Charles Dickens. Nevertheless he did not spare himself. Copies of the funeral arrangements were sent to the hotel at Folkestone for Miss Coutts and Mrs Brown on their arrival, and to Lady Falmouth's house where they were to stay. Mrs Brown's attempt to secure a private ceremony by secretly altering the day of the funeral was firmly thwarted.

The ceremony on 7 November was simple, such as Dickens wanted for himself, and appropriate for so simple and unaffected a man as Dr Brown. There was to be 'no preposterous show of horses and feathers'.[18] Affectionately considerate though Dickens had been to Mrs Brown, his remarkable effort was made not so much for her but for Miss Coutts. 'God bless you,' he wrote to Mrs Brown, 'only think what a friend you have beside you, in the noblest spirit we can ever know, and what an inestimable blessing you possess in her.'[19] Mrs Brown was grateful to Dickens all her life. For the next few years, on the anniversary of Dr Brown's death, she embarrassed him with her effusive letters of thanks. On 7 November 1856 she held a faintly macabre memorial service, after which twelve widows, dressed in black, were each given £2 by the veiled Mrs Brown, and a copy of the book *Footsteps of Jesus*. A florid and elaborate alabaster mural on the north wall of St Stephen's commemorates Dr Brown but the inscription is simple. Dickens probably wrote it. He certainly arranged for a memorial scholarship at St George's Hospital on Mrs Brown's behalf. A kind, simple and cultured man, Dr Brown was sorely missed. He had quietly undertaken much of Miss Coutts's charitable work, both at the Home and at St Stephen's Church and Schools.

A week after the funeral, Miss Coutts asked Dickens to find her a secretary. Dickens, overworked as he was, was reluctant to let another take his place. He suggested W. H. Wills, so that Miss Coutts's affairs would still be under his eye. After some delay this was arranged, at a salary of £200 a year and for the next eleven years Wills was Miss Coutts's principal secretary. He was discreet, hard-working and totally reliable, and though he could never take Dickens's place, he was a pillar of support.

Latterly Dr Brown had been helping Miss Coutts with a new project, a scheme to encourage the teaching of practical subjects in schools. His loss meant a long delay in the publication of the report of her experiments at Whitelands Training College which finally appeared in 1856, under the awkward title of *Common Things*. (Dickens suggested 'Good Housekeeping'.)

She was not the first to realize the importance of practical education – Lord Ashburton had in a recent speech drawn attention to the need for such teaching; she had, she wrote, 'joined his campaign'. But in fact, her little book and her subsequent encouragement had a far-reaching effect on both domestic science teaching and technical education. Dickens wrote to Miss Coutts on 11 July 1856, 'I think Shuttleworth and the like, would have gone on to the crack of doom, melting down all the thimbles in Great Britain and Ireland, and making medals of them to be given for a knowledge of Watersheds and Pre-Adamite vegetation (both immensely comfortable to a labouring man with a large family and a small income) if it hadn't been for you.'[20]

Once again, Dickens advised and helped but this time Miss Coutts was on familiar ground and it was she who influenced Dickens. Certainly he wrote *Hard Times*, he told her, partly with the talks he had had with her and Mrs Brown in mind.

Long before she met Dickens, Miss Coutts had been well versed in educational theory. Sir Francis, influenced by Rousseau, had adopted progressive ideas on the teaching of girls. Thomas Coutts was sceptical: Mrs Coutts, he remarked drily, had brought up three girls 'without theories – and having succeeded tolerably I am inclined to prefer her practice to Rousseau's Theory, who for aught I know perhaps never saw a new-born infant in his life'.[21] Then, too, she had learned from Dr Kay Shuttleworth, and her father's friend Lord Brougham, a great deal about the problems of educational administration. The latter, champion of popular education, could even in old age still hold her spellbound with the undiminished fire of his oratory.

Her own education had been privileged. The Burdett girls had always had the best teachers available. Fuseli as an old man taught her eldest sister Sophia to paint and wrote her strange letters in Greek and Latin. From her earliest years she had been taken to the theatre, to operas and to concerts and had been encouraged in her unfeminine interest in science and geology. As Lady Burdett's great cavalcade of coaches rolled through Europe, the best tutors were drawn in to teach her languages and she learned geography the easy way. But it was from Hannah Meredith, her lively and stimulating teacher, that she had learned that there was a time to shut up the 'barren leaves' and, like Wordsworth, to observe nature with an eye that 'watches and receives'. When she confronted the practical problems of education both at the Home at Shepherds Bush and also at her new school at Westminster, she realized the irrelevance of much of the talk of educational reform. The 'march of intellect' could never start in that Devil's Acre until the children were fed, clothed, and housed properly. And they desperately needed practical training to help them get work.

The need for a new approach to education was forcibly brought home as she sat in the classroom at St Stephen's and saw the pupils, dulled by poverty and overwork, being crammed with facts that bore no relation to their lives. Their teachers, though earnest, were inadequate. Subjects like hygiene, cookery, needlework and laundry, which might have been of some use, were unknown to the teachers themselves. It was to give guidance in teaching such practical subjects that she compiled *Common Things*. The book owes much to Dickens. He set some of the questions and wrote for advice to such experts on women's education as Harriet Martineau, who welcomed it, glad that something was being done at last. Miss Coutts sent her manuscript to Dickens asking him to go over it for her and warning him not to make it 'too good'. He added sentences where necessary: but although his fingers itched to make improvements he was careful never to change her meaning. Although much of the report was clearly in the style of Miss Coutts, Dickens's hand is often obvious. One suspects that the following was introduced by him as a joke. 'I most earnestly wish that a better style of handwriting could be introduced into our female schools – that which at present prevails is so extremely bad, as to become confused and almost illegible after the first few lines.' Miss Coutts's appalling handwriting often reduced Dickens to despair. The book included a selection of the girls' prize-winning essays. They were, as

Photo: Angelo Hornak

Dr William Brown's memorial in St Stephen's Westminster. The text
was almost certainly composed by Charles Dickens.

Dickens rightly complained, 'not natural – over-done . . . full of a . . . surface morality – disagreeably like one another and in short, just as affected as they claim to be unaffected. Dickens, of the dazzling waist-coats, found particularly offensive Catherine Stanley's 'if she is fond of gaudy clothes we naturally suppose she has a little mind'. 'I constantly notice', wrote Dickens indignantly, 'a love of colour and brightness to be a portion of a fine and generous nature.'[22] But Miss S. Higginbotham gave an even more powerful reason for avoiding finery – 'many wicked men', she wrote sternly, 'have led girls from the path of rectitude, tempted by a love of fine clothes'.

Not for the first time Miss Coutts disagreed with Dickens on the subject of bright colours – which she always found disturbing. She always felt a certain guilt at her own delight in pretty clothes. It was part of that femininity she was at pains to suppress. She clinched her argument this time by adding as an appendix two quotations from their friends the prison governors Chesterton and Tracy. The former asserted as an un-doubted fact 'love of dress is the cause of ruin of a vast number of young women in humble circumstances'. Tracy agreed, in twenty years' exper-ience he had found the excessive love of dress a cause of 'early lapse into crime – for girls it was equal as a cause of ruin as drink was for men'.

There was one sense in which Miss Coutts and the prison governors showed some realism. There were not many honest ways for a working girl to come by fine clothes – unless as a servant she inherited those of her mistress. A working girl who appeared in satins on the streets of Bethnal Green would be certainly assumed to have taken to the life of pleasure, or at least to be offering a sign that she was willing.

Common Things is a fascinating reflection of Victorian attitudes to morality and station and dress, but the conventional concept of a rigid social hierarchy implicit in them was not Miss Coutts's. Although she certainly accepted the class differences which existed and was afraid of class conflict, she never claimed, as did many of her kind, that one class was morally superior to another. Dickens was pleased with the book. He congratulated Miss Coutts heartily on it. It was indeed sensible and practi-cal, a kind of poor woman's *Mrs Beeton* with notes on weekly expenditure for a labouring man, the most economical methods of cooking, of washing and mending clothes. The recipes were simple and useful, if unappetizing, 'four gallons of soup for one and ninepence out of a cow's head'. There were sample budgets for occupations ranging from clerk to brickmaker, and most of it was written with a practical understanding of the real difficulties ('if there is no water, keep clean by rubbing with a dry cloth, if no stove use a dutch oven'). There were notes on simple first aid and household remedies. In an era when doctors were luxuries, these were certainly of use and probably did no more harm than the doctors.

The book was well received and was later reprinted in a larger edition. *The Times* was enthusiastic. The working men and women to whom it was shown for their comments pronounced it most useful. The Central Committee of the Institutional Association of Lancashire and Cheshire wrote to ask her either to give a box of books for the 'itinerary free library or prizes to young women upon subjects of domestic economy'.

Characteristically she donated books but refused to give the prizes, since she had, she wrote, no knowledge of conditions in that area. Also, she feared the 'excitement' of competition would be too great a strain on working girls.

From 1855 Wills began to undertake much of the work that Dickens had done so cheerfully for more than thirteen years. Dickens still maintained an interest in the Home and attended committee meetings, but there are fewer references to it in his letters. The Home was now running smoothly. There had been a difficult time in January and February 1854 when the bright and kindly matron, Mrs Morson, had left to be succeeded by Mrs Marchmont who, although highly recommended, had nevertheless seemed flabby and unprepossessing to Dickens. The girls had obviously thought so too and had delighted in baiting her until the worst offenders were firmly ejected.

In November 1856 Dickens and Miss Coutts had a cheerful argument about the swatch of patterns for the girls' dresses. Dickens, always ready to plead for more colour in life, was scornful. '. . . I return Derry. I have no doubt it's a capital article, but it's a mortal dull color. Color these people always want, and color (as allied to fancy) I would always give them. In these cast-iron and mechanical days, I think even such a garnish to the dish of their monotonous and hard lives, of unspeakable importance.'[23] Did Miss Coutts not remember that other swatch, of sprigged and striped poplins, sealed in an envelope and marked 'the Duke of Wellington's favourite poplins'? This difference of opinion over dress and colour had a deeper significance. Miss Coutts called on a strong will, reinforced by a sense of duty, to hold back any urge to frivolity. Dickens, however, was at this time torn asunder by the conflict between a sense of duty and the overpowering desire to break out.

Dickens and Miss Coutts were beginning to drift apart. After the death of Dr Brown, as always in times of stress, Miss Coutts looked for a retreat. Dickens had made enquiries for her. Tunbridge Wells, he suggested, was extremely healthy, very beautiful, very accessible – a house on the light sandy soil near the Heath would suit her. Alternatively she could try Croydon, Dorking or Guildford. In the end Miss Coutts settled for Torquay, renting a house in Hesketh Crescent. She and Mrs Brown began to spend more and more time there. There is a hint of jealousy beneath Dickens's bantering tone. Ages, he thought, had rolled by since he had seen her. Now he had 'reverentially' to approach Mr Wills to know how or where she was. What a 'monstrous state of existence' she appeared to be leading. If she did not return home soon, he threatened, he would 'insert a mysterious and pathetic advertisement to ABC in the Times.'[24] But Torquay had caught them and from now on London was for them a 'Babylon' to which they were increasingly reluctant to return.

For Dickens, Torquay was an 'Imposter, a mockery, a delusion and a snare'. His tone was light but he was troubled by her absence. On 7 June he was delighted that Miss Coutts and Mrs Brown were coming to stay at his new house at Gad's Hill. Hans Andersen was to be a fellow guest. Dickens must have remembered that Miss Coutts had first made Andersen's acquaintance ten years earlier, for he wrote, 'You won't mind him, especially as he knows no language but his own Danish, and is suspected of not even knowing that.'[25] It must have been a strange week-end; Andersen, childlike and blindly unaware of the impending breakdown in Dickens's marriage, seeing his wife Catherine as a paragon in an ideal household; Dickens, the perfect host, concealing his impatience with his vague guest, whom his children later called 'a bony bore'; Mrs Brown, who shared with Andersen a passion for paper cutting, mesmerized by Andersen as he snipped away at his caricatures.

Uneasy, suspicious and locked by language and temperament in his own world, Andersen found comfort in Miss Coutts's company. He understood her perfect German and she seemed to comprehend his strange tongue. Sir Henry Dickens remembered the suppressed hysteria at dinner time, and how Andersen greatly embarrassed his father, who was offering his arm to a lady (presumably Miss Coutts), by suddenly seizing his hand, putting it into his own bosom and leading him triumphantly into the dining-room.[26] On Saturday Hans Andersen remembered the walk with the ladies in the cool June morning up to the Monument, from which 'there is a magnificent view . . . we lay upon the grass, the air was warm, the wind cold. I made daisy chains.'[27] After dinner on Saturday Miss Coutts returned to London. To the great delight of the Dickens family she suggested taking Andersen off their hands, and on Tuesday Walter Dickens brought him to stay with her in Stratton Street.

His account of the visit is full of wide-eyed wonder. 'She must be', he wrote, 'fabulously wealthy, lodge keeper, footman in princely livery, carpeted staircases.' Dickens said that her fortune was immense. His banker friend Hambro 'gave her yearly income as so great that I did not rightly understand it; it was, I believe, £100,000. At any rate she is most benevolent, builds churches, gives rich alms, does unending good.'[28]

After dinner to which 'came all London's aristocracy', Hans Andersen retired to his firelit room. It was 'a bedroom as never before, with a bathroom close by, a fire in the grate, priceless carpets, a view over the garden and Piccadilly'. 'Happy and grateful to God', he prepared to sleep, only to find that his bed was impossible – he liked to lie with his head high on many pillows. Terrified of her haughty footman and chambermaid, he crept back to Miss Coutts and 'asked her to change his bed, since the servants were far too grand'.[29] Much amused, Miss Coutts returned with him, together they made up his bed as he liked it. No wonder he was so attracted by her warm-heartedness and thought her 'a noble splendid person'. Her situation was quite like that of a princess in one of his own fairy tales. 'I was told', he wrote, 'that many had courted this rich lady, but she refused every suitor, for she supposed it to be her money which pleased them.' Andersen never forgot the 'straight-forward, kind and good natured' lady who had made him so comfortable.[30]

Miss Coutts could temporarily relieve the domestic strain on the Dickens household by removing Andersen, but she could not save the marriage. She had watched Dickens at Gad's Hill and noticed how near he was to breakdown. 'Yes', he wrote in reply to Mrs Brown's sympathetic letter, 'I certainly was exactly in the state you describe. It belongs to such a life as mine and is its penalty. Thank God while I have health and activity it does not last long, so after a miserable day or two, I have come out of the dark corner into the sun again.'[31] Miss Coutts watched with foreboding as he tore himself to pieces in Wilkie Collins's play *The Frozen Deep*, originally an amateur production involving the Dickens family.

She was not unaware of the attraction he felt for the young actresses who took the place of his daughters in the public performances of *The Frozen Deep*. Ironically, it was Miss Coutts whose delicate hint had helped to decide Dickens to engage professional actresses. While Dickens's daughters Mamey and Katy could properly take part in amateur productions, Miss Coutts felt they ought not to be exposed to the dangers of the public stage. When Dickens wrote from Manchester to tell her of the touching young Maria Ternan who sobbed so brokenly on the stage, she must have wondered whether she had been wise. Wills probably told her that it was not Maria, but Ellen Ternan who was fascinating Charles Dickens. Miss Coutts was also well aware that Dickens was becoming increasingly irritated by his wife. His exasperation with Catherine had exploded when she called on Miss Coutts to ask help for her brother. He had himself written to her and was furious to find that Catherine had been anxiously importuning.

However unsettled his domestic life at this period, Dickens not only continued to manage the Home but was even planning, in July 1857, to enlarge it. With the Reverend William Tennant and Mr Dyer, he still attended committee meetings and during the winter both girls and matron seemed comfortably settled. But on 14 April he wrote to tell Miss Coutts of a deeply disturbing incident. 'Yesterday morning between four and five (to make the matter very short) the police constable *employed to watch the place* was found in the parlour with Sarah Hyam by Mary Lugg whose suspicions had been excited by the early rising of Hyam.'[32] Dickens's letter was simple – written without moralizing. But coming at this most critical time, when the collapse of his marriage was imminent, the affair must have seemed both ironic and poignant. The walls of discipline and morality were crumbling about him.

A month later he wrote to tell her that his marriage was at an end. The publicity and scandal which followed him for the rest of the year made it impossible for him to continue his work at the Home. The Reverend William Tennant and Mr Dyer carried on and Archdeacon Sinclair continued to help but, without Dickens, the heart was dead. Quietly the Home was allowed to run down; the last girls were settled and the matrons comfortably established in a home nearby. By 1862 the 'Home for Homeless Women' was no more.[33]

It was no surprise to Miss Coutts when early in May Dickens's separation from his wife was announced. Both she and Mrs Brown had noticed at Gad's Hill with foreboding the strain between them. Anxious for her understanding and sympathy on 9 May Dickens wrote a long letter of explanation. 'You have been too near and dear a friend to me for many years, and I am bound to you by too many ties of grateful and affectionate regard to admit of my any longer keeping silence to you on a sad domestic topic.' She knew him well enough to discount the exaggeration in his claim that his marriage 'has been for years and years as miserable a one as ever was made'. But she well understood the painful effort he was making to be honest with himself and with her. She knew his weaknesses – they had often joked about those 'impulsive faults', which he claimed 'belonged to my impulsive way of life and exercise of fancy'.

Dickens found great relief in writing to Miss Coutts about his marital problems, pleading 'don't think the worse of me; don't think the worse of her . . . I think she has always felt herself to be at the disadvantage of groping blindly about me and never touching me, and so has fallen into the most miserable weaknesses and jealousies'. Miss Coutts also had sympathy and understanding for Catherine who had more than a little in common with her own mother, Lady Burdett. Both were pretty and in-dolent, each felt herself inadequate to deal with a brilliant husband's driving energy; it might well have been said of Sophia too, 'if she had married another sort of man she might have done better'. But Catherine had not Sophia's intelligence, nor, with those nine children, could she take the grand lady's way out. But with her parents' example in mind, Miss Coutts continued to hope she could bring them to a reconciliation. After all, Sir Francis and Lady Burdett had lived happily together at the end of their days.

Throughout the troubled month of May, while gossip and slander whirled round Dickens's head, Miss Coutts remained steadily kind to both sides. Catherine called to weep and touched her by her simplicity. On 19 May Miss Coutts sent her messenger to Dickens asking him to call, but not even she could change his determination. His reply came back immedi-ately: 'How far I love and honor you, you know in part, though you can never fully know. But nothing on earth – no, not even you, can move me.' Her messenger set out again from Stratton Street and Catherine tearfully accepted the inevitable. Miss Coutts retained Dickens's friend-ship, as others who supported Catherine did not. She was convinced, as she said to Crabb Robinson, that 'there has been nothing criminal – no-thing beyond incompatibilité d'humeur – to require a separation'.[34]

Dickens still felt the need for her approval and understanding. He came to ask her advice; he wanted to give a series of public readings from his novels. He had done so for charity: should he now do so for himself? He was surprised that she immediately replied that 'most people would be glad you should have the money rather than other people'. She had always discouraged the showman in him, but now, practical as ever, she saw that he needed not only the money but also an outlet for that driving energy. Dickens went on tour in 1858. His letters were few but affectionate. No letter for 1859 appears to have survived.

In 1860, Charley Dickens called on Miss Coutts in Torquay to say good-bye before setting off for China. His visit seems to have spurred

Miss Coutts to try to mend his father's marriage. On 4 April she was in London for a brief visit, while Mrs Brown remained in Torquay. So when once again he called on her in Stratton Street they sat together alone. We know little of what they said in that last quiet intimate meeting. We only know that they talked together with the old ease and understanding, that Miss Coutts urged that there should be no secret skeletons between them, but that not even she could persuade him to a reconciliation with his wife. 'It was simply impossible that such a thing can be', he wrote next day. 'That figure is out of my life for ever more (except to darken it) and my desire is, Never to see it again.'[35]

For the rest of Dickens's life the tone of the letters was unfailingly affectionate but shadowed by a sad sense of a lost world. He thanked her for her condolences on his brother Alfred's death, in August 1860, 'the kind remembrance of true friends'. In an unusually faint, small hand he wrote on 12 February 1864 to thank her for her letter on Walter's death. She was still 'my dearest friend', and he 'dearly prized' her 'affectionate letters'.[36] Obviously moved by Catherine's lonely misery at such a time, Miss Coutts pleaded once more but in vain for 'forgiveness and tenderness'. That page in his life he wrote 'has become absolutely blank'. In January 1865 he thanked Mrs Brown for her Christmas card with its 'welcome little redbreast . . . no leaves ever fall or are ever strewn . . . over the remembrances that I have which we share together'.

Hardly a letter has survived from the 1860s. On 11 June 1865, he replied with an 'unsteady hand to her kind, kind letters', after the tragic train accident at Staplehurst in which he was involved. He hoped, he wrote, he could come and recuperate at Holly Lodge, but it was probable that about this time the actress Ellen Ternan became his mistress and he would not have visited Miss Coutts under those circumstances.

He did write in February 1866 to ask her help for a Mr Sawyer, the headmaster of a school in Tunbridge Wells where her nephew and his youngest son were at school. It is possible that he and Miss Coutts did not meet again. But he still sent affectionate messages through Wills. 'Tell Miss Coutts', he wrote to Wills in November of 1866, 'I shall be delighted to try my hand promptly at the inscriptions.'

From 1857 onwards, the occasional breaks under Torquay sky for the sake of Mrs Brown's health gradually turned into long periods of residence. When Dickens came to Torquay on his reading tour in January 1862, a crowded audience heard on the morning of 9 January his moving reading from *David Copperfield*. The evening performance of *Nicholas Nickleby* was cancelled. Mr Dickens was indisposed. Such a cancellation was unusual. Perhaps Miss Coutts and Mrs Brown were in the morning audience. Perhaps the reading had been too painfully nostalgic and the story of Little Emily too sharp a reminder of the bright hope of their Home.

In October 1862 they were both in Paris, though Miss Coutts was with other friends. Dickens looked up at her window in the Hôtel Bristol but passed without calling. He did send through Mrs Brown his 'most affectionate and grateful regard to Miss Coutts' and assured her that he continually 'lived over again the years that lie behind us'.

Dickens now accepted their separation with sad resignation. In the last years of their friendship he had noticed the fresh Torquay faces among her entourage, had met her bright new young men at her dinners, had seen them beside her at his readings. When she had met him in London in 1860 he was aware that she had come to London not for his sake but on business for her new hero Rajah Brooke of Sarawak. Charles Dickens's life was almost done but Angela Burdett-Coutts had stepped out into new worlds.

CHAPTER FIVE

Calm Anchorage – Torquay
1856–77

LONDON, IN the late 1850s, was becoming increasingly intolerable, with fog in winter, stench in summer, and all the year round, the lurking fear of cholera. The smell from the Thames was so offensive that the Honourable Members hung gauze soaked in disinfectant at the windows of the House of Commons. Torquay, in contrast, was sparkling fresh. Here as a child Miss Coutts had spent an idyllic holiday with her parents and cousins. In the 1820s, Torquay had been a little fishing village and although there were rather too many 'novel reading cottages' for Sir Francis's taste, he had found the hills and rocky creeks wild and romantic, and the mild, warm climate had suited Lady Burdett.

In the spring of 1857 Miss Coutts had rented Meadfoot House, 1 Hesketh Crescent, and for the next twenty years spent many months of every year in Torquay. Dazzling in the clear air, Hesketh Crescent was as clean and white as childhood. Here she found peace after London's turmoil. For the next three winters she and Mrs Brown lived in the house at the end of the sweeping crescent. Behind, the bare hills were golden with gorse, below them the blue sea beat on the rocky cliffs.

And there was, too, a new friend to replace Charles Dickens. William Pengelly was a seaman's son who had roughed it as a boy on his father's fishing vessel. He had taught himself and now taught others, becoming one of the most stimulating lecturers in the West Country. Miss Coutts and Mrs Brown had listened enthralled to his lecture on physical geography at the Torquay Museum and had gone up to the platform afterwards to congratulate him. From that moment a firm friendship was established which lasted until his death in 1893. Pengelly was tall, handsome, with intelligent eyes, a mobile mouth and an engaging sense of humour. He was also an enthralling talker. He had once held a gang of roadmenders spellbound as he explained to them the history of the fossils among their broken stones. They persuaded him to give a course of lectures for working men and he kept their interest and affection for the rest of his life.

In 1861 Miss Coutts looked for a more permanent house in Torquay and leased the newly built Ehrenberg Hall. If Hesketh Crescent was Bath by the sea, Ehrenberg Hall was Belgravia. Comfortable rather than grand, it became Miss Coutts's home in a sense that no other house ever was. From the cosy drawing room, warmed by the afternoon sun, or from the big windows of her bedroom above, she could look down across the terraced gardens to the sea, watch the tall ships sail into Torbay Harbour or the sun go down over the bay that always reminded her of Italy. Much as she loved Holly Lodge and its gardens, Ehrenberg Hall had the sea, and all her life, particularly when under stress, she found a benison in water. It drew, she said, the electricity out of her frame.

In Torquay too she found a pleasant community life. There were the

quiet activities of country church bazaars and Easter and Harvest festivals. She could enjoy theological arguments with her friend Phillpotts, the formidable Bishop of Exeter. At this period Torquay was attracting interesting people. Disraeli had made friends there with his wealthy admirer Mrs Brydges Williams – who left him a handsome inheritance and her Torquay house. Later, in the 1860s and 1870s, the Empress of Russia discovered this English paradise, and Queen Sophia of Holland and Louis Napoleon were among the distinguished guests Miss Coutts entertained at brilliant dinners and receptions. Queen Sophia was so delighted with Torquay that she came twice in 1868 and 1870. Miss Coutts was her guide and hostess, arranged for Pengelly to give her children tutorials, conducted her to the little lecture hall to hear him lecture and to his house to see his famous collection of fossils.

In 1860, she bought Pengelly's fine collection of Devonian fossils and presented them to the new museum of the University of Oxford in connection with the foundation of the Burdett-Coutts Geological Scholarship.

Miss Coutts took up botany and natural history again and in the study of plants, seaweeds and shells she found relief. She joined the Natural

Hesketh Crescent, Torquay, which was almost a replica of the Royal Crescent in Bath. Angela Burdett-Coutts rented No. 1.
Borough of Torbay

History Society and bought a collection of rare seaweeds and shells from the local expert, Mrs Griffiths. These she presented in September 1862 to Kew and the British Museum. In 1863 she helped finance research into the fossil flora of Bovey Tracey and paid for the publication of a beautifully illustrated volume. But it was geology that she found most exciting and she was quick to understand its double importance – its impact both on religious belief and on the development of industry. It was not a new interest; she had been fascinated by her mother's collection of fossils and rocks but in William Pengelly she had a stimulating guide to this infant science. Moreover, she encouraged Pengelly not only in his researches into the past, but also to look for useful minerals. She sent him to Ireland hoping that he would find coal or natural resources more profitable than the potato.

The new geological discoveries were disturbing. The publication in 1859 of Darwin's *The Origin of Species* shook the foundations of conventional religious belief; but, like Faraday, Miss Coutts managed to preserve a simple faith in the midst of these revelations.[1] In the religious controversies that rocked the 1850s and 1860s, though her instincts were all for stability and conformity, her understanding of the new science gave breadth and tolerance to her faith.

She shared another interest with Pengelly, in that they were both concerned at the state of rural education. He had been taught in a country dame school and encouraged Miss Coutts in her scheme which she developed at Torquay to raise the standard of village education. For Miss Coutts could not remain long in the past; driving round the muddy villages around Torquay she noticed with concern the ragged children running wild.

In 1864 she began an experiment, the results of which she later published in a pamphlet called *Ambulatory Schoolmaster*. On 19 January 1865 she explained the plan in a letter to *The Times*. 'It consisted', she wrote, 'in the schoolmaster being the ambulatory centre of unity to a group of schools carried on under his superintendence.' The trained and certificated teacher was to keep up the standards of the dame schools in his group, assembling them once a year in one centre for examinations. She suggested that grants of public money should be made but meanwhile the experiment was begun at her expense. *The Times* gave the scheme its blessing: 'We are disposed to think that a lady has won the prize for which so many statesmen and legislators have been contending.' At the beginning of 1865 the Torquay Group of United Schools was set up – an impressive title for the little groups of children in five scattered villages near Torquay.

144

The teachers were untrained, one was a labourer's wife. At Cockington they met in the kitchen. The travelling master, Mr Dicker, spent at least two hours a week in each school. HM Inspector, after his annual visits, proclaimed the experiment a success. As a result other groups of schools were set up in York, Carlisle, Norwich, Oxford and Exeter. The Education Act of 1870, however, by bringing in compulsory education, made her scheme less necessary. The idea was also adopted in Scotland with some modifications. In the Scottish project, as in all others, she was not content merely to donate money; she visited the Torquay Schools regularly and the other groups when possible. After 1870 she visited Scottish country schools and even gave demonstration lessons in a rough village school.

Florence Nightingale had made nursing a respected profession; Miss Coutts wished to do the same for teaching. Just as middle-class girls were encouraged to take the place of the 'Sairey Gamps', so she hoped to see the transformation of Mr Wopsell's great aunt – the archetypal dame of the village dame schools.

William Pengelly, geologist, naturalist and popular lecturer: a photograph taken in Torquay in November 1869.

Mansell Collection

CHAPTER SIX

The Wider World
1857-67

IN THE quiet of Torquay Miss Coutts began a new life. Until now she had been influenced and directed by her father, by Wellington and by Dickens. Now it was she who began to take the dominant rôle. The girl whose angelic temperament and shy modest nature had been so generally admired was beginning to show both power and edge.

In the years when they were so close, Dickens channelled Miss Coutts's energy into building model houses, clearing up slums, promoting sanitary reform and picking up fallen sparrows. But Miss Coutts secretly longed to unleash eagles. . . . Fired by the travellers and missionaries who brought back to mid-Victorian England the excitement of uncharted Africa, she wanted to play her part in a new and exciting world. Dickens had always held her back. He had created Mrs Jellaby as an awful warning. Now, she was free to explore. Wellington had discouraged her interest in Ireland. But now, with the memory of her father to spur her on, she began her work there.

Her interest in Ireland had roots in the years between 1796 and 1798 when her father had been perilously involved in Irish politics. He had built up a reputation which lasted well into the next century. The 1860s were famine years in Ireland and Miss Coutts decided to involve herself seriously. She sent Wills on a mission of enquiry and, appalled by his report of the conditions on the islands of Sherkin and the Skibbereen area, she sent copies to the Government – who did nothing for three years. In the meantime Miss Coutts set up relief centres where corn, flour, meal, sugar and tea could be bought cheaply. When she found that her stores were being distributed free she wrote to her agents a firm letter explaining

146

her policy clearly. 'I Sincerely hope the efforts made to prevent the demoralising effects of aid and help, may be secured by avoiding gratuitous distribution of food, money or clothes.' Although she recognized that some such distribution was necessary in emergencies she considered that 'it would be . . . quite an insult to the hard-working, willing islanders to be treated as mendicants. . . . My object is not to make dependence on my bounty or on that of anyone else, but to bring them comforts which can be secured by their own industry hereafterwards.'[1] Though her first aim had been to save life and afford relief, she firmly believed that stop-gap charity was no answer in the long term; such aid degraded the poor.

Emigration was one solution – in 1863 she sent three parties to Canada. But she continued to believe that the ultimate answer for Ireland lay in agriculture and fisheries. She lent money for the purchase of boats and nets and when pessimists reported that the rugged coasts made sailing in the long, narrow creeks impossible, she provided a cart to transport boats overland. But most of all she encouraged industrial training schemes.

In 1880 she made her most spectacular donation to Ireland. It was an attempt to solve both the potato problem and at the same time to lift that permanent millstone round Irish necks – debt. She offered to her friend W. H. Smith, First Lord of the Admiralty, a grant of £250,000 for the purchase of seed potatoes.[2] W. H. Smith was staggered and wrote to make sure he had really understood the sum involved.[3]

*   *   *

Just as Wellington had done over Ireland, Dickens had observed her fascination with Africa with apprehension. In the winter of 1856 she wanted to know who had written an article on Africa in *The Times* and Dickens had put out a cautionary hand. He did not know. He would find out. On 3 February 1857 he wrote to discourage her. 'Without at all disparaging Dr Livingstone or in the least doubting his facts I think however that his deductions must be received with great caution. The history of all African effort, hitherto, is a history of wasted European life, squandered European money and blighted European hope.' It was a sentiment worthy of Wellington himself. But just as Miss Coutts had quietly listened as the Duke told her how impossible it was to change the nature of wicked women, and then just as quietly set about establishing a Home for them, so now she read Dickens's letter and turned to aid Livingstone in his dogged determination to overcome the 'tremendous obstacles'.

On 12 December 1856 Livingstone returned to England to a wildly

Ehrenberg Hall, Torquay, showing the great elm uprooted in a hurricane in October 1877.

enthusiastic welcome. His heroic two-year journey from coast to coast across the dark half of Africa, had caught the imagination of Victorian England. In his two years in Britain, by lectures and writing, he encouraged statesmen and geographers, churchmen and industrialists to share his vision of Central Africa as a fertile land rich in minerals. He was firmly convinced that God had shown him the pathway, the Zambesi River flowing from west to east through the heart of central Africa. A chain of commercial stations, he thought, could bring prosperity to the African and 'strike an effective blow at the slave trade, the scourge of Central Africa'. Miss Coutts, like many others, caught his confidence and shared his vision. She attended his lectures, read his book and invited him to Stratton Street. By the end of 1857 she was determined to back him.

They had much in common. Like her he had been fascinated by geology long before it was fashionable. He too had a passion for botany, scouring the countryside collecting herbs. And like many other shy and awkward men he could relax with Miss Coutts. In the bundles of letters from him

148

that have survived he writes with unusual humour; only in his journals is there a comparable lightness of touch.

In Livingstone, Miss Coutts saw those qualities which she admired in all her heroes: a fundamental simplicity combined with a powerful will and a driving energy of mind and body. Like her other famous friends, Livingstone was convinced he was directed by 'the hand of God'. Wellington had talked of 'the finger of God', Louis Napoleon of his 'star', Dickens of his 'genius'. So now, as Livingstone prepared for another expedition to Africa, she was eager to help. Her part in the Zambesi expedition of 1858 has been hitherto unrecorded and is even now not entirely unravelled. By December 1857 Livingstone felt confident of her financial support. His brother Charles wrote to his wife 'the richest lady in the world, probably, Miss Burdett Coutts will probably give David a steamer if Parliament does not sanction it'.

In the weeks before their departure Dr and Mrs Livingstone were overwhelmed by her generosity; 'the evidence of your Christian sympathy and kindness softened my heart', wrote Livingstone, '. . . my dear friend . . . I think by your spontaneous liberality you have taken part in what I humbly hope may be a great blessing to Africa'.[4] She ordered for him the best microscope available which, he wrote, 'with other souvenirs will be heirlooms in my family'. She and Mrs Brown packed up boxes of rugs and medicines and gifts: a little silver drinking cup for David and for his brother Charles Livingstone there was 'a beautiful Duelte concertina'. Nothing was to be spared to make this expedition a success. *The Times* on the eve of Livingstone's departure reported with pride that 'the Government has advanced £5,000 for this fresh expedition into the interior of Africa. A Government vessel will take them to the mouth of the Zambesi – they will travel 300 miles up the Zambesi in a steam launch and not until the travellers are about to explore will the watchfulness of the British Government be withdrawn.'

The Queen granted Livingstone a farewell interview and on Saturday, 13 February 1858 a great farewell banquet was held in the Freemason's Hall. Sir Roderick Murchison, President of the Royal Geographical Society, toasted Livingstone, praised the competent assistants he was to take with him and then, amid loud cheering, raised his eyes to the gallery. There, in the front row beside Miss Coutts and Mrs Brown, sat Mrs Livingstone in a queer out-moded bonnet and stifling layers of linsey-wolsey. As Murchison sat down, a gentleman in the body of the hall called for three hearty cheers for Mary Livingstone who was accompanying her husband on this expedition. Miss Coutts, who had befriended Mary

David Livingstone with his wife and children, 1857.

in her exile, knew that she was desperate to go back to Africa. Difficult though life was, trudging in the footsteps of a man who had always beat his way 'beyond other men's lines' the alternative was worse. Better Africa with him than England without. As it turned out, she was constantly seasick on the voyage out and discovered she was again pregnant. She was left at the Cape with her parents, eventually returning to England to wait for more weary years.

Livingstone sailed on to the mouth of the Zambesi. He wrote to Miss Coutts,

> as an illustration of the value of your prizes for Common Things, fancy my bungling attempts to convert a pair of my wife's sheets into he-apparel and not having been taught the 'common thing' that one leg is not like the other, I cut *two left legs* instead of a right and a left one. I never knew til [*sic*] then that there was any difference but got out of the scrape by cutting two right legs – the sheets fortunately allowing it.[5]

To no one else did Livingstone write so frivolously.

In Livingstone's early letters to Miss Coutts from the delta of the Zambesi, all the frustrations that destroyed the expedition were apparent. Captain Bedingfield was dismissed – he had found it difficult to share command with Livingstone. The steam launch *Ma Robert*, named in the African way after Mary, was proving totally inadequate – 'the asthmatic', they called it, and they needed to cut a ton of wood daily to keep it moving. And the expedition had to travel during a war raging between the Portuguese and the natives. In his great trek across Africa, Livingstone had followed the Zambesi almost its whole length except for the crucial stretch above Tete, where lay the unnavigable cataracts of Kebora Basa.

He wrote on 20 December 1858 on his return to Tete, after a desperate, almost manic, attempt to prove that the cataracts could be defeated, 'the river is confined by mountains to a narrow bed . . . the walls of this groove rose many feet above our mast head'. They could neither sail the steamer through the rapids nor haul her since 'she is only one sixteenth of an inch thick'. But he would not admit defeat. He convinced himself that 'when the river is full . . . no cataract will then appear'. All they needed, he wrote, was 'a powerful steamer to steam the current when the groove is filled'. The invitation was unmistakable. If the Government refused to buy him a steamer he would buy it himself but 'if you can say a word to any of your Government friends it may do all we need. If not, Government or no Government I shall get the steamer. This is the way into Africa.'[6]

Miss Coutts's Government friends might be forgiven for being sceptical about what they called the impossibility of forcing steamers up cataracts but Livingstone wanted a steamer. She had already been generous, founding at the Cape a college for the sons of African chiefs. Her gifts had been welcomed but when he lost the 'precious little drinking cup' in a deep, 'very rapid and alligatory' river he was sorry 'for the kind donor's sake' but he did not want another. 'I don't deal in hints. All I want at present is your good word for a vessel of sufficient power and nothing else.'[7] Livingstone's letters succeeded in persuading Miss Coutts, and through her, the Universities' Mission, that, though there were great difficulties with a powerful boat, the Zambesi could still be made the highway to Mission stations and that in the fertile and temperate highlands missionaries could lead useful and healthy lives.

Whether or not Miss Coutts used her influence to persuade the Government to send out the second boat, she was certainly responsible for sending Bishop Mackenzie with it. In July 1859 Livingstone was delighted to learn from her letter that she had 'been honoured to send the Gospel simultaneously with the formation of a new English colony'.[8]

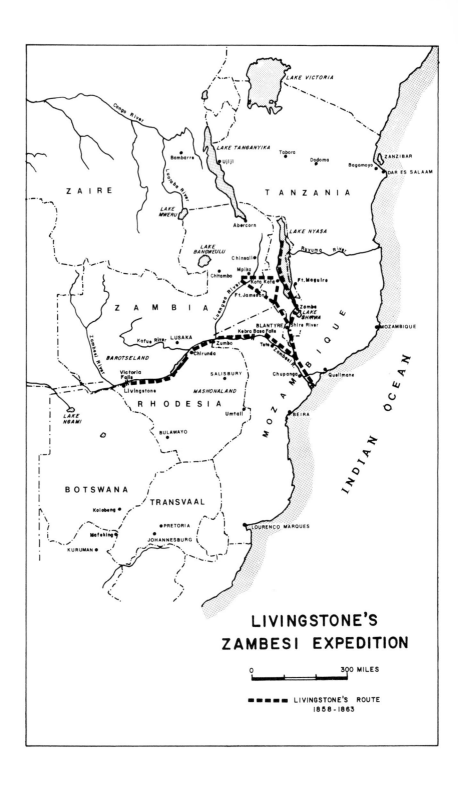

LAKE VICTORIA

Congo River

ZAIRE

Lualaba River

LAKE MWERU

Bombarre

Ujiji

LAKE TANGANYIKA

Tabora

Dodoma

TANZANIA

Bagamoyo

ZANZIBAR

DAR ES SALAAM

Abercorn

LAKE BANGWEULU

LAKE NYASA

Chinsali

Mpika

Ruvuma River

Chitambo

Kota Kota

Ft. Maguire

ZAMBIA

Luangwa River

Ft. Jameson

Zomba LAKE SHIRWA

Kafue River

LUSAKA

BLANTYRE Shire River

MOZAMBIQUE

Kebra Basa Falls

Zumbo

Tete Zambesi R.

Zambesi River

BAROTSELAND

Chirunda

Chupanga

Quelimane

Victoria Falls

Livingstone

SALISBURY

MASHONALAND

MOZAMBIQUE

LAKE NGAMI

RHODESIA

Umtali

BEIRA

INDIAN OCEAN

BULAWAYO

BOTSWANA

TRANSVAAL

Kolobeng

Mafeking

PRETORIA

JOHANNESBURG

LOURENÇO MARQUES

KURUMAN

LIVINGSTONE'S ZAMBESI EXPEDITION

0   300 MILES

▬ ▬ ▬ ▬ LIVINGSTONE'S ROUTE
1858-1863

In a letter of 8 May 1859 he convinced Miss Coutts that he had found the ideal spot for a new mission. 'We have had the honour of discovering a magnificent lake called Shirwa,' he wrote triumphantly, 'and this is the first letter I have written about it. . . . It is surrounded by lofty mountains some 6,000 feet high very grand to behold and is itself 2,000 feet above the level of the sea – there is a mountain in it which is inhabited there is no outlet known, the water is slightly bitter.' Even more exciting was the discovery that only a few miles separated Lake Shirwa from Lake Nyasa. He drew for her the tadpole shape of Lake Shirwa, and added with unusual frivolity 'what a horrid man that is writing about leeches and tadpole'.

Livingstone had in fact, though he did not admit it even to himself, almost given up hope of the Zambesi and was now pinning his faith on the Shire – a tributary of the Zambesi. This should be the new highway. 'We were 22 days on foot – slept only two nights in huts. The elevation made it feel cold but though our beds were always wet with the dew in the morning and the long grass – 8 feet high which hangs over the narrow footpaths – wet us daily we returned in good health – the country is full of people and cotton is cultivated largely – I intend writing to the Church Society to occupy this field.'⁹ Much of this letter to Miss Coutts was dangerous over-optimism, but at least Livingstone is cleared of one charge. He did not underestimate the effects of fever. He was particularly anxious that she should pass on to the Bishop of Oxford a paper he and his companion on the expedition, Dr Kirk, had written on cures for fever.

Thus encouraged, Miss Coutts went ahead. Not only was Bishop Mackenzie to come out with a party of missionaries, his elderly sister was later to join him. This decision is less incomprehensible in the light of the optimism of these letters. Neither Miss Coutts nor the rest of the organizers of the Universities' Mission understood, nor had Livingstone told them of, the desperate problems that would face the missionaries in Africa.

In 1861 the Bishop arrived with his party, bringing with them a portable iron house, and a steamer in sections to be assembled on Lake Nyasa. He was strong, intelligent and anxious to begin work. When they finally steamed up the Shire to Magomero where Livingstone decided to settle them, they found themselves involved against their will in a tribal war, were attacked by slave traders and almost destroyed by famine. The Bishop and a young missionary Burrup died of fever while waiting for Livingstone to return from the coast with Mackenzie's sister and Burrup's young wife.

Back in England, Mary Livingstone had once more enjoyed the benefits of Miss Coutts's kindness. The partners at the Bank had assured her that all her financial needs would be met. They were astonished to discover that Mary was in debt. The truth was that in these miserable years she was finding solace in drink. When she heard that her husband's stay in Africa was to be extended for another three years she wrote desperately to Miss Coutts that she was 'very much inclined to rebel against the higher powers. I should like to ask them what they mean.'[10] But it had been a sentence in Mary's letter to her husband that had persuaded him! 'Even Miss Coutts agrees with me that you are wrong to leave me so long, and so does Mrs Brown.'[11] So, urged by Miss Coutts, Dr Livingstone allowed his wife to come out to join him. The happiness of the reunion, however, was short-lived. Mary Livingstone caught fever. She died in her husband's arms and was buried at Shupanaga on the banks of the Zambesi under a great baobab tree.

After these tragedies nothing prospered, and on 2 February 1864 Lord John Russell recalled the mission. In July 1864, Livingstone was back in England after an extraordinary voyage, 2,000 miles across the Indian Ocean in the little steamer, the *Lady Nyassa*. This time there was no triumphal reception and *The Times* was scathing. 'We were promised cotton, sugar, indigo, and we got none. We were promised trade and there is no trade. We were promised converts and not one has been made. In a word the thousands subscribed by the Universities and contributed by the Government have been productive only of the most fatal results.' In fact the Zambesi expedition was not a total failure. Livingstone had aroused fierce determination to get rid of the slave trade, and had established the existence of healthy, fertile highlands in the heart of Africa.

Miss Coutts did not easily forget her part in the Zambesi tragedy. Had she been partly responsible for sending the excellent Bishop Mackenzie to his death? Had she not intervened, would Mary Livingstone be still alive and in England? Gazing across the sea from her window in Torquay, remembering the last time the Bishop had sat there with her and the gay confidence with which he set out, these were questions which would destroy her peace of mind for many months.

If she was disillusioned, it was not for long. She backed H. M. Stanley in his search for Livingstone. On his return, Stanley was welcomed in Stratton Street, and became her friend for life.

She heard of Livingstone's death while on a visit to Edinburgh. When his remains, brought back by his loyal African servants, were buried in Westminster Abbey, the bier was covered with her flowers.

Livingstone was the most famous of the missionaries who received her financial support and encouragement, but there were many others. Her interest in missionary work was not new. As early as 1841 she had been so impressed by reports from the Lambeth Conference on the Church in the Colonies that she had offered her help. In 1847 she had established episcopal sees in Cape Town, South Africa, and Adelaide, South Australia, and ten years later she had founded the bishopric of British Columbia in Canada. Much was achieved, but one of the greatest disappointments of her life was that these bishoprics were gradually removed from the control of the Mother Church. It was a change that Miss Coutts fiercely and doggedly opposed for many years.

The argument that raged around the colonial churches was intensified in 1863 by the dismissal of John Colenso, Bishop of Natal, by his immediate superior, the Bishop of Cape Town. Colenso, a brilliant mathematician, had found it difficult to reconcile his scholarship with his religion. His controversial articles doubting the accuracy of the Old Testament caused the South African bishops to depose him. He appealed to the Privy Council. Although they confirmed his position as Bishop of Natal, they also established beyond doubt that the Church of South Africa had no power or right under English Church Law.

Miss Coutts was not so much concerned with the theological arguments; but what angered her was the part of the judgement that ruled that colonial churches were not part of the Mother Church. She had provided funds on the firm understanding that the Church of England overseas was under the jurisdiction of the Archbishop of Canterbury.

She appealed against the judgement, threatening to withdraw her endowment. And she approached Gladstone, who was not only particularly close to her at this time but was also the Chairman of the Colonial Bishopric Fund. He warned that 'the restoration of the supremacy of the Crown was practically impossible'. She would, he advised, have to choose between claiming back her endowment or allowing it to remain covered by sanctions and guarantees. 'For', he wrote, 'progress cannot be arrested. There must be more or less unmooring of the Colonial Churches from the old ground of the Establishment.'[12]

She reluctantly followed Gladstone's advice and let the matter rest, but she never forgot. When, in 1888, she made her will she inserted a clause insisting that her endowments had been made to 'the Protestant Church of England now by law established under the supremacy of the Crown being Protestant'. Should the Church of England ever be disestablished, she declared, such endowments should revert to her heir.

She had much in common with Gladstone, but in this case as in others their different temperaments impelled them in different directions. Throughout the long years of their friendship Gladstone was always reluctant to become involved in the affairs of other countries. Miss Coutts, on the other hand, by nature possessive, was always anxious to increase Britain's stake in the world overseas and was always unwilling to see her influence diminished.

In the 1860s Miss Coutts's influence reached out beyond Africa to the kingdom of Sarawak. In December 1857 Sir James Brooke, the White Rajah of Sarawak, returned to England after a sensational escape from death. The news of the revolt of the Chinese in his kingdom of Sarawak, his spectacular swim to safety from his blazing house and his subsequent firm and successful handling of the revolt had filled the newspapers.

Miss Coutts wrote to congratulate him and welcome him on his return. Their friendship, begun ten years earlier, was renewed. For the next decade Sir James Brooke played Wellington's rôle of friend, confidant and hero. Miss Coutts, for her part, was his 'guardian angel', his banker and his unfailing support. Brooke was still extremely handsome, with a remarkable and charismatic personality. Miss Coutts was mesmerized by his dash and glamour and his simplicity and gentleness. He was a man who could lead a charge into battle and tenderly pick and send her the first primula, who could subdue the pirates in the China Seas, make friends of the head-hunting Dyaks and yet write with such simplicity of his tame birds and spring flowers, who could reduce rebel tribes to awestruck admiration by his superb horsemanship yet was happy to trot by her quiet pony carriage through the Devon lanes.

Sir James had left Sarawak in the charge of his nephew, Captain Brooke-Brooke. Exhausted by the adventures of the last years and weakened by the first of a succession of strokes that were eventually to kill him, he was looking for a lonely cottage where he could retire and lead the simple life he loved. He always avoided 'society' but found in Miss Coutts and Mrs Brown sympathetic and intelligent friends who shared his love of informality and quiet. In 1859 he found a house, Burrator, between Plymouth and Tavistock, about twenty-five miles from Torquay. His 'little box' was 'snugly situated under Dartmoor – a stream babbles close at hand – wood is plenty and in all boasts 72 acres of land. I might have searched for ten years without meeting a place within my limits so retired, so near the world and so suited in all respects to my tastes.'

He wrote about a thousand letters to the 'ladies' in the years between

156

1857 and 1868 and many of them were addressed to Mrs Brown. If we are to believe the evidence of Mrs Twining, wife of the Vicar of St Stephen's, Rajah Brooke was in love with Mrs Brown and would like to have married her. Certainly his letters to her show a particular warmth and ease. He called Miss Coutts 'Missus' but his affection was tinged with awe. He put up with Mrs Brown's riddles with affectionate tolerance, and it was to her as much as to Miss Coutts that flowers and verses were sent.

This was not merely a sentimental relationship between two maiden ladies and a retired Empire-builder. The Rajah had not completely retired from Sarawak, he still kept a watchful and perhaps jealous eye on the nephew to whom, as prospective heir, he had entrusted his kingdom. He had three great problems. The first was the economy of his little country; the second was the succession to the throne; and the third, Sarawak's external stability. Miss Coutts, fired by the romance of this Far-Eastern adventure, immediately and generously helped him to solve his first problem. She lent him £5,000 interest free, and strengthened Sarawak's defence system by buying him a steamer, which she and Mrs Brown named the *Rainbow*, and which could serve both as gunboat and transport vessel.

The real stability of Sarawak, however, could not so easily be bought and it was for this that Miss Coutts worked for the next few years. A small territory bordered by rival states, surrounded by the China Seas infested with pirates and riddled with internecine feuds, could only be in the long run secured with the help of a foreign power. It was Miss Coutts's task to persuade the British Government that it was in its interests to keep Sarawak in English hands. The trouble was that Rajah Brooke and his nephew were never quite sure exactly what form this relationship should take, and successive British Governments were exceedingly reluctant to take on a small and remote kingdom that would probably be more trouble than it was worth. Miss Coutts used all the influence she could command to persuade the Government to change its mind. She persistently pleaded with Lord Granville, with her friends at Court and through them, the Queen, but nothing seemed to move her friend Gladstone. He was determined, 'both on imperial and financial grounds' to avoid overseas commitments.

The succession problem also proved difficult to solve. Rajah Brooke had no legitimate heir. There was a mysterious natural son, George, who was acknowledged later in life by Brooke as his son and remembered as such in his will but he was never considered as a possible successor. That left the two sons of his sister Mrs Johnson, Captain Brooke-Brooke and

Charles Johnson. In their different ways both seem to have been competent and adequate young men, but lacked their uncle's personality. Both were brave, and capable of dealing firmly with any military situation and both inherited from their uncle a love and respect for the people they governed. Miss Coutts, however, seems to have taken a dislike to both of them from the beginning. Captain Brooke she had never trusted and Charles she found cold and even hostile. It is not surprising that the nephews regarded her in turn with some suspicion.

Trouble began in 1860 when Captain Brooke suddenly shattered his uncle's rural calm by sending a hostile report from Sarawak, objecting to the Rajah's attempt to secure the protection of France. Despairing of a dilatory British Government Miss Coutts had turned to Louis Napoleon. The quarrel which ensued was complicated and it is probable that it might have been solved if Miss Coutts had been a little more conciliatory.

158

As it was, it resulted in the Rajah tearing himself away from his moorland quiet and rushing off to Sarawak to depose his disobedient nephew and to place his brother Charles Johnson in charge.

He sailed into Sarawak in style on board the *Rainbow*. He had no difficulty in restoring his authority, and he was greeted by a tumultuous welcome. Captain Brooke was banished for three years and the Rajah settled back into his old bungalow. He sent long letters to the ladies at Ehrenberg Hall, enclosing flowers and verses and riddles for Mrs Brown and long reports on the state of his kingdom for Miss Coutts. But his health was poor, he longed for the quiet of Devon and, leaving Singapore on 8 October with Spencer St John[13], he reached England on 20 November 1861.

But Captain Brooke continued to make trouble for him and threatened to take legal action. In December 1862 the Rajah decided to return for the last time to Sarawak and borrowed £500 from Miss Coutts for his fare. He was afraid that Captain Brooke would attempt a coup and was determined to reassert his authority. But, realizing the perils of his journey and that he was no longer young (he was now sixty), before he left England he made a new will. This time he left Sarawak to Miss Coutts.

On 12 January 1863, John Abel-Smith, the MP who was Miss Coutts's friend and agent in her Sarawak affairs, informed Lord Russell of the Rajah's new will, declaring that Miss Coutts accepted the trust 'for and on account of the Government of Great Britain'. Her fitness to be Queen of Sarawak, wrote Abel-Smith, was 'strengthened by the fact that she is the principal creditor of the state of Sarawak. . . .' But Miss Coutts made it quite clear that she would not allow her personal claims 'to be an impediment to the conclusion of an arrangement advantageous to Sarawak either with Great Britain or with any other European nation'.[14] The last proviso was important. If Britain would not take responsibility for Sarawak, Miss Coutts and the Rajah were ready to negotiate with other countries rather than let Sarawak sink back into tribal warfare.

The Rajah left for Sarawak with an easy heart. 'My advice', he wrote from Marseilles, 'is in case of my death to offer it for one month to the British and failing a settlement, place it in the hands of the Emperor of France. A middle course would disturb your peace and end badly. Ever and Ever thine. . . .' He did not stay long in Sarawak. Miss Coutts urged him to return for the sake of his health.

While the Rajah was in Sarawak his friends managed to secure its recognition as an independent state under his rule. The first British Consul was appointed on 9 January 1864. Miss Coutts had used all her influence to secure this decision; she had invited Gladstone and his family to stay. 'I make over Gladstone to your tender mercies,' the Rajah wrote to Mrs Brown, 'He may, thus inspired, look upon recognition in a light more favourable than protection.'

After his return, the Rajah attempted a reconciliation with Captain Brooke. He was feeling old and tired and wanted to live at peace with his sister. It was at this time that Miss Coutts became impatient, hurt and angry. Back in England, the Rajah appeared to neglect his 'guardian angel'. His communications to her, she complained, were made through others and the proposed reconciliation with his old enemies made nonsense of the whole campaign. So for some months Miss Coutts was chilly and formal in her letters to him. She was understandably hurt; if the row with the nephews had been a storm in a teacup, in that case her campaign involving Cabinet Ministers, the Queen, the French Emperor and foreign powers made her look a little foolish. If he was now prepared to let Sarawak continue under his nephew's rule, what had all the fuss been about? Gently but firmly she withdrew herself from Sarawak affairs. She would keep up her missionary and philanthropic work but she made it clear that after the Rajah's death she could not take on the responsibility of the kingdom. The Rajah then made Charles Johnson his official heir and as Charles Brooke he now took charge.

Although by September 1866 she had given up most of her interests in Sarawak she still arranged for the purchase of a new steamer to replace the *Rainbow*, 'but I think', she wrote, 'we both feel this must be my last effort – with the exception of a little money I have invested in a farm there, my relations with this country in whose history I have been so much interested have now closed. It would not be fair in me to go on like a will-of-the-wisp deluding the Rajah with an idea of advancing the interests of his poor people and deluding myself with the idea I am fostering English interests, while in fact I may be gathering a harvest for the stranger.'[15]

There were many differences during the last years of the Rajah's life and often he felt a touch of Miss Coutts's 'Arctic manners'. But when in December 1866 he had a stroke, Miss Coutts and Mrs Brown rushed down from London on Christmas Eve to be at his bedside. Though he recovered, in his last months he was ill and difficult. His last letter to Miss Coutts, on 20 May 1868, wearily ended, 'I say farewell with kind regards to Mrs Brown and yourself until better inclined to write.' On 11 June 1868 the Rajah died. The funeral was quite private – this time 'the ladies' had not rushed to his deathbed. Miss Coutts tried, in vain, to get a memorial tablet erected in Westminster Abbey. The White Rajah had left his small kingdom more stable, more peaceful and more prosperous than he had found it. That was his – and her – memorial. 'Sarawak was struggling and well nigh ruined,' he had written in 1861, 'you gave me life by giving me hope and your help enabled Sarawak to struggle through difficulties that well nigh overwhelmed her . . . would the people could know and acknowledge what they owe you. . . .'

CHAPTER SEVEN

Home Affairs

1867-70

ALTHOUGH UNTIL the end of her life Miss Coutts kept her interest in the world overseas, she never allowed it to divert her from her main concern – the welfare of the poor at home, to which she gave by far the greatest proportion of her financial aid. Dickens's influence proved lasting.

Edinburgh, Liverpool, Manchester, Carlisle and Newcastle all received large sums of money at different times and for different purposes, but it was London, and especially the East End, to which she devoted most of her benevolence. It is impossible to calculate the exact amount she gave. Sometimes she donated large sums in cash, which her trusted steward, Weeden, delivered by hand. Sometimes she conducted her business through her lawyer W. J. Farrer. By 1866 her chief aide Wills was receiving an annual spending budget of £8,000. She used him as her eyes and ears. But also he quietly strolled through the East End picking up ballads on the death of the Prince Consort. Miss Coutts sent his report to the Queen. In the 1860s and 1870s her funds were mostly distributed by trusted almoners and paid out through special accounts in their names. Often she employed in this capacity clergymen friends; Archdeacon Sinclair of Kensington, or Prebendary Barnes of Exeter. Gentle Julian Young, the clergyman son of her old friend Charles Mayne Young, was devoted to her and wrote adoringly of her in his memoirs. In 1867 a lawyer, Mr Hassard, was brought in as an assistant and after Wills's hunting accident in 1868, he took over as her chief minister with a budget of £2,000 a year. The most gifted of her later secretaries was Charles Osborne, who was with her from 1887 to 1898.

She had other 'ministers'. Her architect Henry Darbishire was her

The gatehouse to Holly
Village, a model Gothic
village created by Angela
Burdett-Coutts in 1865.
Angela and Mrs Brown
flank the gateway.

Photo: Angelo Hornak

One of the Gothic houses
designed by Darbishire in
Holly Village.

Photo: Angelo Hornak

Drinking fountain in
Victoria Park, Hackney,
erected in 1867 to
Darbishire's design. The
enormous cost of £7,000
was borne by Angela
Burdett-Coutts.
Photo: Angelo Hornak

Minister of Works, responsible for her buildings in the East End and else-where. Some idea of the scale of her generosity can be seen from Darbi-shire's budget. In the years between 1862 and 1870, when he was in charge of the building of Columbia Square, Columbia Market and Holly Village in Highgate, at least a quarter of a million pounds passed through his hands. She paid him £7,000 for the construction of the fountain in Victoria Park. It was an East End Albert Memorial, magnificently ugly.

From 1857 onwards John Sapsford, a competent accountant, was her bursar. She established him in the abandoned Urania Cottage and was godmother to his children. Later he became a kind of Minister of Em-ployment and Social Security in the East End. His budget varied from £6,000 to £20,000 a year. In 1867, during the cholera epidemic, he organized a complete system of aid, arranging for the distribution of medicines, food and clothing, sending out health visitors and, according to the Duchess of Teck's account, in one week distributed on Miss Coutts's behalf one thousand eight hundred and fifty meat tickets of the value of a shilling each, five hundred pounds of rice, two hundred and fifty pounds of arrowroot, fifty pounds of sago, fifty pounds of tapioca and oatmeal, twenty gallons of beef tea, thirty pounds of blackcurrant jelly, eighty quarts a day of pure milk supplied from her own farms, four hundred yards of flannel, two hundred garments and a hundred blankets, twenty five gallons of brandy and fifty gallons of port wine.

The Duchess of Teck also reported that Miss Coutts regularly employed three nurses in the district and during this epidemic 'she added five more under the direction of a medical officer. She appointed two sanitary inspectors, and four distributors of the disinfectants which she supplied.' Her work for the sick was far sighted and courageous. She used her knowledge of science to help research, seeking always for the cause of the disease. She was one of the first to support cancer research and it was to her generosity that the remarkable Brompton Cancer Hospital largely owed its success. Now the Royal Marsden Hospital, it was named after the surgeon William Marsden who founded it in 1851 to treat 'poor persons afflicted with cancerous disease'. Miss Coutts gave him an interest-free loan which enabled him to build the hospital and in 1859 she laid the foundation stone and continued to give generous donations and an annual subscription of £50.[1]

She championed the costermongers in their battle for the right of street trading, sending her own solicitor to plead on their behalf and though the case at first went against her, the decision was reversed in the Court of Appeal. She had always been recognized as their friend, but from that time onwards she was the 'Queen of the Costermongers'.

Although her administrators were competent and reliable, she did not merely delegate responsibility. She never took on a project without first studying the background, and then followed the work with the greatest care. Even when abroad she was almost daily in touch with her agents. Her travelling desk was filled with their reports. In the 1860s and 1870s she frequently absented herself from the felicity of Torquay to come up to London personally to supervise the work in the East End. In 1863, for example, she was helping to organize the transfer of a hundred families from Spitalfields to their new homes in Columbia Square.

Gradually, round her new buildings, she developed social clubs for young people. But since most of them were at work from an early age she attempted to protect them at work. Flower girls and boot blacks were organized into brigades or societies and put under the protection of the police. And as always her emphasis was on training; flower girls were taught to sew and to make artificial flowers, and boys were given the chance to train for the navy on training ships.

In the East End, as elsewhere, her money was spent on providing good homes, food and health. But the most lasting charity, in her view, was that which provided vocational training, and the chance to work. Her greatest pride until the end of her life was in watching her evening classes for working boys develop into technical institutes. Westminster Technical College was to be one of her finest memorials.

But it was not all success. No one was more aware than Miss Coutts that in attempting to deal with the vast problems of poverty, she was lighting candles in a Stygian night. She knew the limitations of private charity.

Her most ambitious scheme was a monumental failure. Columbia Market, a noble idea splendidly executed, was from the start a tragic disappointment. She had begun building it in 1864, though the idea had obviously occurred to her even earlier. Her model buildings had brought to the three hundred families a 'dutch-like cleanliness and tidiness', nevertheless infection and epidemics still swept the area. She was one of the first to accept that infections were not inhaled through pestilential air, the common belief even after 1869 when Dr Snow proved otherwise, but carried through viruses in water and food. The breeding places of infection were all around, in the unhygienic food stalls and barrows, in the little streets where the pavements were 'green with refuse leaves'. In an attempt to bring order and hygiene to the haunts of costermongers, a new police regulation threatened to drive them from the streets. Miss Coutts's idea was to move street traders to a splendid covered market where hygienic conditions could be enforced and cheap and wholesome food sold fresh.

Although she attempted to understand the needs of the people of the East End, she did not entirely succeed. One of the reasons for the failure of Columbia Market was that it attempted to draw the East Enders into a pattern of life that was totally alien. No swearing was allowed and, more disastrously, no Sunday trading. Sunday was then, as now, traditionally market day in the East End. The most important factor was the determined hostility of the rival and old-established market, Billingsgate.

A further reason for failure may have been the very magnificence of the concept. The market building was described by *The Times* as 'almost a Cathedral Pile'. The great hall outdid 'Les Halles' of Paris and the Central Market of Brussels. The gates were 'masterpieces of scroll wrought iron

166

Gustav Doré's drawing of a
flower girl from *London
Pilgrimage,* 1872. Young flower
sellers in Covent Garden were
often molested, so Angela
Burdett-Coutts formed them into
brigades, under the protection of
the police.

Silver model of a watercress
seller, presented to Angela
Burdett-Coutts by the Watercress
and Flower Women of London
'as a token of their profound
respect and gratitude for the
interest and sympathy shown by
her ladyship in their welfare'
May 1879.

*By kind permission of Mrs Elizabeth Coxon.
Photo: Blinkhorns*

work, corridors roofed with carved, groined arches of polished teak. Every pillar is of polished granite and the capital of every pillar is a little carved chapter of ornament in itself . . . rich towers, belfries and pointed arches, carved deeply with appropriate texts from Scripture.' This magnificent Gothic pile was opened in April 1869 by the Prince of Wales with the most grandiose kind of ceremonial. The Duke of Cambridge attended, as did the Duke and Duchess of Teck, the Archbishop of Canterbury and the Bishop of London. But within six months the Market was closed.

Miss Coutts refused to be defeated. In February 1870 she reopened the Columbia as a fish market. But again, the machinations of the Billingsgate traders doomed the project. In 1871 she handed the market over to the City Corporation. In December 1874 the Council threw in its hand and gave Columbia back to Miss Coutts. With characteristic stubborness, she tried again. In 1879 a Columbia Meat Company was an experiment that failed. In 1881 she tried a London Fish Market and National Fishery Company, but this too went into liquidation in 1884. The next year even Miss Coutts acknowledged defeat: in 1885 Columbia Market was closed for the last time.

*   *   *

Not all Miss Coutts's money, however, was spent on charity and good works. She lived and travelled in great comfort and, though she never played 'the great lady', she did everything in style. Her clothes were simple, embroidered silks and fine old lace, but always of the finest quality. She bought them in Paris and was one of Worth's first customers. Her banquets were memorable for the rare fruits and exotic flowers provided by her glass-houses at Holly Lodge, and the table set with Sèvres china and gold plate. Her balls were brilliant but rarely lively. There were always far too many serious old men and too many bishops.

She loved to give concerts and play readings in the great drawing-room at Stratton Street but, remembering Harriot, always received the artists as friends rather than as performers. When Liszt came to luncheon in 1886 she tactfully had the piano removed lest he should feel compelled to perform. The great pianist asked to have it brought back so that he could play for her.[2]

Perhaps her greatest personal extravagance in these years was the collecting of china, pictures and rare manuscripts. She sent agents all over the Middle East in search of the latter. At the same time she loved browsing in 'old Curiosity Shops', finding quaint trifles for gifts to friends. She was a familiar figure in auction rooms; Harry Furniss drew her at an auction, sitting, head on one side, amused and interested.

Gustav Doré's engraving of Columbia Square, Bethnal Green.

The quadrangle of Columbia Square: an engraving from *The Illustrated London News.*

She had acquired many of her grandfather's great paintings, but it was Samuel Rogers who had started her on her career as a serious collector. In 1856 at the sale after his death she bought a number of paintings which were to form the nucleus of her remarkable collection. Two of her three Gainsboroughs came from the Rogers sale, as did three of her eight paintings by Sir Joshua Reynolds. From Rogers too came the Turner seascape, the Wilson landscape, *The Mill* by Claude Lorraine and Poussin's *Campagna of Rome*. But her greatest prizes from that sale were Raphael's *Agony in the Garden*[3] and Rembrandt's *Forest Scene*. Among the more famous of her later acquisitions were the portrait of William Pitt by Hoppner (which she bought in 1885), Raeburn's *Sir Walter Scott*, two paintings by Hobbema and three by Holbein including his outstanding portrait of Sir Thomas More.

It was her father who inspired her to collect Shakespeariana. She had four Shakespeare portraits, the 'Felton' which she bought in 1873, the 'Lumley' and the 'Zuccharo' which Wills bought for her in 1862. A fourth, known as the 'Burdett-Coutts' portrait, she inherited. To her Shakespeare collection she added a second First Folio; the first had been left to her by her father.[4]

Although for more than twenty years Torquay was the calm anchorage to which she returned every winter, in summer Holly Lodge was her favourite retreat. Much of her entertaining was done in the beautiful gardens. Her fêtes champêtres were as popular as Harriot's extravaganzas, though more sober. The house became shabby and rather dilapidated, but it was comfortable and welcoming and many of her famous friends came to relax there.

Holly Lodge was, as Rajah Brooke wrote, 'the spot on earth that suits you best'. Sitting in the basket chair on the sloping green lawn under the cedars, watching the fountain play among the high rhododendrons, she read the letters that came to her from all corners of the globe. Or she would walk up to her favourite herb garden on the crest of the hill and enjoy the spectacular view down across London to the Surrey hills, or wander through rose and honeysuckle walks, glades and sunny terraced gardens down to the model farm and the meadows below. Here the herd of prize Anglo-Nubian goats and champion pigs and cows were to be joined by a sleek white Egyptian donkey – the gift of costermongers – and the two llamas that Spencer St John brought her from Peru. On summer nights the nightingales sang in the shrubberies until bird-fanciers from Kentish Town smuggled them away.

Not all her guests at Holly Lodge were famous. She greeted many

170

Raphael's *The Agony in the Garden,* the pride and joy of Angela
Burdett-Coutts's art collection.

parties of East End school children there, meeting them at the West Hill
entrance gates and taking them on a tour of her pleasure grounds. In 1866
when a school party ended a glorious summer day with a strawberry feast
in the meadow, 'two hundred and sixteen pottles of strawberries were
eaten'. How like Disraeli's Adriana, whose mother feared she would
never be persuaded to 'receive' but would retire to a villa and hand round
'pottles of strawberries'.

In May 1869, six hundred and fifty of Mr Cubitt's workmen were invited to a dinner in tents in the high meadow at the edge of the pleasure
grounds, where they could look down eastwards to Bethnàl Green and the
magnificent Columbia Market they had just completed. A service of
silver was presented to the first three workmen and a Prayer Book to every
man employed. They, in turn, presented her with an illuminated Address
and, at her request, instead of silver plate, a portrait of the Market's
Management Committee.

But the most spectacular of her Holly Lodge fêtes was that which she

171

gave to two thousand six hundred Belgian Volunteers. Miss Coutts had offered her hospitality for many reasons – it was a particular favour to the Queen and to her friend Lord Granville. Also her grandfather, Coutts Bank and she herself had had long and close connections with the Belgian royal family. But most important there was, at the time, a danger that France would invade and annexe Belgium. The fêting of the Volunteers was intended to demonstrate the military resolve and the solidarity of England and Belgium. Lord Granville himself gave the address of welcome at Miss Coutts's garden party – in witty and excellent French. The Belgians were given a party they would never forget. Harriot herself could not have done better. The day is amusingly described in M. Bertram's Journal.[5] 'You would have thought', he wrote, '. . . we had delivered the Crimea, reduced Bismarck into dust, subjugated Mexico and discovered the answer to the Eastern question,' such was the enthusiastic welcome they received as they marched from Albany Barracks through Kentish Town. Crowds lined the streets, hung from the windows, climbed to the roof-tops and showered them with smiles and kisses. 'A funeral procession stopped to let us pass, only regretting they could not raise the dead in our honour.'

Through the triumphal arch with its banners 'Welcome to Highgate', up the drive they marched and for two hours filed past Miss Coutts, who stood in the midst of 'a brilliant circle on the steps of her modest villa'. She carried an immense bouquet sent that morning from Belgium. Bertram noticed her air of resigned melancholy as though, he said 'she needed consolation for the *malheur d'être riche*'. And, thought Bertram, Belgian bankers would have painted the shutters and whitewashed the walls of Holly Lodge. The banquet was held in the tents whose mirrored walls reflected the magnificent views. Bertram describes the feast in mouth-watering detail. 'Oh the beef and the lamb, the salmon and lobsters, the baskets of fruits, the creams and the jellies! . . . Six hundred waiters . . . and then the cider, the ale and the wine!'

*   *   *

Miss Coutts's farm and her animals became increasingly important to her as she grew older. In 1870 she was made President of the Ladies' Committee of the RSPCA and much of her popularity in the 1870s stemmed from her campaign against cruelty to animals. Her concern was not, as is so often the case, a substitute for care for people. It was part of the principle which always guided her, that 'life, whether in man or beast, is sacred'. As she wrote in 1871, 'All that relates to animal life affects indirectly the

The Illustrated London News for July 1867, showing the Belgian volunteers cheering Angela Burdett-Coutts as she stands on the steps of Holly Lodge.

welfare and safety of man and the close connection should never be lost sight of'; and moreover, 'inhuman treatment of animals should be held to be a wrong and a sin'. She used every means in her power to further her campaigns, persuading her friends in Government to improve the law and to make sure that the new laws were carried out. On 17 June 1872 she wrote to Gladstone to persuade him to give his support to an amendment clause in the Wildfowl Bill for a close season for all birds. Her love of animals went back to early childhood and to her father's campaigns against cruelty in all its forms. Sir Francis had been one of the sponsors of the first Act designed to make cruelty to animals illegal – the Martin Act. There were pet birds and animals in all her houses and there is scarcely a painting, photograph or sculpture of her in which her pets do not appear.[6]

Her parrots were legendary. She had inherited from Harriot a wicked old grey parrot whose raucous insults and cry of, 'What a shocking bad hat!!' amused her royal guests. When he died he was replaced by Cocky,

173

the remarkably intelligent bird sent by Rajah Brooke from the Far East. The parrot, swinging on his perch in the window in Piccadilly was, like the Queen's standard at the Palace, a sign that Miss Coutts was in residence. When Cocky and his less intelligent partner at Holly Lodge died, their places were taken in the respective windows by porcelain cockatoos, to the perpetual amusement of the passers-by.

She was devoted to her dogs, particularly to the intelligent Fan whose biography she wrote and whose death distressed her deeply. The story of Edinburgh's faithful dog, Greyfriars Bobby, inspired her to erect an imposing seven-foot drinking fountain in his honour.[7] Designed by the sculptor Brodie, it was typically elaborate but also provided much needed water for man and beast.

Sentimental though she and Mrs Brown undoubtedly were over their pets, she was also practical and aware of the importance of animals as man's working partners. The Industrial Revolution had deprived not only men but working animals of the food, water and shelter that were more easily available in the country. She brought these comforts to city animals, building stables for costermongers' donkeys near her model buildings in Columbia Square and providing drinking troughs in many cities. These latter were not merely a rich woman's whim but a practical necessity in Victorian city life.

Animals were not only, in her view, companions and workmates, they were the source of food, the gift of an all-wise providence. So all her life she encouraged the search for this natural source of food and encouraged its use. She financed fishing schools in Ireland and hired fishing smacks at Yarmouth to bring in cheap food for London's poor. She introduced sheep on to Irish islands and bred pigs and kept fine herds of cattle on her Holly Lodge model farm. At Holly Lodge, too, she kept champion goats (the most famous was oddly called after Lord Wolseley). She tried to popularize goats' milk and encouraged the poor to keep 'the poor man's cow'. She was not only President of the National Goat Society, the National Bee Keeping Association also made her its President. Honey, she insisted, was the poor man's sugar.

An engraving of the gardens at Holly Lodge shows two llamas in the foreground – this was not eccentricity. In the first half of the nineteenth century the Bradford wool manufacturer, Sir Titus Salt, had discovered that a handsome cloth – alpaca – could be made from the wool of llamas. In the 1860s Miss Coutts introduced a pair from Peru hoping to persuade them to breed at Holly Lodge. They did not, and finished their days stuffed, in glass cases.

174

One of the porcelain cockatoos that replaced Angela's live parrots. These birds were hung in the window of Stratton Street to indicate that Angela Burdett-Coutts was at home.
By kind permission of Sir Anthony Wagner. Photo: Angelo Hornak

Christmas card by Edmund Caldwell, showing the pets of Angela Burdett-Coutts.

Cocky proposes a toast. "Her Ladyship with musical honours."

Fan, Angela's favourite dog, from a *carte de visite* in her collection.
Mansell Collection

Her financial support for the RSPCA was comparatively small, but in every other way she furthered its cause. She was prompt to protest in letters to the press at any example of cruelty, and in 1869 she led the attack on conditions in the cattle trade, providing patent cattle trucks at her own cost. In Edinburgh, in 1873, she ran a successful campaign against the over-loading of horses on tram-ways. She wrote pamphlets for coster-mongers on the care of donkeys and encouraged schools to give lessons on animal welfare. Education, she believed, was most important: 'The earlier children learn to be kind and gentle the better for society . . . and in the tearing of a butterfly's wings may lurk a future monster.'[8]

Invitation to a reception for Belgian volunteers at Holly Lodge, 19 July 1867. The llamas in the foreground were brought to Angela Burdett-Coutts from Peru, as she hoped to breed them in Highgate and use the alpaca in weaving.

CHAPTER EIGHT

Public Honour – Private Stress

1868-78

FOR THIRTY years Miss Coutts had given unsparingly of her time, her energy and her money. The next ten were years of fame, of cheering crowds, civic honours and royal approval. She had earned not only the respect but also the affection of a remarkably wide range of admirers both at home and abroad. Whenever she travelled in England, the cry went up: 'God bless the Queen of the Poor!'

In December 1866, thousands of working men who had tramped through the mud of Piccadilly on their way to the great Reform demonstration cheered the slight figure at the bow window of the familiar house. Sir Francis had fought to secure the passage of the first Reform Bill in 1832. Now his daughter watched the men marching to a demonstration for wider suffrage. Their cheers echoed those earlier shouts, 'Burdett for Ever!', but in the main it was a genuine and spontaneous tribute from working people who had benefited from thirty years of her practical and kindly help. As twenty-five thousand men, arms linked together, six or eight abreast, marched in orderly ranks through mud and rain past the house at the corner of Stratton Street, even the most cynical reporters were impressed. Julian Young described the scene: 'A glimpse of a face at the window and the cry went up "Three cheers for Miss Coutts".' For two and a half hours as each rank filed by the air rang with reiterated hurrahs unanimous and heartfelt as if representing a national sentiment. Grey heads cheered Burdett's daughter, but the young men took up the cry: Miss Coutts by her own work had earned their cheers.

Five years later, it was the Queen's turn to honour her.[1] In 1871 Miss Coutts became the first woman to be made a Baroness in her own right.

The royal honour was not accepted lightly nor without some thought. Gladstone wrote in some surprise to the Queen, 'Miss Coutts took two days to consider it.' She hesitated at first, perhaps remembering how often her father had been offered similar honours and how consistently he had refused them. However, she finally accepted, probably encouraged by Mrs Brown who wrote an effusive letter of gratitude to Gladstone.

She found some difficulty in choosing her title.

> I will at once ascertain with what land I could associate my name and will lay the same before you. The *Coutts* are of the gypsy families of the lowlands of Scotland, and I suppose the wandering instincts of my tribe has prevented my attaching myself to the soil and I have only pitched a tent here and there. So you have caged the wild bird. I will do my best to give it a local habitation and a name. . . . The other place to which I could connect myself was Ancoat in which the first Burdett founded a priory. He was that excellent and wise soldier to whom I am under such infinite obligations who came from Normandy with the Conqueror.

Gladstone approved her final choice. She became Baroness Burdett-Coutts of Highgate and Brookfield. *Punch* celebrated the occasion in excruciating verse.

IN ANGELAE HONOREM

Sweet names there are that carry sweet natures in their sound;
Whose ring, like hallowed bells of old, seems to shed blessing round:
Such a name of good omen, Florence Nightingale, is thine;
And hers, our Angela's, for all in want and woe that pine.

But what can gold, or silver, or bronze, or marble, pay;
Of the unsummed debt of gratitude owed her this many a day?
What record, parchment blazoned, closed in golden casket rare;
Can with her love, in England's heart, for preciousness compare?

If we needs must find her symbol, then carve and set on high
A heavily laden camel going through the needle's eye;
Gold-burdened, by a gentle yet firm hand wisely driven——
Our Angela's, that on it rides, riches and all, to heaven.

Or if a painted record be by the occasion claimed,
Paint up Bethesda's Pool, and round, the sick, the halt the maimed,
Waiting until our Angela through Earth's afflicted go
To stir wealth's healing waters, that await her hand to flow.

Christmas and New Year card for Baroness Burdett-Coutts and
Mrs Brown, 1871–2.

London Guilds also honoured her. On 10 January 1872 the Turners
decided to offer her the Freedom of their Company and on the 10 July it
was presented. She took the responsibility seriously, wore her badge with
great pride at all subsequent civic receptions and was an active and useful
member of the Company. On 18 July 1872 the City of London, with suitable ceremony, made her their first woman Freeman. In 1873 the Clothworkers, recognizing her long connection with the textile industry made
her an Honorary Freeman, and in 1888 the Haberdashers followed suit.
No woman had better earned this honour. Thirty years earlier, she had
been among the first to encourage the teaching of needlework and handi-
crafts and technical subjects. Later in her sewing school on Brown's Lane
in the East End she founded a small but model workshop for women.
She had long supported the silk weavers of Spitalfields, helping to find
work for them and when that failed assisting in their emigration to the
colonies. In 1869 she helped 1,200 weavers from Girvan in Ayrshire to
emigrate to Australia. The people of Girvan marked their gratitude with
a memorial – but they forgot to repay the loan.

The full history of her attempts to revive the cotton trade in Lancashire
will probably never be known. But she never forgot that her grandmother

was a working girl from Lancashire and among her many schemes for bringing prosperity to that county was her encouragement of cotton growing in Africa. She sent a cotton gin to the mission of Abeokeuta on the Gold Coast. A special correspondent reported to the Duchess of Teck that since she had presented the gin 'the cotton trade which is almost entirely in the hands of the natives, has wonderfully increased. The approximate yearly export being upwards of 10,000 bales.' So the Clothworkers and Haberdashers had reason to be proud of their honorary Freeman. But it was the Turner's badge she wore when on 15 January 1874 Edinburgh followed London in making her the first woman Freeman.

It was a moving and nostalgic ceremony. In Edinburgh's flower-filled Music Hall, Mrs Brown at her side, she heard the Lord Provost speak of the familiar names among her predecessors: Dickens and Disraeli, Sir Walter Scott and her grandfather Thomas Coutts. She had discovered only that morning that he had been made a Freeman in 1813. But she was most touched that, in praising her work for the RSPCA, the Provost should have reminded the audience that it was Sir Francis who had helped to bring in the Martin's Act in 1824.

In a graceful reply, the Baroness thanked the Council. She had been, she said, the first woman to be made a Baroness in her own right, the first woman Freeman of the City of London and now the first to be enrolled in the list of Edinburgh's Burgesses. It was because this was an honour for women that she was proud to accept it. She paid a tribute, of which Harriot would have approved, to Thomas Coutts. 'From my grandfather I derived that position which has placed me under such gracious and kindly notice today and has placed in my hands the ample means which alone have enabled me to further those public objects to which you have referred so kindly.'[2]

Her simplicity and eloquence touched her Scottish audience, and she herself was deeply moved. At last she had found her roots.

*   *   *

The 1870s were certainly triumphant. Upright, spare, she received her honours with grace and calm composure. On royal occasions her curtsey was unmatched – Harriot and the French Court between them had long ago given the lanky girl an eighteenth-century style. No longer nervously shunning the limelight, she had become an eloquent public speaker. Her voice, like her father's, was clear and silvery, her manner direct, simple

Angela Burdett-Coutts and Mrs Brown in Edinburgh: a painting by
Drummond, showing them at their hotel window, overlooking
Princes Street

and unaffected. She appeared to speak spontaneously but Osborne, one of
her secretaries, remembered the careful preparation and how she shut
herself away in her boudoir beforehand.[3] Long ago Dickens had written
of her gift of 'seeing clearly with kind eyes'. Now she was becoming increasingly autocratic though the kindness was always there. Her deepest
eyes were lively and humorous but in repose her face was lined and in-
expressibly sad. This was her natural expression and, even when she was
young, painters and photographers had caught this melancholy.

Certainly her wealth brought worry in this decade but it was also a time
of loss. One by one, heroes and devoted friends fell away. Rajah Brooke
died in 1868; old Mr Marjoribanks in 1869. Dickens died in 1870 and so
did Sir Edmund Antrobus, nephew of her grandfather's trusted friend,
who had been a partner in the bank since 1816. In 1873 came the death
of Louis Napoleon.[4] When, in 1877, kindly old Mr Coulthurst died, it
was the end of a chapter. He more than the other partners had understood
her philanthropy, and had himself built a church, St Matthew's, in Sur-
biton. Now only her cousin Lord Harrowby and Mrs Brown were left

to give her the frank advice of long friendship. And Mrs Brown was approaching eighty, failing in sight and health.

In 1877 there was trouble at the bank and the responsibility fell heavily on the Baroness. The Coutts family half-share in the bank was clearly allocated. Her elder sister, Clara Money, would succeed her should she die first, and Clara's son, Frank, was next in line. Frank was a worry. Now aged twenty-five, he had, Angela thought, surrounded himself with people of a 'flashy mercantile kind'. He could, under the terms of the partnership agreement, bring in partners of his choice, and they might be unworthy. Her strong sense of duty to the bank, her desire to keep Frank under her control made her unfair to him. Old Mr Marjoribanks had always urged his sons to keep an eye on Frank Money. Understandably, Frank resented the watching eyes of aunt and bankers.

But the real difficulty came from her own relations with the Marjoribanks family. The seeds of the trouble were planted long before. Old Mr Edward was, after Thomas Coutts, the most influential of the partners and he was anxious through his sons to keep that influence strong. In 1836 Edward, the elder, was working his apprenticeship in the bank and Dudley Coutts, godson of Thomas, was a bright boy of sixteen. Harriot, at this time preparing her will, was anxious to be fair to the Marjoribanks family. She had been impressed by the intelligent and vigorous Dudley, and now she sent for Edward to spend his summer holidays at Southampton with her. But Edward clearly failed her test. It was the second son, Dudley, who was chosen to succeed to the Coutts family half-share should the Burdett girls die childless. So Dudley had from boyhood expected at least a career as a partner in the bank and at best had hoped he might succeed to Thomas Coutts's fortune. In 1843, when Edward married, his father tried to persuade the other partners to allow Dudley to join Edward as a joint partner. But Miss Coutts and the trustees refused. Her lawyer Parkinson had known that Thomas Coutts had been determined to keep the 'supremacy' in the Coutts family. If the Marjoribanks family became over-represented it would set a dangerous precedent. Dudley felt he had been thwarted and, seething under the injustice, from time to time exploded in fury. But it was a family feud, for the Marjoribanks and the Coutts were distantly related.

In 1843 it seemed likely that the Burdett daughters would remain childless. No one then could have foreseen that Clara, in middle age, would marry and in 1852 bear a son. It was possible that Dudley could himself succeed. But in refusing Dudley's application Miss Coutts gave the reason that Dudley was not suitable for 'he had not been trained in business

Photograph from Angela Burdett-Coutts's album of the Mediterranean cruise, taken aboard the steam yacht *Walrus* in 1879. The drawings and paintings that surround the photograph could well have been executed by the Baroness.

habits'. It was a tactless phrase that rankled for the rest of Dudley's life.[5]

When in 1865 Miss Coutts brought in her cousin Henry Ryder as a partner, Dudley wrote sarcastically of his non-existent 'business habits'. Miss Coutts was justified in taking part in the selection although by the terms of the will she was not permitted to interfere with the running of the bank. Thomas Coutts had made it clear that those who succeeded him should have the chief voice in the selection of partners. In this and subsequent troubles she was persuaded that she was acting from a high sense of duty to her grandfather's memory. By 1868 Dudley had almost accepted the inevitability of his own exclusion, but wanted to secure for his sons a promise of a future partnership. In this year his father was dying and the old man wanted to have Miss Coutts's promise, if possible in writing, that his grandsons would become partners. Dudley rushed up to Harrogate where Miss Coutts and Mrs Brown were staying with the express purpose of securing a letter of promise to show his dying father. But although she received Dudley kindly and wrote an affectionate letter to the old man there was not a word of promise for Dudley's sons' future. Dudley chose to regard it as an insult and wrote her an explosive reply.

His father died before his return. Dudley assured Miss Coutts that he had destroyed her wicked letter and would never hold it against her, but the letter remains among his papers with the pencilled word 'destroyed' in the corner.

It is easy to understand both sides. Dudley, the godson of Thomas Coutts, chosen by Harriot, not only was barred himself from the bank but so were his sons. Miss Coutts acting, as she believed, in the interests of the bank and the family must have taken Dudley's flying visit as moral blackmail. But there was more than this. In 1843 it had been a conference of partners and trustees at Stratton Street that had considered Dudley unsuitable. Perhaps the hot-tempered outbursts that flashed through his letters had given additional reasons for his exclusion. Quiet courtesy was the rule at Coutts Bank.

But there was more trouble to come when the old man's will was read. His considerable fortune went not to the elder son Edward but to Dudley. Mr Marjoribanks had for some time been aware of the justice of Dudley's complaints. Edward, as Dudley had written to him bitterly, had inherited the partnership, had married a wife with a fortune and as elder son stood to inherit the family fortune. Wishing to redress the balance, their father had decided that Dudley should be compensated by having the bulk of the fortune. This time it was Miss Coutts who was furious, both on behalf of her wronged 'excellent friend Edward', but also because, by unexpectedly removing his fortune she believed that his father had endangered the interests of the bank. Mr Marjoribanks had disappointed Edward and let the bank down. Therefore, she wrote coldly, she felt she could not accept the legacy of £2,000 that Mr Marjoribanks had left her. She would, however, take it if it could be transferred to Edward's account. Dudley's sisters wrote to each other, their letters sizzling with anger against 'Couttsy'. Their fury bears all the signs of a long-suppressed jealousy. Their father, they wrote, had given her thirty years of devoted service, had worshipped her and now she had dishonoured his memory. They were even more furious when, calling at Stratton Street hoping to discuss their father's will, they found Miss Coutts courteous but blandly determined to avoid the subject. This again was typical. She never fudged an argument. She either discussed it or totally ignored it. Dudley and his sisters remained furious, Edward basked in her approval.

But the story did not end there. Hardly had the dust settled than a new storm broke. In July 1877 the Baroness became uneasy about the reserve fund at the bank. With the deaths of Marjoribanks, Antrobus and Coulthurst, their several fortunes had been withdrawn to pay their legacies. Therefore the reserve fund had been distributed and reduced, she wrote, 'to the original £200,000 share capital'. Following a suggestion Marjoribanks had made before his death, she proposed that she should contribute the £76,000 just paid to her as her share of the distributed reserve fund and that the other partners should do the same pro rata. Mr Edward Marjoribanks Junior replied, tactfully pointing out that this was an internal matter and that they were in fact about to do as she suggested. But he could not have been comfortable at the prospect, for in February 1877 the gossip had already been heard in the City that his own financial position was shaky, that he had been speculating in Russian shares.

The Baroness heard the rumours and attempted to elicit the truth. Her solicitor questioned Edward, who retired to his sick-bed and sent furious missives through his wife. What right had she, to ask about his business? Should they not just as well ask her about Columbia Market?[6] A shrewd thrust! But the Baroness's suspicions were justified. Mr Edward was in deep trouble. He had, he confessed, involved himself in larger building operations than he could afford but it took some time for her to discover that in fact his debts were almost half a million. He had borrowed from the partners at the bank and from the Bank of Scotland. The Baroness was generous but firm, she paid his debts to the partners but would do no more. His family must pay the rest. The situation strained Dudley's generosity. He wrote fierce letters to the Baroness, attempting to bully her into taking over all his brother's debts. But she dug her heels in and the only concession, and that reluctantly made, was that the bank should make an allowance to Edward's wife in the event of his death.

There was a swift and skilful operation to save the reputation of the bank. In September the partnership was quietly dissolved and reconstituted without Mr Edward. A diplomatic paragraph in *The Times* smoothed the ruffled surface, 'Mr D. C. Marjoribanks has done a noble thing, he has paid off his brother's debts. The Baroness was anxious to have done it for him but he nobly refused, saying it was for the family to make restitution.'

Edward's son, George, was brought in as a partner in his father's place but neither Dudley nor his sons ever came into the inheritance they so dearly wanted. After this disturbance the team needed strengthening. Two partners were brought in from outside, Robert Pym from the Bank of England and William Rolle Malcolm from the Colonial Office. Though the Baroness, Dudley and his sisters remained, as he said, 'at scissors' she kept a friendly and affectionate relationship with the rest of the partners. Lord Archibald Campbell, Lindsay Antrobus and her cousin Henry Ryder were all her protégés, as were George Robinson, the senior clerk who became a partner in 1869, and Mr Malcolm.

*   *   *

The years 1877 and 1878 brought the most exotic honour of them all. Abdul Hamid, Sultan of Turkey offered the Baroness the First Class and Star of the Order of the Medjidiyeh; no other woman except Queen Victoria and Lady Layard had been so honoured. It was a reward for her remarkably successful campaign for Turkish relief during the Russo-Turkish War of 1877.

Her passionate support for the Turks, at a time when Gladstone was shipping up a frenzy of hatred against them following the brutal massacres in Bulgaria, needs some explanation. Turkey and the Orient had fascinated her since childhood. Long ago as a little girl of seven she had been taken to see *Il Turco in Italia* with her mother. After the performance they had met 'il Turco' himself in full regalia in the theatre corridor.[7] Later Sir James Morier had stirred her imagination with the story of his life in Turkey and Persia. She was also prepared to dislike the Russians, not only for their part in the Crimean War, but for their earlier ill treatment of the Poles. Her cousin Dudley Coutts Stuart had given his life in the service of the Polish refugees.[8] Lastly, if brutality was reprehensible in the Mohammedan Turk, it was doubly so when practised by the Christian Russians. She had other reasons for supporting the Turks. In 1877, the new British Ambassador in Constantinople was none other than her old friend and turcophile, Sir Henry Layard. On the day Layard presented his credentials to the Sultan, Russia declared war on Turkey. The advance of the Russian army provided the Bulgarians with an opportunity of revenging themselves on the Turks.

Layard's harrowing account of the ensuing massacres prompted the Baroness to undertake the organization of the Turkish Compassionate Fund. *The Daily Telegraph*, whose correspondent was passionately pro-Turk, was her ally and in August 1877 the *Telegraph* published a letter from her. As a result, the Fund grew in days from her initial £1,000 to £30,000. The Baroness commissioned a yacht, the *Constance*, and stocked it with flannel, quinine, stocking and socks, cottons, rugs and medicines. By October the relief stores were being unloaded in Constantinople.

She appointed as Commissioner to the Fund a young friend, William

Ashmead Bartlett, giving him the job of organizing the unloading and distribution of the stores. She first met Bartlett when he was a schoolboy in Torquay. His mother, a widow, had returned from America with two young sons and was living nearby. Miss Coutts had felt sorry for Mrs Bartlett and had paid for Ashmead's education first in Torquay and later at Highgate School in London, and had supported him during his days at Oxford. His bright face, ready tongue and eloquence had deeply attracted her and he came to be called her godson: even today, descendants of her household remember him as such. In September 1874, concerned that he was wasting his time at Oxford, she asked him to stay, and Mrs Brown remembered exactly for how long.

> Mr Bartlett left us for Oxford after a visit of five weeks and two days – and never once relaxed in his daily of reading – giving eight hours and a half daily – never saw him til luncheon – then not again til dinner – and whatever company there might be – he always left the drawing room before ten o'clock. I hope all this may be of some avail! But what a pity he had been so neglectful.

After Oxford he read for the Bar, at the same time being drawn into the circle of young men that made up the Baroness's secretariat. In sending him out to Turkey, the Baroness was testing his mettle.

> I hope [she wrote anxiously to the Layards] you will find him all I always have and I am sure you will find his heart in whatever you will find him to do. I am sure you will, as far as possible assist him with advice and means to avoid the dangers, and should he be ailing from change of climate and the excitement that both you and Mrs Layard will look after him. He has a mother and though he went with her consent still she is of course *very anxious* so any news you can write of him which I can repeat will be very welcome.

It was clearly not only the mother who was very anxious. The Baroness decided he should come home. 'He is reading', she wrote, 'for the Bar and should keep Term and pass an examination. I have entered into all this as I feel, as you will understand, rather responsible.'

At the beginning of April 1878, Mr Bartlett caught typhus and she was beside herself with anxiety. 'I am of course anxiously expecting the next account', she replied to Layard's telegram, 'and earnestly pray that it may confirm the favourable report of yesterday. If all in God's providence goes well with Mr Bartlett, it is clear that the time is come when he must return.' The Baroness sent Ellis Bartlett, Ashmead's elder brother, out to Constantinople to take care of him and bring him home.

Only now, when he was in danger, did she realize how much young Bartlett meant to her. 'Whenever Mr Bartlett can return', she wrote, 'it may be consoling to him and cheering that, in my opinion, his being here would be useful to the winding up of the fund, which, under your direction, has saved so many lives and rendered a much needed help to Christ on Earth.'[9] The Compassionate Fund could now be closed, she wrote to Layard – though they would still have to decide what to do with the balance.

*   *   *

Throughout the years of triumph Mrs Brown had shared the honours; but the tours, the cheering crowds, the speeches and receptions, took their toll. 'We return here tomorrow', she wrote to Henry Wagner in September 1875. 'Oh how thankful I am it is over. These great successes are charming and I am thankful, but these *publicities are trying.*'[10]

She was now approaching eighty and to the mysterious ailments from which she had suffered for the last forty years was now added the loss of sight. The sharp little governess had mellowed over the years. Rounded, lapped in furs she was the 'dear Mrs Brown' to whom an Empress and two Queens sent their affectionate greetings. For her social position was no longer uneasy; the Baroness had placed her firmly among the ladies. In Torquay especially she was accepted. The doctor's widow had her own status, and the governess was quite forgotten.

Miss Coutts and Mrs Brown had always enjoyed mothering bright young men. Two of their particular favourites were Henry and Arthur Wagner, sons of Henry Michell Wagner, the wealthy and autocratic vicar of Brighton. The Wagner family were bound to the Baroness by many ties. She had known the father when, as a young man, he had been tutor to the sons of the Duke of Wellington. His two sons attracted her from the moment she had first seen them. Henry, the gentler of the two, was devoted to her – indeed the Wagner family believed that he was more than a little in love with her.

But Mrs Brown's greatest favourite was Mr Henry Irving, the young man who was to brighten her last days. She had watched his career from the very beginning. Miss Coutts admired his genius but Mrs Brown totally lost her heart to the awkward shy man whose difficult childhood had made him particularly susceptible to older women. He was to call himself her 'shadow son' and her his 'shadow mother'. She saw his Hamlet thirty

188

Tea in the garden under the cedars at Holly Lodge: from left to right, Angela Burdett-Coutts, the Rev. Baber (chaplain at Whitelands), Mr Darbishire (architect of Columbia Square), Mrs Brown, Henry Wagner, Dr Pope-Hennessy and Prof. Tennant (the geologist).

Mansell Collection

times, and in 1877 was mesmerized by his Richard III. After the first night, the Baroness presented him with Garrick's ring with the message 'in recognition of the gratification derived from his Shakespearean representations, uniting to many characteristics of his great predecessor in histrionic art (whom he is too young to remember). The charm of original thought giving delineations of new forms of dramatic interest power, and beauty.'[11] The gift was from the Baroness but the convoluted style was Mrs Brown's.

In the spring of 1877, Mrs Brown's health and sight failed and her letters became more and more difficult to read until the Baroness became her secretary adding illegibility to illegibility. In April the Baroness sent for Critchett, the distinguished eye surgeon, and iridectomy was performed on both eyes. For a while her condition was precarious. She had caught a cold in Edinburgh and her cough made the operation dangerous. But she partially recovered and Edmund Johnson, another eye specialist, reported to Henry Wagner that she could now distinguish the colour of flowers. She was even well enough to risk the train journey back to London, where in July she underwent a second eye operation. But although, as William Sinclair wrote to Wagner in September, 'there is nothing in the condition of the eyes which would prevent the sight returning', the two operations had taxed her strength. By September she was almost completely blind. 'She comes down and moves from room to room and stays till ten or eleven at night,' Sinclair wrote to Wagner. 'But as her strength improves the sense of inactivity and imprisonment becomes more irksome. She is never free from the oppressive sense of darkness and is sometimes much depressed; at others cheerful and argumentative as usual.'[12]

There was no hope now of returning to Torquay. Walks in the Duke of Devonshire's garden next door were the most she could manage. Autumn was to prove a sad time. All their friends had left London. Neither the skill of the best doctors nor the constant care of the Baroness could save Mrs Brown. At 5.30 on the afternoon of 21 December 1878 she quietly died.

For the last two years the Baroness had been prepared for this. It was the agony of the prospect that had driven her with uncommon urgency in her Turkish relief campaign. But as Bartlett wrote later to Layard, 'it has been even a greater blow to her than those who knew the relations between them could have expected: and though the state of Mrs Brown's health for the past year must have prepared her friend in some way, it does not seem to have lightened her grief or to have relieved her of the sharpness which suddenness always adds to death.'[13] She was incapable of writing letters in the first days. Even the Queen's letter which came, as she later wrote, 'in the first hours of my grief', remained unanswered for days.

Her friends understood the depth of the Baroness's affection for Mrs Brown but even they were amazed at the profound effect on one whose self-control had been legendary. Unable to face them on 27 December, the morning of the funeral, she sent them a printed message which was read by the Reverend Reginald Barnes.

My dearest kindest Friends

I am deeply grateful for your loving kindness to *us* in being here to-day, and to all who have whether from afar or near ministered to my poor Darling in her darkness and affliction. . . . Could any wish of my dearest earthly Friend – the companion and sunshine of my life for fifty-two years – be known, it would be that you should all be here in our Home to support and comfort me, in the midst of our Household.[14]

It took all her resolution to get her through the funeral service in St Stephen's Church. Blinded by grief, she remembered little of the ceremony.

Bartlett observed the service with a new awareness. 'Lady Burdett-Coutts was in one way quite overcome', he wrote to Layard, 'and yet her great strength of character and self-control pulled her through the first part of the ordeal. The funeral was to all who had known the two together most impressive and painful, and when, having stood close behind it all the time, she knelt down and placed both hands on the coffin as it was being lowered into the grave, there could have been few in the church who did not feel deeply for her.' It is a poignant, sensitive letter and the affectionate support of its writer was desperately needed. 'With regard to Lady Burdett-Coutts herself', Bartlett added, 'she seems now to have recovered from the physical effects of the trial and I suppose she will resume her former life and throw herself with redoubled vigour into her manifold charitable schemes. . . . I saw the letters from the Queen, the Empress Eugenie and the King of the Belgians to her on the subject and those, especially Her Majesty's, were most warm and sympathetic.'[15]

Not many Victorian governesses could have been so mourned or could have found so special a place in the affections of the famous.

CHAPTER NINE

The 'Mad Marriage'

1878-93

IN THE spring of 1879 the Baroness picked up once more the threads of her charitable work. But it was duty without joy, all was dark and burdensome, she wrote, now that her 'poor Darling' was gone. Loneliness inevitably brought restlessness. For the past years she had been anchored in England by Mrs Brown's illness, travelling vicariously through her friends. Now, as in the past, she turned to the sea for solace. She asked her Devon friend Prebendary Barnes to look for a suitable ship and in the summer of 1879 she chartered a steam yacht, the *Walrus*, and set sail for the Mediterranean. Her ship-mates were Mr Edwin Long the artist and his wife, and her old friends Admiral and Mrs Gordon. Henry Irving, the actor manager to whom Mrs Brown had been so devoted, joined the ship off the Isle of Wight. So did Ashmead Bartlett.

It was as much for Henry Irving's sake as for her own health that the cruise had been planned; he needed a rest and the holiday was her recompensation for his kindness to Mrs Brown. Irving seized the chance to absorb ideas for Mediterranean settings for the productions he was planning of *Othello*, *The Corsican Brothers*, Otway's *Venice Preserved*.

The shipmates were not altogether happy. Long and Irving vied with each other competing for the Baroness's attention and both were jealous of Bartlett. For a month they sailed in calm weather, calling in at Spain, Tangiers and Tunis. Irving was considering a new interpretation of Shylock in *The Merchant of Venice*. The Baroness encouraged him. She had many Jewish friends and knew how deeply they were offended by the caricatured Jew of stage and literature. She had been most impressed by Sir Moses Montefiore, the great Jewish philanthropist, and wanted Irving to present a dignified Jew.

192

So, as they sailed into Venice, a new Shylock was haunting Irving. He would recreate those magical first moments in the tremulous grey light when the gilded domes rose out of the level sea, and the strident magnificence of the Rialto in bright morning. Against this background, Shylock would appear dignified, complex, a man of mood changing as subtly as the Venetian light.

Irving certainly found a new Shylock in Venice. Was it there that the Baroness found a late love? Certainly somewhere on the cruise Bartlett made love to her, allowing the affection of a mother for a son to change into something more. And however innocuous the love-making, as far as the Baroness was concerned it was proof of a binding and genuine love.

The yacht called at Sorrento and Corsica. Irving, his mind bursting with ideas, could not wait to get home. He was set down at Marseilles and took a fast train back to the Lyceum. Meanwhile as the yacht sailed up the coast of Spain the Baroness, radiant as a young girl, planned her future with Bartlett. He would dispel her loneliness. She could offer him luxury for life and a career. With her help he could get the nomination as Conservative member for Westminster, her father's old seat.

But by the time they reached Guernsey, Bartlett must have been having second thoughts. Here they picked up some young friends, a Miss Shirley and Miss Braddyll. 'The new ship-mates', the Baroness wrote to Irving, 'are nice girls rather of *the* period – who would be pretty if they would only leave their poor hair to grow as Nature meant. Life on board you know does not admit of much vanity.'[1]

Miss Shirley found Bartlett tantalizingly attractive especially since, as he told her, he was engaged to an unnamed other lady. Photographs taken on the cruise show the young man reclining on his Turkish rug with undeniable, sultry charm. Bartlett, it would seem, after the heat and close confinement of the long voyage, found Miss Shirley refreshing.

There were other excitements. The yacht, on entering Jersey Harbour, drove on a reef, and the Captain decided to make for the nearest port, Cherbourg. 'It was a very big sea, rougher while it lasted than the Bay,' wrote the Baroness to Irving. 'Your bed mattress outside the deck saloon and the chairs were all thrown about and Mr Bartlett, a young lady and myself nearly followed. The dinner table on deck walked about and all sorts of other casualties. . . .'

The Baroness was due at St Malo where she had promised to inspect the lifeboat she had presented to the town. So with the *Walrus* out of action they made their way there overland. It was a nostalgic journey. Once again she lived over 'the old French life quite past. . . . Even at this

Pictures from the album of the

Mansell Collection

Ashmead Bartlett and Henry Irving, plus symbols of Shylock.

Below: left to right, Ashmead Bartlett, t Baroness, Henry Ir Prof. Tennant, Adr and Mrs Gordon.

...ean cruise of the *Walrus*.

The dining room: left to right, Miss Shirley, Dr Stoker, Miss Braddyll,
Ashmead Bartlett and the Baroness.

Ashmead Bartlett in his cabin.

Henry Irving in his new interpretation of Shylock in 1879, on his return from the cruise.

Raymond Mander and Joe Mitchenson Theatre Collection

moment the horses neighing as the diligence enters the old French court-yard carried me back such years and the bells jangling, links that long ago with the bells of today in a curious unison.'[2]

On 1 November, after their return to England, Irving's production of *The Merchant of Venice* opened with Ellen Terry as Portia, Irving as a compelling Shylock, and costumes and scenery of what the critics called 'surpassing beauty'. It was an immediate and triumphant success.

The cruise had restored the Baroness's health but the homecoming was desolate. Life without Mrs Brown was unbearably lonely. Had it not been for the constant and solicitous attention of young Mr Bartlett she would

196

have found it difficult to face the future.[3] In the New Year she sent him to oversee her charities in Ireland, but she was glad to have him back. She could not bear to be without him. 'If I have struggled through', she was later to write to Lord Harrowby, 'it has been mainly if not solely through Mr Bartlett's being constantly there.'[4] But her increasing dependence on him disturbed her other friends. The Reverend Prebendary Barnes decided that he would see her no more. The Baroness sent him a formal note of regret. She may have revealed her secret plans to him, or even asked him to marry them privately. But, for whatever reason, it was to be many years before their friendship was renewed.

There was more sadness in the early summer of 1880. On 5 June her brother Robert died. Now only Susan and Clara were left and both were old and ill. Once again came the harrowing aftermath of death and family papers bringing painful memories. There were legal difficulties, a vain search for a will; there were passages of an undistinguished life which must be erased. All through the autumn she was harassed by Robert's affairs, of which she was the administrator. She and her two sisters were co-heirs and there were family posesssions to be divided.

In June she visited her old friend Wills and she found him 'sick of death'. (He was to die on 1 September.) She needed support. Stratton Street was unbearable, Holly Lodge too full of memories. She looked for a house near Hungerford and all the time dread of the lonely future preyed on her mind.

On 4 July 1880 the incredible news leaked out. Baroness Burdett-Coutts the good, the charitable, the honoured lady, was to marry. She, who could at any time in the last forty years have chosen a partner of distinction had instead selected William Ashmead Bartlett, an obscure young American, half her age.

She expected that the marriage would take place quickly and quietly. But she reckoned without her solicitors Farrer and Ouvry. On 4 July, although pledged to secrecy, they found a way to signal warnings to W. R. Malcolm and H. L. Antrobus, two partners at the bank. Henry Ryder recorded, 'On Saturday 4 July Malcolm told me he had casually met W. J. Farrer at the New Life Office who had asked him if Ouvry had said anything particular in the Strand. The Baroness had an idea in her head from which he had vainly tried to turn her and which was very foolish. His lips were sealed, he could say no more.'[5]

The partners began guessing. Was it a foolish endowment, the foundation of a colonial bishopric or some fancy charity? Henry Ryder, who knew her best, immediately guessed that it might be a marriage. Gradually they extracted the truth from Mr Arnold White, her sister Clara's solicitor. 'Come', they said, 'it is no use concealing it. Is it matrimonial, is it Ashmead Bartlett?'[6] Arnold White nodded his head, at the same time saying that the matter was most secret and must on no account be divulged. William Ashmead Bartlett? The young man who had been a kind of junior clerk in the Baroness's secretariat? Malcolm and Antrobus were incredulous. Bartlett had a certain indolent charm and his trim moustache and 'Imperial' gave him quite a look of Louis Napoleon. But in no way was he worthy of 'our lady'. The Baroness's friends at the bank moved into action. Apart from their private concern there were serious implications for the bank. Bartlett was quite clearly an unscrupulous fortune hunter, they considered.

The marriage must be prevented, and, knowing how obstinate the Baroness could be, there was only one person who could persuade her. A whisper was passed to the Queen. 'Lady Burdett really must be crazy,' Victoria exploded, 'since poor Mrs Brown's death she seems to have *lost* her balance.'[7] With her customary shrewdness Victoria had seen the cause of the trouble. However, she was unwilling to intervene directly – it was to Lord Harrowby that the letter from Windsor was sent.

> The Queen is anxious to learn from Lord Harrowby privately whether a report that has reached her as to Lady Burdett-Coutts's marriage is true, as the Queen has been told there are circumstances which make the marriage an unusual one. She trusts that Lady Burdett-Coutts has given the fullest consideration to this step before making her final decision. The Queen knows too little respecting the subject to offer an opinion on it but it would grieve her much if Lady Burdett-Coutts were to sacrifice her high reputation and her happiness by an unsuitable marriage.[8]

Lord Harrowby immediately forwarded the Queen's letter to the Baroness with a note from himself. 'You may suppose that I have been much startled by the receipt of the enclosed letter – what answer am I to give?'[9] Her reply was brief, 'I think you had better say (what is true) in reply to the enclosed rather singular letter that you have no information on the subject alluded to. . . .'[10]

The partners at the bank were perturbed. Antrobus wrote to Ryder, 'I wish our Lady had come back to her senses and would wait until after her death to bestow £10,000 a year on Mr A.B. – I should not object to that – far more respectable than bestowing it with her hand.'[11] On 12 July Harrowby replied to the Queen that he regretted to say that, 'Lady

Burdett begs him to reply that he had no information on the subject.' 'It looks', said Ryder, 'like a snub to her Majesty; this is a pretty kettle of fish.'[12]

Now her friends tried another tactic. Under the terms of Harriot's will, by marrying an alien, she forfeited the inheritance. Bartlett was an American. But she had forestalled this difficulty by persuading her sister Mrs Clara Money to waive her claim. If the partners could now persuade Mrs Money and her son to insist on their rights, then Bartlett might believe the game not worth the candle. On 15 July Antrobus wrote to Ryder, 'I pin my faith on the efficacy of Mrs Money's move far more than on her Majesty's remonstrance.' Antrobus, like the others, felt protective, 'I should be really grieved to do anything to hurt B.C.'s feelings as in former years she stood my firm friend against old E.M. [Edward Marjoribanks] which I can never forget and since then she has always been most friendly and kind.'

No one at the bank dared raise the subject. It was left to Lord Harrowby to offer help.

> Dear Angela [he wrote on 16 July, and it is a measure of her loneliness that he was almost the only one left to call her Angela], I do not like to let this crisis of your future pass without seeing whether I can be of any use to you. You have had recourse to me at different times, and it has been a pleasure to me to comply with your requests. Now that you have lost your faithful friend of childhood almost, I looked round in vain for an adviser for you. Can I be of any use to you? At least I do not think you should be without the offer. Your position is not one which you can think so unimportant to yourself or others as to make the advice of a friend indifferent or superfluous. I will not knock at your door or go further in the matter without your leave. I am, dear Angela your affectionate cousin, Harrowby.

Such a kind and affectionately friendly letter she gratefully acknowledged and for the first time made an attempt to explain her position. She had intended to tell him, she wrote, but 'the will of my poor Duchess had made it extremely desirable that for the present nothing should be said or known beyond the few absolutely necessary. I was deeply grieved when your letter and enclosed came to me last Sunday. It is an entire mystification to me how anything connected with *me* (and known to only two or three) should by publicity have got talked of in that quarter most unfortunate (not for me but for the interests of others).'

Only to Lord Harrowby could she write openly. Marriage, she wrote, offered her the only chance of comfort, and now that she 'could never be a *first* object to anyone (except a husband)', Bartlett's constant presence was essential to her. Only his support had enabled her 'to struggle through' and 'this would not last, and to lose all this now leaves me a future from which I not only recoil but which I feel I cannot face'.

On 16 July Bartlett called on Farrer and told him that 'finding so many difficulties in the way, he had given up the idea of marriage and had released the Baroness from any engagement to him'. The partners were delighted, especially since they could happily deny press rumours. The relief at the Baroness's escape was universal. On 20 July Malcolm rushed off to the Duchess of Teck with the news. 'I went up to Kensington and told her the matter was at an end for which intelligence I thought she was going to embrace me.' Queen Victoria breathed a sigh of relief.

But the joy was short-lived; they had reckoned without the Baroness. On 22 July Farrer reported to Malcolm that the Baroness was surprised to find Lord Harrowby treating the affair as all over and asked what it meant. Farrer said he concluded it was after the communication Bartlett made to him. 'But', said the Baroness, 'that may be so, but I don't release him and I mean to carry it out.'

There was one other card to play. The Baroness would not release Mr Bartlett but she might reconsider her decision if she were persuaded that Bartlett was already engaged. And so Miss Shirley was produced with evidence that Bartlett had made love to her on board the *Walrus*. Mrs Gascoigne, a friend of the Baroness, wrote breathlessly to Henry Ryder:

> Miss Shirley came here yesterday and this was what she told me. . . . On board the yacht this man had made violent love to *her* and told her over and over again that he couldn't marry her though he gladly would. He was under very peculiar circumstances. He could not explain them but he felt obliged to marry a lamp-post of a woman (his very words) repeated again and again. And that her money would help on his ambition! Miss Shirley apparently had his presents but no letters as proof of Bartlett's wooing. . . . She [the Baroness] is like a girl of 15. She does not *know* the storm of censure, indignation, grief, amazement that is going on everywhere. She is quite unaware of what she is going to bring on herself.[13]

Not even this succeeded. The Baroness found it understandable that the young lady was in love with Ashmead, but was perfectly confident in his fidelity. Nothing could persuade her. The difference in their ages did not matter – she had, all her life, had close friends of widely differing ages. Her grandfather's second marriage had been happy and Harriot had genuinely loved a very old man, and had married the Duke of St Albans though he was half her age. She herself, at Bartlett's age, was more than willing to marry Wellington.

Her own view of her proposed marriage she made clear to Mr Hassard, her secretary at that time. The draft of the letter of 10 August is in Bartlett's hand and some of the phrases are in his style. But most of the letter is in her unmistakable crisp style.

No marriage, however 'singular or if you like eccentric', she believed was a matter of scandal. And no one, she insisted, had a right to judge of her behaviour but herself, nor had they a *right* to offer her advice or remonstrance. Society might be shocked but, she believed 'in *low* life it would be regarded as more respectable' and her friends of this class regarded her husband-to-be as 'a good liver'. She understood her own singular nature: 'My position', she wrote, 'was, and always was, peculiar',[14] echoing Dickens's words of 1854: 'You are always like yourself and nobody else.'

Nevertheless in September, desperately in need of support, she turned to two men she could trust to be honest, Gladstone and Dudley Coutts Marjoribanks. Dudley, she wrote, would be surprised to hear from her but she had at this time instinctively turned to him. Dudley replied that he too had had an instinctive feeling that she would write. 'Instinctive feelings', she had now decided, were 'a more reliable guide than the sense of duty.' Dudley could not let the opportunity pass and rubbed salt in the wound – she had after all, he believed, ruined his life. Even so he spent days with solicitors in an attempt to find a way for her to keep her income and her marriage. He advised her to marry first and argue the alien clause afterwards.

On 6 September she wrote to Gladstone, 'I should have hesitated to intrude private (or what ought to have been private) matters on you at the close of this heavy session but as from what Sir James said you were kindly interested and my situation is marked by such peculiar circumstances and may pass quite soon openly into public question I feel a great wish to see you and speak to you upon it before you leave tomorrow. It may be of considerable importance and you should I feel know all connected with it.' It was a rare occasion – she who all her life had been ready to help others now needed help herself. And Gladstone, characteristically, was unwilling to get involved. Just as in the past she had tried in vain to get him involved in affairs of colonial churches and of Sarawak, now he declined to interfere in her private life. He immediately replied in a typically evasive letter, 'If I were thought to understand and concur, my concurrence would have little value. If it happened on the other hand that I was not able to declare a similarity of judgement, the issue of the conversation might give us both unnecessary pain, without any prospect of compensating advantage.'[15]

She retreated to St Leonards. Here, where eighteen years ago her sister Joanna had died, she was poignantly reminded of her isolation. She drove up to the grave in the little churchyard at Fairlight and wrote the sad lines which are now almost illegible on the mossy tombstone. Some lines can still be read:

> *Memory repaints each group around the stone*
> *Where now one woman stands and stands alone.*

By the end of September her friends realized that the marriage would certainly take place. W. H. Smith wrote to Lady Ely, the Queen's Lady-in-Waiting, 'I am afraid there is no doubt the marriage will take place.' By October it was clear nothing would shake her resolve. It was fortunate that few of her friends knew of the bombshell which was tossed into her lap in November 1880. Farrer, her faithful lawyer, brought news that a young lady was claiming that Ashmead was responsible for the baby she was expecting at the end of the year. Her uncle had come to him on her behalf. The Baroness's reaction was immediate and characteristic. It could not possibly be true. Just as years ago she had refused to believe the reports of her father's affair with Lady Oxford so now she was convinced of the 'utter falsity' of the charge. It is possible that Bartlett was not guilty, although the affair certainly does not show him in a favourable light. The Baroness, however, revealed once more her particular character –an inflexible will combined with vulnerable innocence. As always she could steadfastly and obstinately refuse to believe something she did not wish to know.

She could not live without Bartlett, who accompanied her as her fiancé throughout January, to the astonishment of society. In February 1881 Prince Arthur of Connaught saw them together at the Albert Hall and marvelled that so handsome a young man should be engaged to an old woman. Neither Disraeli nor Dickens could have invented so improbable an ending for the story of Agnes or Adriana. Disraeli, who had of late renewed his friendship with the Baroness, listened to the gossip with fascinated disbelief. 'Next to Afghanistan', he wrote to the Queen, 'I think the greatest scrape is Lady Burdett's marriage. I thought Angela would have become classical and historical history, and would have been an inspiring feature in your Majesty's illustrious reign. The element of the ridiculous has now so deeply entered into her career that even her best friends can hardly avoid a smile by a sigh!'[16]

On Saturday morning, 12 February 1881, William Ashmead Bartlett led his bride to the altar but not in her own church of St Stephen's, Westminster. The thought of Dr and Mrs Brown buried beneath the chancel, the sight of the Duke of Wellington's altar cloth, would have spoiled the day. The wedding took place at Christ Church, Down Street, a few minutes away from Stratton Street. The incumbent, the Reverend William Cardell and her old friend the Reverend Henry White, Chaplain of the Savoy, performed the ceremony.

The bridegroom, tall and sleek, was accompanied by his friend, Mr Macaita, and the bride was attended by three bridesmaids – Maud and Mae, the two daughters of her cousin Sir Francis Burdett, and Miss Maria Keppel. The Baroness was approaching her sixty-eighth year but in the dim light of the church the slender figure in white velvet, veiled in delicate old lace, was a snow maiden, ageless and immaculate.

They left the church for the wedding breakfast at her sister's house in Chester Square. Above the rattle of wheels on the cobbles, faintly across the Park, came the sound of her own bells. The bell-ringers of St Stephen's, puzzled and disturbed, nevertheless wished her well. Her sister, Susan Trevanion, received her with affection. All through the trying months she had steadily supported her, and now, as she said, she could die happy, knowing that Angela had a protector.

In the early afternoon the bridal pair left London in high style. They were driven to Kings Cross in a carriage and pair. They were received at the station by Sir Edmund Watkin MP, Chairman of the Company, and led across a carpet of red cloth to the royal saloon in the special train that would take them to Headcorn. They were to spend their honeymoon at Ingleden, Ashford, the home of Admiral and Mrs Gordon.

Was the marriage a success? Bartlett's enemies, and he had many, asserted that the Baroness's useful life ended with her marriage, that he destroyed her happiness and wasted her inheritance.

By marrying an alien she had forfeited her right to her inheritance. Her sister Clara had invoked the old clause in Harriot's will in a vain attempt to dissuade Bartlett. In September 1880 in order to avoid the scandal of a legal battle an agreement was reached whereby the Baroness retained her position in the bank but took only two-fifths of the income. The other three-fifths went to her sister Clara Money.[17] From now on her income

The marriage of Baroness Burdett-Coutts and Ashmead Bartlett at
Christ Church, Down Street in 1881.

was much reduced. In the last years of her life the two-fifths interest was
settled at a regular £16,000 a year; out of this she allowed herself a budget
of £1,000 a month for household expenses. This left comparatively little
for charities. She gradually transferred most of her stocks and shares to her
husband and bought Holly Lodge out of the estate for him. She had
already, before their marriage, given him her third share in her brother
Robert's estate.

Bartlett managed her financial affairs with little apparent skill. Certainly by 1903 he had found it necessary to mortgage Holly Lodge to the Earl of Jersey. Mrs Twining, whose husband was the vicar of St Stephen's from 1889 to 1923, believed that her happiness like her wealth was diminished, if not destroyed, by her marriage. Bartlett's tastes were certainly expensive. The vicar and parishioners of St Stephen's might justly have thought that the Baroness's money would be better spent on the church and schools than on racing or on the stud for improving the Old English breed of horses that he set up at Brookfield. He bred Cleveland bays and Yorkshire coach horses until, in 1910, the arrival of the motor-car put him out of business.

But Mrs Twining, though well-intentioned, was not a reliable witness. Most of the evidence suggests that of the twenty-seven years of marriage, most were contented and many very happy indeed. Friends and relations frequently remarked how young and well the Baroness looked. The marriage brought Bartlett an impressive name, a career, a comfortable life and a chance to indulge an expensive hobby that he would otherwise never have had. He took the name of William Ashmead Bartlett-Burdett-Coutts.

As the Baroness had planned, in 1885 Bartlett became Conservative Member of Parliament for Westminster. He was competent and assiduous as an MP – mostly leaving controversial party politics to his brother, Ellis, the MP for Eye. She took no part in his elections, nor appeared on his political platform, and indeed left London during elections lest it should be thought that her charities were intended to buy him votes. He worked hard, though in vain, to keep Columbia Market going. Under her direction he introduced into Parliament the Hampstead Heath Act which preserved Parliament Hill and three hundred acres of Hampstead Heath as an open space. Again on her behalf in 1900 he went to South Africa to observe the conditions of soldiers in the Boer War. His letters to *The Times* drew attention to the appalling hospital conditions there and resulted in a commission of enquiry.

In 1921, he was made a Privy Councillor. He died at Holly Lodge on 28 July 1921 and was buried at Frant, Sussex. Rudyard Kipling was among his mourners there and King George V was represented at his memorial service at St Margaret's, Westminster.

*   *   *

The Baroness began her married life with a dignity that, in time, silenced the gossips. Although for the next two years she appeared less frequently she did not withdraw from public life.

Cartoons from *Vanity Fair,* 1881,
depicting the Baroness and
Ashmead Bartlett.
The rather scathing text describes
Ashmead as 'a smart young man,
bold, shrewd and practical; energetic
and intelligent, and not destitute of
a certain ambition. He is of good
address, fond of shooting, hunting
and other field sports, and he has a
sufficient sense of the importance
of the husband of the Baroness'.
Photo: Angelo Hornak

In April 1881 she unveiled a memorial in Hackney Church and on 4 May she was presented with her husband to the Queen at the Drawing Room. Surprisingly, she appeared in a blaze of jewellery. Victoria raised her eyebrows. 'That poor foolish old woman Lady Burdett-Coutts', she wrote in her journal on 3 May 1881, 'was presented on her marriage with Mr Bartlett 40 years younger than herself. She looked like his grandmother and was all decked out with jewels – not edifying!' This may not have been a direct result of her marriage, for, although normally modest in appearance, at Court Miss Coutts could dazzle. On the morning after a large ball given by the Queen in 1845 Thomas Moore

called upon Miss Coutts, whom I had seen in all her splendours the night before, and found her preparing to send it all back to the bank. 'Would you like', she asked, 'to see it by daylight?' and, on my assenting, took me to a room upstairs, where the treasure was deposited. Amongst it was the famous tiara of Marie Antoinette; on my asking her what, altogether, might be the value of her dress last night, she answered, in her quiet way, 'I think about a hundred thousand pounds.'[18]

However much the Queen disapproved, there was no sign that the Baroness's popular appeal was diminished. On 30 July a delegation of thirty brought her a memorial address of good wishes on her marriage from St Stephen's Church. In the afternoon a thousand parishioners joined them for a party in the grounds of Holly Lodge.

By June 1883 her life was returning to normal. She held a succession of summer parties at Holly Lodge and Society accepted, if it did not approve, the tall young man at her side.

By 1884 she was ready to battle once more, this time on behalf of the last of her heroes, General Gordon. The man Gladstone called 'The hero of heroes', had been a friend of the Baroness since 1858.

As a young man of twenty-five he had returned from the Crimea with a reputation for exceptional courage and daring. In 1863 he had, as a Lieutenant-Colonel in the Chinese Service, taken command of the 'Ever Victorious Army'. Under his leadership it earned its name; in two years Gordon achieved his objective, the crushing of the Taiping Rebellion. He became world-famous as 'Chinese Gordon'. He was the classic Victorian hero, restoring order in the land of the heathen armed only with a rattan cane. Gordon disdained reward, and, like Livingstone, disliked his fame. On his return to England, he spent six years obscurely in Gravesend as Commander of the Royal Engineers, constructing forts for the defence of the Thames. Few people ever reached the man behind the legend, he

A garden party at Holly Lodge, from a painting by A. P. Tilt, 1882.
The Baroness and Ashmead Bartlett are shown receiving their guests
in front of the conservatory.

kept himself aloof and solitary and the Baroness was one of the few with
whom he felt at ease and who could draw him out. For Gordon the hero
she shared the Victorian admiration; but she was even more in tune with
Gordon the deeply religious philanthropist who spent much of his spare
time training and housing the Ragged Boys of Gravesend, his 'scuttlers',
'his kings'.

In 1872 Gordon was appointed to take Sir Samuel Baker's place as
Governor of the equatorial province of Central Africa. The Baroness was
delighted. She saw him as continuing the work of Livingstone in com-
bating the slave trade. Certainly by 1875 Gordon had, temporarily at
least, achieved one of Livingstone's ambitions. He had established a chain
of fortified posts a day's journey apart and had for a time at least dispersed
the slave traders.

Gordon resigned his post in 1880 and for the next four years restlessly
travelled through Ireland, India, Palestine and Mauritius, and by October
1884 he was prepared to take service in the Congo for the King of the
Belgians. On 2 January 1884 he had accepted a blank cheque from King
Leopold and was preparing for the mission. It was at this time that Gladstone's Government sent for him and asked him to go out to the Sudan to
208

effect the evacuation and the withdrawal of the garrisons there. Gordon accepted.

In 1882 Britain had come to the aid of the Khedive in Cairo, put down an army rebellion and virtually taken over the military and political control of Egypt. Baring, who was nominally appointed HM Consul General in 1883, was, in fact, the ruler of Egypt. Gladstone hoped this would be a temporary situation – he hated foreign involvement. When a new rebellion, led by the fanatical Mahdi, broke out in the Sudan, Gladstone's instinct was to get out, not only from Khartoum and the garrison towns but even from Cairo itself.

From the beginning the Baroness was in close touch with all the players in the drama. Gladstone and Lord Gordon were her friends. She knew and frequently corresponded with King Leopold of the Belgians. Gordon consulted her before deciding to postpone his Congo expedition. He found time to visit her in the frantic hours between his acceptance of the Government's Commission in the afternoon of 18 January 1884 and his departure for the Sudan in the evening. The Duchess of Teck reported 'barely an hour before leaving England for the last time [he] went to see her. Expressing a desire to receive some little memento from her hands she gave him a letter case which always lay on her table and it is known that he always carried this about him to the last.'[19]

In accepting the Commission, Gordon had explicitly committed himself to a policy of evacuation and abandonment. From Cairo he wrote, in an official memorandum to the Foreign Office, that he understood his mission was 'to arrange for the evacuation and safe removal of the Egyptian employees and troops from the Sudan'. But though Gordon, at home, was prepared to see the Sudan abandoned, in Khartoum, confronted by a fanatical adversary, he changed his mind.[20]

In the first month he did evacuate some sick, widows and children, but by March, he decided that with £100,000 and two hundred Indian troops he could easily 'smash up the Mahdi'. From then on he convinced himself that his mission was a different one – that he must bring stability to the Sudan before he left and that for this the destruction of the Mahdi was essential.

On 12 March the telegraph line to Cairo was cut. The difficulty of communicating provided the excuse for both Gladstone and Gordon to act in character – the Prime Minister to delay involvement and the General to prepare for the forbidden battle.

Gordon's request for troops was refused, the Government insisting once again that he must evacuate Khartoum. In their defence it must be

William Ewart Gladstone at his books: a portrait by S. P. Hall.

said that they were misled by his early over-optimistic reports, some of them sent out to confuse the Mahdi's spies. Those like Baring, who understood the real danger Gordon was facing, surrounded as he was by tens of thousands of the Mahdi's fervent followers, sent repeated warnings to the Government. As early as March, the Queen asked Gladstone to send Indian troops to rescue Gordon. When the contents of Gordon's last telegram were received, his friends in England began to campaign on his behalf.

On 8 May 1884 the Baroness wrote, from Paris, a fierce letter to *The Times*. She had, she said, been entreated to organize, by public subscription, a volunteer movement to attempt the relief of General Gordon. Poor men had offered their support, 'a French workman offers you his 20 francs with an English lady who would send £5,000'. She realized that it would now be difficult to know from what direction such support should come. 'General Gordon looks to the equator as his only point of refuge. Providence may shield him along that wonderful and dangerous path,' but it was with some 'bitterness of heart' that she reflected that it was not to England that he turned for hope in his abandonment. The Baroness was not so much appealing for a volunteer rescue force as sending a letter of encouragement to Gordon. She made sure that her letter and the response to it got through to Khartoum. According to the Duchess of Teck 'when General Gordon was shut up in Khartoum and no effort was made to rescue him she joined with a few other private friends in engaging an English merchant, resident in Morocco, to undertake the perilous enterprise of finding his way into Khartoum, in disguise, with a packet of letters and English newspapers, which were the last words Gordon ever had from England and which told him how deeply the national heart was stirred on his behalf.'

In spite of public and private appeals, the Baroness herself sending on to the Government letters suggesting routes for rescue expeditions, it was not until August that Gladstone moved in Parliament that a sum of £300,000 should be allotted for the relief of Gordon. The expeditionary force that was finally sent out under the direction of Wolseley reached Khartoum too late.

The Mahdi had expressly forbidden his followers to kill Gordon, indeed at the last moment he sent Gordon a remarkable offer of escape, 'I understand that the English are willing to ransom you alone from us for £200,000 . . . if you agree to join us it will be a blessing to you. But if you wish to rejoin the English, we will send you back to them without asking for so much as a farthing.'[21]

But in the bloody heat of battle Gordon was cut down on the steps of his palace. His head was cut off and taken to the Mahdi. When the brutal details of his death reached England, public outcry was ferocious and there were those who would happily have sent Gladstone's head to the Mahdi.

The Baroness watched with double anguish the tragedy that moved so inevitably towards the final catastrophe. She would, if she could, have been a 'dea ex machina' – the ransom offer of £200,000 must have come partly from her. But she must have known, better than anyone else perhaps that, given the characters of the players in the tragedy and the African setting, the outcome was inevitable. Surprisingly she did not subscribe to Gordon's memorial. In a letter to Cardinal Manning of 18 March 1885 she explained why. The public, who idolized him after death, had no understanding of his aims. Her memorial to Gordon was not a contribution to a statue but continual support for those who carried on Gordon's work in equatorial Africa.

Gordon was the last of her heroes. Wellington, Dickens, Louis Napoleon, Layard, Livingstone, Brooke and Gordon had each a potent combination of simplicity and brilliance, humour and a sense of mission. What drew her most to her famous friends was the almost manic energy with which they sought their destinies, releasing and directing an answering force in her. Yet, in the quiet of her drawing-room, these restless spirits could be at peace, the shy and awkward could be at ease.

1885 brought the death of many friends. It is not surprising that photographs of the Baroness show a sad, thin face, the skin taut over the strong jaw, the eyes weary. But only the camera and her closest friends caught that mood. The Baroness of the *Spy* cartoon, upright and gracious, eyes quizzical and full of humour, faces the world with intelligent, unfailing curiosity. She took a keen interest in Bartlett's political career. For his sake, in August, she rented Heydon Hall, Norwich, where he could hunt and shoot.

Heydon Hall was, she wrote to Henry Wagner, 'a charming antique place that belonged to the elder branch of the Bulwer family'. She had known it in her youth and found it interesting for that reason but Bartlett's energetic sporting friends were not particularly congenial and the sight of the sportsmen returning with limp, dead birds can scarcely have given much pleasure to the President of the Ladies Committee of the RSPCA. She always returned with relief to London, the 'land of the living'.

Once again, as in her childhood, she began to move restlessly from place to place. Paris continued to be her second home. Some part of every year was spent there, usually at the Hôtel Bristol. In October 1886, she found a magical retreat. She took a long lease on the Château de Chantilly, home of the Duc d'Aumale, the fifth son of her old friend Louis Philippe. The Duc d'Aumale had inherited it in 1830 when a small boy, from his godfather, the last Duc de Condé. During his years of exile, in Louis Napoleon's reign, others had enjoyed the elegant, gilded salons, and the 'singeries' – rooms decorated with Chinese wallpaper in which the world of fashion was peopled by monkeys. The old Duke had restored both the château and the lakes and gardens with loving care.

It must have been with painful nostalgia that she showed her young husband the château she had known so long. There were portraits, reflected in the great looking-glasses, that Ashmead could never understand: Louis Philippe, curled and pompous, his Queen, Marie-Amelie, plain and long-faced, and his sister, Madame Adelaide. Almost sixty years had passed since she had received Angela Burdett so kindly, had talked so wisely to the quiet young girl who listened, wide-eyed, to her tales of

Revolution and exile. But Bartlett had no eyes for the past. From the windows of the château, across the lake he could see the most magnificent stables in Europe.[22] Never would his beloved horses be more grandly housed.

* * *

In the first twelve years of marriage there was genuine happiness for the Baroness in once more having a partner who appeared to share her interests and was prepared to work hard for them. Bartlett was no Charles Dickens, but the Layards had praised his efficiency in Constantinople.

In 1887 he accompanied the Baroness to Ireland. She had been known, reported the Duchess of Teck, as 'Lady Coutts' and occasionally as 'Your Lordship Lady Coutts' but now she was hailed, with wild enthusiasm, as 'Queen of Baltimore'.

On the yacht *Pandora*, lent to her by W. H. Smith, Bartlett at her side, she sailed into Baltimore harbour and watched as 'a hundred small fires twinkling far in the air on the wild hillsides, signalled a welcome that was repeated in the booming of a salute from the shore'.[23] She had come to open the Baltimore Fishery School, a project which from the beginning she had supported and encouraged.

Her welcome was the climax of her own work for Ireland over the last twenty years; but it also echoed an Irish enthusiasm for Sir Francis Burdett which went back nearly ninety years.

* * *

It would seem that, after what she called 'the *mad* marriage', Queen Victoria never again visited the Baroness at home. In past years the Queen had enjoyed sitting at the bay window in Stratton Street, discreetly watching the passers-by, and she adored the gardens at Holly Lodge. However, she still wrote to the Baroness as she always had done, through her lady-in-waiting, Lady Ely. The Baroness always replied with a particular personal note of affection to her 'ever dear and cherished lady'.

On 28 March 1883 she wrote to console with the Queen on the death of John Brown. 'Dear Lady Ely, I should so much like to know how Her Majesty's health bears the sudden strain on her nerves and feelings . . . the loss of a tried, faithful, intelligent servant united as, in a sense, servants only can be with one's life and its joys and sorrows, is no slight trial to anyone, how much more to the Queen.'[24] The Baroness shared with Her Majesty the royal isolation; she too had lost a faithful Brown.

Princess Victoria Mary of Wales, later Queen Mary: a photograph taken in 1903 and presented to Angela Burdett-Coutts.

Victoria Mary

With the Cambridge family and especially the Duchess of Teck and her daughter, Princess May, later Queen Mary, the Baroness remained on the friendliest of terms. From childhood she had had an amused affection for the eccentric old Duke of Cambridge, watching wide-eyed the odd old face under the great yellow wig and listening aghast to his stentorian asides during church services. He was almost the only son of George III who had not been permanently in her grandfather's debt. In fact, rigid old Tory though he was, he had always been a generous supporter of her charities.

She had known his daughter, Mary Adelaide, as a girl in neighbouring Cambridge House, Piccadilly, and had always been particularly kind to the immensely fat girl with the beautiful face. For years it had appeared that poor Mary was doomed by her enormous size to a life of dull spinsterhood and nobody was more delighted than Miss Coutts when she had finally caught a handsome but penniless husband, Prince Francis of Teck. It was Miss Coutts who drew Mary Adelaide into charitable work. Nothing

214

Princess Mary of Cambridge, Duchess of Teck: from a *carte de visite* in the Baroness' collection.

Mansell Collection

delighted her more than to see the spontaneous demonstrations of affection that always greeted 'fat Mary' in the East End.

The Duchess's daughter Princess May, later Queen Mary, was similarly drawn to the Baroness's work in the East End. The Baroness supported the Duchess and her family discreetly in financial crises over a period of years, often lending them Stratton Street or Holly Lodge. Her unconventional marriage did not affect their friendship. To the Tecks she was always 'our dear Baroness' and Bartlett, who was generally disliked in Court circles, was held in warm regard. It is not surprising, therefore, that the American organizers of the Chicago Exhibition of 1893 should have turned to the Duchess of Teck for a biography of the Baroness.[25]

In 1892 the Baroness began her last important project, a report on the philanthropic work of British women, to be presented at the Great World Fair opening in Chicago in May 1893.

Her report was published two months earlier under the title of *Women's Mission. A Series of Congress Papers on the Philanthropic work of women by*

In 1887, Angela Burdett-Coutts opened an industrial fishing school at Baltimore in Ireland. The school was designed to accommodate four hundred boys, who were to be trained in navigation, sail, net and rope making, and boat building. These two photographs were taken shortly after the school opened, and show net making and the work room.

eminent writers . . . with a preface and notes by Baroness Burdett-Coutts. The book is a reflection on and a summary of her own career in charity. It contains a Preface, written by the Baroness, an introductory poem, thirty-two papers, including two of her own and one by Florence Nightingale, a statistical survey, and an appendix in which she summarized the work of over two hundred and twenty organizations and individuals in England, fifty-two in Ireland and forty-four overseas. Her secretary, Osborne, did much of the work but the book is unmistakably her own. It is an illuminating and at times touching picture of that much-mocked figure, the Victorian lady doing good.[26]

The Baroness looked back with nostalgia to the country houses of her youth. In pre-railway times they were often like distinct little settlements. They were moved by a conscious sense of responsibility, influencing in turn their villages and groups of farms, they formed centres of thought and consideration for all within a certain area about them, dispensing the kindnesses that are now recognized under the broad word 'philanthropy'. It was, as she remembered it, a world in which the lady of the house 'lived under the influence of traditional duties', in which boys found their technical training on workshop and farm, where girls learned their domestic science in the dairies, the kitchens and the workrooms of the great house. When the Industrial Revolution drove workers into the big cities they were cut off not only from their communities but from an education that had been an accepted part of life. They were cut off too from the natural world. The Baroness had spent a lifetime attempting to bring back these technical skills, recreating the old links between town and country, and between rich and poor.

She described how the social classes were interdependent, their lives interwoven, sharing country amusements and attending church together. In the old-fashioned libraries of the country houses there was, she claimed, a source of learning denied to the slum dweller. So she had built one library in her workmen's flats, another for the use of the clerks at Coutts Bank.

Though she felt nostalgia for this idealized past, she nevertheless accepted that it was dead. Her father's favourite quotation was her own: 'Man's eyes were given him to look forward not backward.' She had no wish to put back the clock, neither did she 'under-estimate the enormous blessings of the growth of trade'. It had, after all, given her the means to do good. But with it had come the evils she knew so well, 'overcrowding, feverishness of factory work, temptation to spirit drinking as a goad to exhausted energy, dissociation of labour from nature, and from common sympathies . . . not to speak of other evils that breed in crowded courts and reeking towns'.

In compiling the book the Baroness's methods of enquiry were her own; her choice of examples was equally characteristic. Throughout the book the emphasis is on 'work, not alms'. The truly generous, she repeated 'enabled the destitute to help themselves'. Only by this kind of reproductive charity could you create dignity, independence and self-reliance.

The heroines of her own two papers were typical. In 'Women the Missionary of Industry' she described the work of Mrs Bernard, who gave up her career as Superior of the Convent at Ballaghaderin in Ireland to set up a woollen mill at Foxford. In the wretched area round the convent, girls had no skill other than that of hoeing potatoes and when that crop failed they either starved or emigrated. Starting with a worm-eaten old hand loom, with the help of four Sisters of Charity Mrs Bernard established a water-driven woollen mill.

Her second heroine was Mrs Rogers, who in February 1880 set out to teach the Irish women of Carrick to knit gloves. At first besieged in her cottage by a thousand women desperate for work, she finally and after much difficulty established a glove making industry that by the end of the year earned £1,000 in wages. It had taken, however, three months and the bribery of a gallant priest before the totally unskilled women could produce a single pair of gloves.

The second paper dealt with the work of Miss Ormerod of Sedbury Park near Chepstow. At a time when agricultural entomology was virtually unknown in this country, she had, by patient research, identified the injurious insects which destroy crops and cause disease in animals. Her work on the cause of the potato blight was of particular value at this time. This was the Baroness's ideal philanthropist. Miss Ormerod was a 'patient enquirer and investigator where ignorance is pain and loss'.

The most distinguished contributor to *Women's Mission* was Florence Nightingale, whose paper was a vigorous appeal for 'missioners of health at home'. County Councils had been given, by Act of Parliament, the power to encourage the teaching of 'nursing and sanitary knowledge'. Miss Nightingale insisted that such education should be practical. She was preaching the gospel that the Baroness had practised throughout her career.

The Baroness included reports on the work of the RSPCA, the NSPCC and the YWCA, and among the hundreds of other charitable projects listed, there was scarcely one for which she had not worked from the beginning. The first meeting, in London, out of which grew the Society for the Prevention of Cruelty to Children, took place in her drawing-room. Her whole working life had been devoted to the care of children. Her father had been a founder member of the RSPCA in 1824 and it was her own letter to *The Times* which inaugurated the Society's educational work. She had been one of the first to organize the outings for what Mrs Molesworth in her paper called 'food, fun and fresh air for the little ones'. Waggon-loads of children had regularly been transported to the fields and farm at Holly Lodge. It was her abiding concern to bring town and country together again for she had watched with regret the Industrial Revolution driving them apart.

Above all she had been one of the first of the philanthropists to reach to the roots of distress. Forty years ago she had recognized that the slums bred vice and disease. Her well-ventilated homes, with their clean water and good sanitation, had set the standard for the century. Philanthropy was always for her the service of the rich to the poor, and it was given, in her case, without condescension. To have submerged herself in squalor, would have seemed hypocritical and unpractical. But for those late Victorian ladies like Miss Mary Steer, who lived and worked among the fallen, she had the greatest admiration. Miss Steer's paper on 'Rescue work by women among women' she read with an expert eye. Though she had never considered living and working among the poor, she was one of the first to buy houses in poor areas where her assistants could live in comparative comfort.

Victorian women and their good works have been underestimated. It is true that some were impelled by doubtful motives, some snobbishly followed in the train of royal ladies like the Duchess of Teck and Princess May. Many too were inspired by a desire to boss, some by a *'nostalgie de la boue'*. There were many who warmed their chilled and repressed spirits in the vitality, colour and humanity of the East End. But together they created that intricate network of voluntary work on which, even now, the State relies.

With customary modesty, the Baroness scarcely mentioned her own work in *Women's Mission*. In January 1893 the American President of the Ladies Committee asked the Duchess of Teck to set the record straight. A slim volume was quickly produced by 'a competent and accurate hand'; it remained for many years the only biography of the Baroness.

In her introduction the Duchess praised her as a powerful example to others but even more because she had 'ever sought to increase the usefulness of women in their homes, to extend the opportunities of self-improvement, and to deepen the sources of influence which they derive from moral worth and Christian life'. The Duchess was overwhelmed by 'her vast work' which was 'one of which no living hand can ever write the history, and she herself would probably be the first to desire that it should remain unwritten'.

CHAPTER TEN

The Noblest Spirit We Shall Ever Know

1893–1906

ALTHOUGH, WITH her income diminished after her marriage, the Baroness could no longer give large donations, she kept an interest in those causes that had always been important to her. The charity bazaars, so fashionable in the 1890s, had little appeal, though she was occasionally persuaded to help the royal princesses and the Duchess of Teck. On 18 April 1894 she helped the Duchess organize a bazaar for the Great Central Hospital. But at no time did she play the conventional Lady Bountiful. As President of the Destitute Children's Dinner Society she continued to organize their work and made an annual appeal for them through the columns of *The Times*. She still served on committees: the Grosvenor Hospital for Women, the Stafford House committee which helped soldiers overseas, the RSPCA and, until policy differences made her withdraw, the NSPCC. Her greatest pleasure was in the success of her technical institute in Westminster. In 1892 two of the four prize-winners in a national competition for metal plate work came from the College.

In 1894 she was eighty, deaf and a little lame and her eyes troubled her. Her portraits show her at this time, sad-eyed as ever, but always beautifully dressed in black silks, stiff and ruched but softened at the throat and wrist with fine old lace. She had outlived many of her friends. Not only Charles Dickens but even some of his children were dead, so were her two remaining sisters, Susan and Clara. But some friends still survived from the old days. Admiral Keppel, old friend of Rajah Brooke, bluff and cheery but completely deaf, was a frequent companion and so were

Admiral and Mrs Gordon. She needed her friends, for there were troubles in these years which are only hinted at in her letters. Mrs Twining wrote darkly of Bartlett's flirtations and of how in 1890 the Baroness, in an unusual state of agitation, brought her most precious archives in three wooden boxes to the Reverend Twining, for safe keeping.

Nevertheless, there were still happy times. When she attended services in St Stephen's Church, the congregation stood, as they would to the Queen. And in Westminster Technical Institute in 1894 when she presented prizes to working boys, the *Strand Magazine* described the event.

> When Her Ladyship stood up to commence, the ovation was simply tremendous. . . . When at length it did subside the immense audience (and hundreds had been turned away) although the hour was late, sat and stood in perfect silence eager to catch every word that fell from her lips. The entire affair . . . had resolved itself into an unmistakable tribute of affectionate regard; for when the Baroness had entered the hall . . . everyone present had sprung to his feet and continued standing until she herself was seated. No greater respect could have been paid to majesty itself. . . .

Henry Furniss was among the crowds outside her house in Piccadilly as she watched Queen Victoria's Diamond Jubilee from her window.

> Suddenly a hush spread over the vast sea of people. A slim form, supported by several ladies and men, was seen silhouetted against the light; it stepped on the balcony and stood there leaning tremulously against the window. A great hoarse roar spread over the night, cheers, snatches of songs and wild cries of welcome and delight, . . . in the tiniest of tiny barrows a fat woman struggled to her feet . . . and yelled above all the clamour – 'The best woman in London – God bless her!'[1]

But it was not all idolatry. There was an extraordinary story at the time which was taken up with ribald enthusiasm in the East End. Compton Mackenzie remembered it: 'There was a fantastic domestic legend current during my youth that Lady Burdett-Coutts was afflicted by lice self-generated. I have heard this repeated over and over again but I was too young at the time to be ready with the right response and remind the tellers of this ludicrous tale that any woman with as much money as Lady Burdett-Coutts was liable to be afflicted by parasites.'[2]

The story, fiercely denied by the descendants of her servants, possibly originated in the skin complaint from which she had suffered since girlhood. However ridiculous the story, it was accepted as true. Even today a cockney will use the word 'couttsy' for 'lousy'.

*   *   *

In the last decade of the century she spent some months of every year abroad. The Mediterranean cruise of 1879 had revived her passion for travel. Until her late eighties she crossed over to Paris as easily as she moved from Stratton Street to Holly Lodge, and Boulogne as always was a favourite resort. But her favourite island was Corsica, where she had called on the cruise with Irving. In 1896, at the age of eighty-two, she spent March and April in Ajaccio in Corsica, returning the next year for three happy months. The bay before her grand hotel reminded her of Torquay. Ashmead fished in the crystal streams, together they drove up the winding mountain roads. She wrote home in rapture of the sea, the mountains and the wild flowers. In the clear bright air her English friends noticed she looked 'wonderfully young for her 82 years'. She had many links with Corsica. She visited the relations of Lucien Bonaparte there. She was a popular figure, for she had arranged for the ashes of General Paoli to be returned to his village in the mountains.[3]

The new century came in. She was eighty-six and not even she could face the long journey to Corsica. She turned again to Brighton as she had done in her youth. The last Brighton days were never sad, there were still Wagners there to keep her mind alive. She was remembered as lively, intelligent and humorous to the last. Harry Preston, manager of the Royal York Hotel, where she stayed, recalled how she would take the whole of the first floor for herself and her suite. Although over ninety, she retained her clarity of mind and sharpness of wit. Every night she enjoyed a specially prepared four-course dinner. 'It was an epicurean repast. With the fish she would take a half-bottle of excellent old vintage champagne. Later on she would take a pot of strong black tea, and then retire for the night and sleep like a baby.'[4]

Brighton was a town rich in memories. Long, long ago she had seen her mother's friend, old King William IV, leaning against the wind on the Chain Pier, breezily chatting to the passers-by. In the 1830s she had watched Harriot's dazzling assemblies at St Albans House. In the 1840s she had spent long weeks looking out to sea from their house in Eastern Terrace and watching her mother's last, langorous approach to death.

On Thursday, 21 April 1904 Ashmead invited a few friends to celebrate her ninetieth birthday. Among the guests were her godson, Prince Francis of Teck, the Duchess of St Albans, Lord and Lady Wolseley, Mr and Mrs Herbert Gladstone, Archdeacon and Mrs Wilberforce and Mr and Mrs George Marjoribanks. The dining room was filled with flowers, but the only ones on the luncheon table were placed in the pair of silver vases to the right and left of the Baroness. They were the gift of the members of her household and bore the inscription, 'To the Baroness Burdett-Coutts, the best mistress and kindest friend in all the world, with the respect and affection of her household. 21 April 1904.'

The new century brought new worries. Ashmead had extravagant hobbies and for the first time in her life the Baroness was concerned about money. In 1901, to the dismay of her friends at St Stephen's Church, she had to cut her contribution to their costs and she handed her schools over to the London County Council.

One after another her last friends were falling away. In January 1901 Queen Victoria died and the Piccadilly house was wreathed in black crêpe, but in the summer, with the coronation of Edward VII, her adored Princess May was one step nearer the Throne.

On Friday, 13 October 1905 Henry Irving died in Bradford. After his last appearance as Shylock earlier that week he had murmured, 'it's a pity, just as one is beginning to know a little about this work of ours it's time to leave it'. Sir Henry's body was brought to 1 Stratton Street and lay in state in the long dining room under the portrait of Mrs Brown.

The Baroness was now very deaf, lame and her sight was failing. Her spirit was still strong, but the snowy December of 1906 defeated her. When the 'day of sad remembrance', the anniversary of Mrs Brown's death, came round again she was ill with bronchitis. On Friday, she rallied and on Saturday she received her household for the last time. 'Giving them each her hand,' as her husband reported. There were last quiet words for the Bishop of London, a sad, kind message for her friends the Twinings at St Stephen's. Like a child who asks forgiveness before she goes to sleep, she said 'tell the Vicar and Mrs Twining I am so grievously sorry for what I did over the schools and to the Church and that I behaved so badly to the Vicar who did all in his power to help me. They were both such true and good friends to me.'[5]

Her mind was clear to the end. At 10.30 a.m. on Sunday, 30 December, quite peacefully, she died.

CHAPTER ELEVEN

Finale

SHE LAY in the house where she was born, and, as at her birth, so in her death, there was controversy and scandal. Her tomb had long ago in 1850 been prepared in St Stephen's Church and she herself had wished to be buried there beside Dr and Mrs Brown. It is as well she was spared the jealous acrimony which accompanied the arrangements for her burial in Westminster Abbey.

Bishop Henson told part of the story in his *Retrospect of an Unimportant Life*. On Monday, 31 December 1906, the Dean, after consultation with the Canons, offered interment in the Abbey. But there was a stipulation that 'the remains of the deceased Baroness should be first cremated'. Ashmead, having accepted the offer with this condition, on the day before the funeral announced that there would be no cremation. The furious Canons telegraphed the Dean, who was away. Should they refuse to accept the coffin? He left the decision to the sub-Dean who decided to proceed with the burial. Canons Henson and Barnett, still fuming, refused to attend the ceremony. It was Canon Duckworth, the sub-Dean, who finally officiated.

Bishop Henson did not publish the sad sequel to the story, whose only record is a note in the journal of Mrs Twining. She reported that in the afternoon, the Dean returned and sending for the Manager of Bantings, the funeral directors, had the coffin removed from the tomb to the back of the Abbey. The coffin shells were removed (there had been three, the first elm, the second, hermetically-sealed metal and the outside, oak). The body was covered in quick lime and then returned, at dead of night, into the tomb. Mrs Twining recorded that this was made necessary because the space prepared was only three foot square and therefore not big enough for a coffin. The truth of this story is not confirmed, but the details are circumstantial and convincing.

Nothing of this had spoiled the spontaneous demonstration of respect and affection or the people's last salute to the 'Queen of the Poor'. Mourners queued outside the house in Stratton Street and were admitted, fifty at a time, to follow along the purple drugget to the catafalque beneath the great chandeliers. At the head of the coffin was a full-length portrait of the Baroness; on the opposite wall a portrait of Mrs Brown. When on Friday evening the doors were finally closed, twenty-five thousand people had filed past the coffin.

On the next morning a great crowd gathered outside the house, keeping watch in silence. A chill wind stirred the manes of the four black horses and unfurled the flags flying at half-mast. Slowly the polished oak coffin was carried out to the open carriage. In the grey morning light the brass plate gleamed with the legend 'Angela Georgina Baroness Burdett-Coutts born 21 April 1814 died 30 December 1906'. As the funeral cortège drew off through the slush of Piccadilly a passing omnibus driver, his whip tied with black crêpe, saluted. It was the last exit of one who in that house had for seventy years welcomed the age's greatest names. The last carriage rumbled towards Westminster Abbey and the whisper of the name died away. The crowds were six deep in Victoria Street, among them working men in black ties and their wives with black ribbons on their bonnets.

Outside the Abbey in a sudden blaze of colour a group of costermongers stood with their banners. Inside only the dark purple and gold capes of Canon Duckworth and Archdeacon Wilberforce relieved the mourning black of an immense congregation. The King and Queen, Prince and Princess of Wales and Prime Minister were represented. There were famous names among the pall-bearers, Prince Francis of Teck (her godson), Viscount Peel, the Duke of Wellington and Mr Herbert Gladstone. Diplomats and statesmen, the Lord Mayor of London, the Mayor of Westminster were among the congregation. But there were also flower girls from Bermondsey and working men and women from Westminster and Bethnal Green.

She was buried at the foot of the memorial to her friend Lord Shaftesbury. Not far away was the black stone which marked Livingstone's grave and around in the flickering candlelight were the shadows of Charles Dickens and Henry Irving, Gladstone and Disraeli. Angela Burdett-Coutts had joined her friends.

There were no flowers now, only the Queen's lilies and on the coffin a simple posy of sweet herbs with her husband's message 'For my best and dearest, from the "Garden on the Hill" '. Only a plain stone with letters of brass marks her grave but the epitaph to Shaftesbury on the wall above

226

The lying-in-state of Angela Burdett-Coutts at Stratton Street in January 1907. In the background can be seen E. R. Long's portrait of the Baroness, showing her wearing her insignia.

might well have been her own: A long life spent in the cause of the help-less and suffering, Love and serve.

*   *   *

What remains of that long life of giving? Some of the Baroness's buildings still stand, splendid Gothic memorials to Victorian taste, Highgate's Holly Village, St Stephen's, Westminster, and the Burdett-Coutts School still thrive. In the little village of Bayden near her father's estate at Ramsbury her model cottages still stand – neat, sturdy and a credit to her planning. Columbia Market has been demolished and Columbia Buildings replaced. Trees and flowers grow around the bright new flats and tower blocks. No one now remembers whose vision it was that first created the model buildings, the earliest of their kind. Only the street names echo the past; Angela Gardens, Georgina Gardens, Baroness Road, Burdett Road.

Two towns in Canada, Burdett and Coutts, bear her name – though the inhabitants have long forgotten who financed the first emigrants there. There are few memorials; there is no blue plaque on the site of 1 Stratton Street. The portrait that Mrs Brown commissioned Swinton to paint hangs on the stairs at the Royal Marsden Hospital though few remember her part in its foundation. Liverpool has given her a place in a stained-glass window in the Cathedral and there are tablets recording her generosity in towns and villages in Scotland. Torquay placed a plaque on Ehrenberg Hall but even that was recently stolen. London, the city to which she gave so much, has strangely neglected her memory. Although no one did more than she for the nineteenth-century Church in England and over-seas, she scarcely gets a footnote in Church history.

At home and abroad her response to social need was always prompt and practical. She set a standard; her charity was given with style, without condescension and with kindness. Into her quiet drawing-room she drew friends of different temperaments, different backgrounds, different epochs. There were those who had lived through the French Revolution; and those who had merely drifted through quiet back-waters of Georgian England. The turbulent spirits of the Victorian era, inventors, explorers, rulers and reformers, mingled there with bishops and artists, writers and actors and were at home. Though she could walk easily with queens, many of her friends were of humble origin and she never forgot that her grandmother was a working girl. Much of her life, her work, her charity remains undiscovered, and she herself still is, as she would have wished, something of an enigma; a lady forgotten, a 'lady unknown'.

228

to: Angelo Hornak

The memorial above Angela Burdett-Coutts's tomb in Westminster Abbey by the great west door and beneath the feet of the great philanthropist, Anthony Ashley Cooper, Earl of Shaftesbury.

Select Bibliography

MANUSCRIPT SOURCES

Bodleian Library, Oxford: Burdett-Coutts Papers
British Library, Department of Western Manuscripts: Letters from Rajah
 Brooke to Angela Burdett-Coutts, Add. Mss
   Gladstone Papers, Add. Mss
   Layard Papers, Add. Mss
   Osborne Papers, Add. Mss
(B-C.) Burdett-Coutts Collection
Chantilly Archives, Musée de Condé, Chantilly
The Archives of Coutts and Co: The Reverend Barnes Papers, Marjoribanks
 Papers
   Lord Latymer Papers
Harrowby Mss, Sandon Hall
Henry E. Huntington Library, California
Lambeth Palace Library
(P.M.) Pierpont Morgan Library, New York: Letters from Charles Dickens to
 Angela Burdett-Coutts
P.M.(E.J.) As quoted in Edgar Johnson's *The Heart of Charles Dickens*
Sir Anthony Wagner Papers
Wellington Archives, Stratfield Saye
Westminster Public Library: Records of St Stephen's, Mrs Twining's Journal
(R.A.) Royal Archives, Windsor

PRINTED SOURCES

ANDERSEN, Hans Christian: *Diary of his Visit to Charles Dickens* (ed. E. Breds-
 dorff, Cambridge 1956)
   Correspondence with Charles Dickens (ed. F. Crawford, London 1891)
   see also BREDSDORFF and MUNKSGAARD
BAMFORD, Samuel: *Passages in the Life of a Radical* (2 vols, London 1844)
BARON-WILSON, Mrs: *Memoirs of the Duchess of St Albans* (2 vols, London 1844)
BLACKMANTLE, Bernard: *The English Spy* (London 1826)
BREDSDORFF, Elias: *Hans Christian Andersen: The Story of his Life and Work,
 1805–1875* (London 1975)
BRIGGS, Asa: *The Age of Improvement* (London 1965)

BROUGHTON, Lord (J. C. Hobhouse): *Recollections of a Long Life* (4 vols, London 1910)

BURDETT-COUTTS, Angela: *Noble Workers* (London *sine anno*)

CHESNEY, Kenneth: *The Victorian Underworld* (Harmondsworth 1972)

COLERIDGE, Ernest H.: *The Life of Thomas Coutts, Banker* (London 1920)

COUTTS, Thomas: *The Life of the Late Thomas Coutts by a Person of the First Respectability* (London 1822)

CREEVEY, Thomas: *The Creevey Papers* (ed. Sir H. Maxwell, London 1904)

CROKER, John Wilson: *The Croker Papers, 1808–1857* (ed. L. J. Jennings, 3 vols, London 1884)

DICKENS, Charles: *Letters of Charles Dickens to the Baroness Burdett-Coutts* (ed. C. Osborne, London 1931)

(*Nonesuch Letters*) *The Letters of Charles Dickens* (ed. W. Dexter, 3 vols, London 1938)

(*Pilgrim Letters*) *The Letters of Charles Dickens* (ed. M. House and G. Storey, 3 vols, Oxford 1965–1974)

see also FORSTER and JOHNSON

DICTIONARY OF NATIONAL BIOGRAPHY

ELLIS, A. C.: *A Historical Survey of Torquay* (Torquay Directory Office 1930)

ENGELS, Frederick: *The Condition of the Working Class in England* (London 1892)

FORBES, William: *Coutts: Memoirs of a Banking House* (London 1860)

FORSTER, John: *The Life of Charles Dickens* (3 vols, London 1972)

FURNISS, Henry: *Some Victoria Women* (London 1923)

GREVILLE, *Leaves from the Greville Diary* (ed. Phillip Morell, London 1929)

HAHN, Emily: *James Brooke of Sarawak* (London 1953)

HARE, Augustus: *In My Solitary Life* (ed. Malcolm Barnes, London 1953)

HAYDON, Benjamin Robert: *The Life of Benjamin Robert Haydon from his Autobiography and Letters* (ed. T. Taylor, London 1853)

IRVING, Laurence: *Henry Irving* (London 1951)

JEAL, Tim: *Livingstone* (London 1973)

JOHNSON, Edgar: *The Heart of Charles Dickens* (New York 1952)

LAZARUS, Mary: *Victorian Social Conditions and Attitudes 1837–1871* (London 1969)

LIEVEN, Princess Dorothea: *The Private Letters to Prince Metternich 1820–1826* (ed. Peter Quennell, London 1937)

LONGFORD, Elizabeth: *Victoria, R. I.* (London 1964)
Wellington: The Years of the Sword (London 1969)
Wellington: Pillar of State (London 1972)

MORLEY, John: *The Life of William Ewart Gladstone* (3 vols, London 1903)

MOORE, Thomas: *Memoirs, Journal and Correspondence* (3 vols, London 1856)

MUNKSGAARD, Ejnar: *Visits of Hans Andersen to Charles Dickens as described in his Letters* (Copenhagen 1937)

MUSGRAVE, Clifford: *Life in Brighton* (London 1970)

NUTTING, Anthony: *Gordon* (London 1966)

PATTERSON, Clara: *Angela Burdett-Coutts and the Victorians* (London 1953)

PATTERSON, M. W.: *Sir Francis Burdett and his Times* (London 1931)

PEARCE, Charles E.: *The Jolly Duchess* (London 1915)

Select Bibliography

PENGELLY, Hester: *A Memoir of William Pengelly, F.R.S.* (London 1897)
POPE-HENNESSY, James: *Queen Mary* (London 1959)
RICHARDSON, Ralph: *Coutts and Co* (London 1900)
ROBINSON, Ralph: *Coutts: The History of a Banking House* (London 1929)
ROGERS, Samuel: *Recollections of Samuel Rogers* (ed. W. Sharpe, London 1859)
RUTTER, Owen: *Rajah Brooke and Baroness Burdett-Coutts* (London 1935)
ST JOHN, Spencer: *The Life of Sir James Brooke* (London 1879)
SETON WATSON, R. W.: *Disraeli, Gladstone, and the Eastern Question* (London
    1935)
STEVENS, The Reverend William Bagshaw: *Journal* (ed. G. Galbraith, Oxford
    1965)
TECK, Duchess of: *The Baroness Burdett-Coutts* (Chicago 1893)
THOMSON, E. P. and YEO, Eileen: *The Unknown Mayhew* (Harmondsworth 1973)
WATERFIELD, Gordon: *Layard of Nineveh* (London 1961)
WELLINGTON, Duke of: *Wellington and his Friends: Letters of the First Duke* (ed.
    7th Duke, London 1965)
YOUNG, The Reverend Julian: *A Memoir of Charles Mayne Young, Tragedian, with
    Extracts from his Son's Journal* (London 1971)

Principal Dates

in the Life of Angela Burdett-Coutts

1814	**21 April** Birth of Angela Burdett-Coutts
1815	**14 January** Death of Mrs Coutts (Susannah Starkie). **18 January** Thomas Coutts's secret marriage to Harriot Mellon. **March** Marriage announced
1819	Peterloo Massacre. Sir Francis Burdett attacks the Government
1821	Sir Francis Burdett condemned to three months imprisonment in the Marshalsea
1822	**22 February** Death of Thomas Coutts
1826–9	Lady Burdett and her daughters tour Europe
1827	**16 June** Harriot Coutts marries the Duke of St Albans
1836	Angela tours the north of England with the Duke and Duchess of St Albans. Summer at Portsmouth
1837	**6 August** Death of Harriot. Angela inherits Coutts fortune. Moves to Stratton Street
1838	Persecution by Richard Dunn at Harrogate
1843	Angela and Charles Dickens begin Ragged Schools scheme
1844	**12 January** Death of Lady Burdett. **23 January** Death of Sir Francis Burdett. Marriage of Hannah Meredith to Dr Brown
1845	Irish potato famine. Angela offers to pay for Charley Dickens's education
1846	Duke of Wellington retires from politics, begins friendship with Angela. Dickens consulted on proposed home for fallen women
1847	Angela founds bishoprics of Cape Town and Adelaide. **7 February** Angela proposes to the Duke of Wellington. **November** Urania Cottage opens
1848	St Stephen's School opens
1849	Death of Sir James Morier. Death of the Duke of St Albans. Angela moves to Holly Lodge
1850	**24 June** Consecration of St Stephen's, Westminster
1851	**August to November** Angela tours Germany and visits Paris
1852	Angela witnesses Louis Napoleon's *coup d'état*. **14 September** Death of the Duke of Wellington
1854	Angela offers support to wives of Crimean soldiers

1855	**13 March** Death of Masquerier. **23 October** Death of Dr Brown. **18 December** Death of Samuel Rogers
1856	**November** Angela takes up residence in Torquay. Meets Livingstone on his triumphant return to England
1857	**January** Angela helps destitute children at St Peter's, Stepney. **February to March** Works with Dickens on *Common Things*
1858	Angela offers endowment for bishopric of British Columbia. Financial aid to Rajah Brooke. Begins friendship and support of Livingstone
1859–61	Correspondence with Livingstone during Zambesi Expedition
1860	Sends out corrugated iron church (St John's) to British Columbia
1861	Aid to East London weavers. Gifts to Bermondsey tanners. Sends Bishop Mackenzie to new colony, Central Africa
1862	**May** To Paris Exhibition with Rajah Brooke. Sees Louis Napoleon in connection with Sarawak. Columbia Square model flats opened. Named as Rajah Brooke's successor. Wills's report on Irish famine. Relief organized
1863	Sends one hundred emigrants from Ireland to Canada
1864	Sewing school in Dr Brown's name opened. Columbia Market begins
1866	**3 December** Cheered by Reform demonstration
1867	**19 July** Fête at Holly Lodge for two thousand Belgian volunteers
1868	**7 May** Death of Lord Brougham. **11 June** Death of Rajah Brooke
1869	**3 June** Death of Edward Marjoribanks
1870	**9 June** Death of Charles Dickens. Angela becomes President of the Ladies Committee of the RSPCA.
1871	**May** Peerage bestowed by Queen Victoria
1872	**July** Granted Freedom of the City of London. **August** Welcomes Stanley on his return from finding Livingstone.
1873	**9 January** Death of Louis Napoleon. **1 May** Death of Livingstone
1877	Turkish Compassionate Fund opens
1878	**22 December** Death of Mrs Brown
1879	**July to October** Cruise on the *Walrus*
1880	Death of Robert Burdett. **1 September** Death of W. H. Wills. Marriage rumours
1881	**April** Death of Disraeli. **29 May** Marriage to William Ashmead Bartlett
1884	Campaign through *The Times* for the rescue of General Gordon
1885	**26 January** Death of Gordon
1886	**17 May** Death of Susan Trevanion
1887	**April** Visits Baltimore, Ireland. Opens fishing school
1888	**April** Visits Cannes and Paris. **December** The Reverend Twining is inducted vicar of St Stephen's
1890	Westminster Technical Institute opened
1891	**January** Visits Abbazia. **April** Visits Paris and Boulogne. **September** Coaching tour of Westmorland and Northumberland
1893	Prepares report for Chicago World Fair

1894	**January to April** Visits Paris and Rome. **5 July** Death of Layard
1896	**March to April** Visits Corsica. **May** Visits Paris
1898–1900	Appeal for Destitute Children's Fund
1904	**21 April** Celebrates ninetieth birthday at Stratton Street. **10 May** Death of H. M. Stanley
1905	**13 April** Death of Sir Henry Irving. Lying-in-state at Stratton Street
1906	**30 December** Death of Angela Burdett-Coutts at 10.30 a.m. in Stratton Street
1907	**5 January** Funeral, Westminster Abbey

Notes and References

Preface
1   *Autobiography of John Hays Hammond*, New York, 1935, pp. 438–40.

Chapter One. THE DOUBLE INHERITANCE: 1814–1837
1   Quoted in Robinson, p. 29.
2   Ibid., p. 31.
3   Patterson, vol. I, p. 17.
4   Robinson, p. 60.
5   6 January 1793, B-C.
6   Patterson, vol. I, p. 11.
7   21 January 1818, Bodleian Ms. Eng. lett., d. 94 fols 13–14.
8   13 February 1793, Stevens, *Journal*.
9   21 April 1793, ibid.
10   12 February 1793, ibid.
11   21 October 1796, ibid.
12   28 January 1798. Quoted in Patterson, vol. I, p. 34.
13   Quoted in Patterson, vol. II, p. 255. 'She resembled a landscape by Claude Lorraine with a setting sun.'
14   Quoted in Coleridge, vol. II, p. 289.
15   Quoted in Pearce, p. 99.
16   Haydon, *Memoirs*.
17   On 17 January Harriot obtained a special licence and she and Thomas Coutts were married the next day at St Pancras Church. It was not until February that he told his daughters and on 2 March the marriage was announced in *The Times* as having taken place 'on Wednesday'.
18   Lady Guilford could hardly complain. Her father had, in addition to the £43,000 settled on her in 1812, allowed her the free rent of the house in Piccadilly (which he reckoned at £700 a year) and an annual allowance of £4,000. The house in Putney cost £8,701 and its furniture £7,000.
19   Fuseli was as devoted to the Burdett girls as he had been to their mother and her sisters. He had a strange sentimental affair with Angela's eldest sister Sophia and painted many portraits of her. He died in the house in Putney in 1835.
20   Moore, *Memoirs*, vol. 2, pp. 158–9.
21   Sir Francis violently attacked the Government over the Peterloo Massacre. After a long drawn out lawsuit he was indicted, fined, and imprisoned in the Marshalsea in February 1821. Sophia's letter to her father on her husband's imprisonment was supremely nonchalant and once again Thomas noticed how she blossomed when her husband was in prison.
22   *The Journal of Sir Walter Scott*, Edinburgh 1891, vol. 1, p. 278.
23   Quoted in John Gibson Lockhart, *The Life of Sir Walter Scott*, Edinburgh 1902, vol. 8, pp. 68–70.
24   B-C.

Chapter Two. THE LEARNING YEARS: 1837–1843

1 The Trustees transferred to her account on 24 June 1838 a residue of £51,425 18s 10d, which included the profits of the Coutts half share in the Bank for 1837–8 of £50,676 17s 6d. In the year 1838–9 a further £44,019 2s 1d was put into her account by the Trustees so that for that year her total credits were £97,795 0s 11d, and in June 1839, having spent £40,149 7s 10d, she carried forward a balance of £57,645 13s 1d.

2 From the inventory of Holly Lodge, Coutts and Co.

3 22 September 1838, Bodleian, Ms. Eng. lett., d. 98, f. 131 and 27 August 1837, Bodleian, Ms. Eng. lett., d. 98, f. 127.

4 Hare, *Life*, vol. 1, p. 17.

5 *Punch*, 21 November 1846.

6 5 December 1833, Royal Archives, Windsor.

7 15 March 1838, Royal Archives, Windsor.

8 Bodleian, Ms. Eng. lett., d. 98, f. 233.

9 Bodleian, Ms. Eng. lett., d. 98, fols 143–4.

10 Broughton, vol. 6, p. 149.

11 Quoted in Waterfield, p. 18.

12 19 January 1847, B-C.

13 Young, p. 397.

14 8 August 1839, B-C.

15 17 August 1839, B-C.

16 5 November 1839, B-C. Babbage to Angela Burdett-Coutts. 'I have been favoured by the loan of a specimen of Daguerre's new art, as I know you are interested in the subject I leave it with you and will call for it tomorrow.'

17 5 September 1857, P.M. (E.J.).

18 Francis Burdett to Angela, Bodleian, Ms. Eng. lett., d. 98, f. 147.

19 Pilgrim Letters, vol. 1, p. 473.

20 6 August 1840, P.M. (unpublished).

21 22 January 1841, P.M. (E.J.).

22 Forster, vol. 1, p. 225. There is no record that Angela was present but it was customary for Lady Burdett and her daughters to join the guests after dinner. Certainly Angela's offer to Dickens of her box at the theatre dates from this period.

23 20 April 1841, P.M. (E.J.).

24 16 April 1841, P.M. (E.J.).

25 Huntington Library. Quoted in the Pilgrim Letters, vol. 2.

26 2 July 1842, P.M. (E.J.).

27 24 March 1842, P.M. (E.J.).

28 Forster, vol. 2, p. 37. She was, he wrote, 'a most excellent creature' and he had 'the most perfect respect for her'.

29 5 September 1843, P.M. (E.J.).

30 16 September 1843, ibid. (Martin Chuzzlewit, Chapter XXV in the October number).

31 5 October 1846, ibid.

32 24 October 1843, B-C.

33 27 December 1843, P.M. (E.J.).

34 13 January 1844, ibid.

35 Sinclair Letters, Coutts and Co.

36 27 January 1844. *The Times* reported that Miss Coutts had refused to allow further experimentation by a water-cure specialist on the Saturday before her father's death. She told the physician that the water treatment had already 'destroyed one of the noblest constitutions ever given to man'.

37 May 1844, Harrowby Ms, Sandon Hall.

38 28 June 1844, B-C.

39 17 November 1851, P.M. (unpublished letter to Dr. Brown).

40 23 March 1851, P.M. (E.J.).

41 5 May 1856, Nonesuch Letters.

42 4 February 1850, P.M. (E.J.).

43 31 March 1835, *New Letters of Thomas Carlyle*, ed. Alexander Carlyle, London 1903.

44 Undated, B-C.
45 Carlyle, *New Letters*.
46 Undated, B-C.
47 18 March 1845, P.M. (E.J.).
48 22 August 1851, ibid.
49 *Household Words*, 1857.
50 26 May 1846, P.M. (E.J.).
51 Ibid.

Chapter Three. THE PEN AND THE SWORD: 1846–1852
Unless otherwise stated, all letters from the Duke of Wellington are in the Wellington Archives, Stratfield Saye.

1   30 October 1846.
2   28 November 1846.
3   26 November 1846.
4   12 October 1839, Haydon, *Memoirs*.
5   1 January 1847.
6   5 January 1847.
7   10 January 1847.
8   12 January 1847.
9   P.M. (E.J.).
10 8 February 1847.
11 As always *Punch* took an interest in Miss Coutts's affairs:
    Marriage of the Metals   Scene: Room in Royal Institution
Professor Smith (reading *The Morning Post*). Very extraordinary!
(To *Professor Jones*) Have you read this? No! Well, then, the Post says that the DUKE OF WELLINGTON – the Iron Duke – is going to marry MISS BURDETT-COUTTS!
Professor Jones. Nonsense! It can't be true.
Professor Smith. But if it should be true, what would you think of such a match?
Professor Jones. Think of it! Why, with the Duke and the heiress, I should think it a most extraordinary union of Iron and Tin.
12 24 September 1847, *Lieven – Palmerston Correspondence 1828–1856*, ed. Lord Sudley, London, 1943, p. 297.
13 3 May 1847.
14 27 June 1847, P.M. (E.J.).
15 27 June 1847, P.M. (unpublished).
16 Ibid.
17 14 August 1847.
18 Ibid.
19 30 October 1847.
20 20 October 1847.
21 25 October 1847.
22 27 October 1847.
23 30 October 1847.
24 20 November 1847, P.M. (E.J.).
25 26 August 1847, ibid.
26 Ibid.
27 4 March 1850, P.M. (E.J.).
28 3 November 1847, ibid.
29 20 November 1847, ibid.
30 29 December 1847, ibid.
31 27 January 1841, to Lady Wilton. Quoted in *Wellington and his Friends*, p. 155.
32 30 January 1848.
33 1 April 1853, P.M. (E.J.).
34 20 October 1848.
35 8 January 1850, P.M. (E.J.).
36 August 1850, P.M. (E.J.).

37   29 August 1849.

38   31 January 1851. Wellington's postscript is characteristic, 'I wonder whether Radetsky is as fortunate.' The Austrian general, his old companion in arms, was still winning battles and Wellington could just bear this if he was not also lucky in love.

39   His letter to her of 9 November 1847 reveals the depth of his involvement, 'I have been entirely alone now nearly a week my companion constantly with me, day and night, with whom I think aloud whom I look at and caress, who is happy and delighted and smiles on me in return! . . . Tell me that you feel your companion near you as I do mine that you converse with him! think with him! God bless you my dearest.'

40   7 January 1852.

41   14 September 1852, P.M. (E.J.).

42   *Household Words*, 27 November 1852.

43   19 November 1852, P.M. (E.J.).

Chapter Four. AT WORK WITH CHARLES DICKENS: 1852–1855

1   10 July 1855, P.M. (E.J.).

2   22 April 1861, ibid. Nonesuch Letters.

3   31 March 1853, (unpublished).

4   *Household Words*, 23 April 1853, 'A HOME for Homeless Women'.

5   17 April 1850, P.M. (E.J.).

6   Letter to Dr Brown, 7 November 1849, P.M. (E.J.).

7   15 November 1856, P.M. (E.J.).

8   Sir Henry Smith, who had fought with Wellington in the Peninsular Wars, was given financial help by Miss Coutts when he became Governor of the Cape. His wife Juanita (whom he had rescued from the battlefield) wrote to Miss Coutts warning that it was dangerous to send girls out to her while the colonists were seething with fury over the Government's decision to send convicts to the Cape. Nevertheless, she reported on the good progress of two girls from the Home.

9   18 April 1852, P.M. (E.J.).

10   *Household Words*, 24 March 1855.

11   10 March 1853, P.M. (E.J.).

12   15 July 1856, P.M. (unpublished). Dickens also described Dunn's persecution in *Household Words*, 8 October 1853: 'Things that cannot be done.'

13   Ibid.

14   To Miss Coutts he left a legacy to be spent on the education of the poor. It was used to build the Burdett-Coutts and Townshend School next to her own school in Westminster and Mrs Brown laid the foundation stone on 13 September 1876.

15   3 February 1857, P.M. (E.J.).

16   P.M. (unpublished).

17   Nonesuch Letters.

18   3 November 1855, P.M. (E.J.).

19   Ibid.

20   11 July 1856, P.M. (E.J.).

21   Stevens, *Journal*.

22   5 March 1857, P.M. (unpublished).

23   15 November 1856, P.M. (E.J.).

24   22 May 1857, P.M. (unpublished).

25   3 June 1857, P.M. (E.J.).

26   Sir Henry Dickens, *My Father as I knew Him*, London, 1934.

27   Andersen, *Diary*, 13 June 1857.

28   Bredsdorff, *Story*, p. 58.

29   16 June 1857, Andersen, *Diary*.

30   Bredsdorff, *Story*, p. 58.

31   7 June 1857, P.M. (unpublished).

32   14 April 1858, P.M. (unpublished).

33   The lease had not yet expired and Miss Coutts established her bursar, John Sapsford, in the house, where he and his large family lived for many years.

34   *The Diary of Henry Crabb Robinson*, ed. Derek Hudson, Oxford 1967, p. 297.
35   5 April 1860, P.M. (E.J.).
36   Walter Dickens had been a favourite with Miss Coutts and she had helped to get him a cadetship in the Indian Army. She saw little of Charley after his marriage in 1861 but he called his daughter Angela and Miss Coutts continued to be generous. In 1863 she gave him £3,000 and in 1864, £5,000.

Chapter Five. CALM ANCHORAGE – TORQUAY: 1856–1857
 1   Miss Coutts had already a distant connexion with Darwin who came to stay in Hesketh Crescent. His grandfather, the great botanist Sir Erasmus Darwin, had been old Sir Robert Burdett's doctor and had prescribed medicine for Angela's mother and aunts.

Chapter Six. THE WIDER WORLD: 1857–1867
 1   Quoted in Teck, p. 136.
 2   Ibid., p. 143.
 3   B-C.
 4   14 February 1858, B-C.
 5   6 May 1858, B-C.
 6   B-C.
 7   20 December 1858, B-C.
 8   5 July 1858, B-C.
 9   10 October 1859, B-C.
10   1 September 1860, B-C.
11   On 18 March Livingstone wrote, 'These words ran into me like a dose of smelling salts and I promised forthwith to send for my *worse* half as soon as I can get up a house for her. But I think that I have decent materials for a quarrel with you for turning against me.' This is the last letter from Livingstone to her that has been preserved.
12   British Library, Gladstone Papers.
13   Spencer St John is described on the title page of his *Life of Sir James Brooke* as being, 'Formerly Secretary to the Rajah, Late Consul-General in Borneo, H.M. Minister-Resident to the Republic of Peru and author of "Life in the Forests of the Far East".' A close friend of Rajah Brooke and Miss Coutts, he was in constant contact during the Rajah's last years.
14   British Library, Brooke Letters.
15   Charles Brooke inherited Sarawak and was punctilious in repaying his uncle's debts to Miss Coutts. She had lent the Rajah £2,500 for the purchase of Burrator; Brooke transferred the house to Miss Coutts who later sold it to a neighbour. She remained an executor of the sovereignty of Sarawak clause in the Rajah's last will until 1898.

Chapter Seven. HOME AFFAIRS: 1867–1868
 1   Royal Marsden Hospital Annual Report.
 2   Augustus Hare, *Life*.
 3   Her favourite painting, part of the predella of the altarpiece painted in 1505 for the nuns of St Anthony at Perugia. At the same time she bought a number of engravings of it. One, by Samuel Rogers himself, she gave to Gladstone as a Christmas present. Another she sent to Florence Nightingale in the Crimea and a third was presented to the Duc d'Aumale at Chantilly.
 4   The Folger Shakespeare Museum, Washington acquired one of her First Folio Shakespeares after her husband's death. It is enclosed in a carved chest made from the wood of Herne Oak in Windsor Park – the wood a gift from Queen Victoria. The author discovered a note giving these details in Miss Coutts's hand beneath the Folio in Washington.
 5   Bertram, *Les Belges à Londres*, Ghent 1867. Translated here by E. M. Healey.
 6   Brodie's bust of her in Coutts and Co. shows her wearing a locket engraved with a dog's head.
 7   Bobby refused to leave his master's grave for sixteen years and in 1867 the Lord Provost of Edinburgh presented him with a handsome collar and exempted him from dog tax.
 8   Address to the RSPCA.

Chapter Eight. PUBLIC HONOUR – PRIVATE STRESS: 1868–1878

1   It was Gladstone who proposed that Miss Coutts be made a Baroness. Among the Gladstone Papers in the British Library there is a scrap of paper, possibly passed during a meeting, recording this exchange; 5 May 1871, 'Is there any way in which the remarkable services of Miss B.C. to her public could be acknowledged? W.E.G.' Underneath is another pencilled note from Lord Granville, 'Like notion of peerage. G.'

2   The *Scotsman*, 16 January 1874.
3   Osborne, Letters, Introduction, p. 17.
4   She had remained a close friend throughout Louis Napoleon's life. She visited him at Compiègne in 1861 and when he was exiled to England in 1870 she welcomed him and sent him fruit and flowers from Holly Lodge in his last illness. She was also a friend to the Empress Eugènie until her death.
5   Marjoribanks Papers, Coutts and Co.
6   Harrowby Mss.
7   Sinclair Letters, Coutts and Co.
8   Wagner Papers.
9   British Library, Layard Papers.
10   Wagner Papers.
11   Irving, *Henry Irving*, p. 284.
12   Wagner Papers.
13   British Library, Layard Papers.
14   Wagner Papers.
15   British Library, Layard Papers.

Chapter Nine. THE MAD MARRIAGE: 1878–1893

1   18 September 1879, Irving Papers. Quoted in Burdett Patterson.
2   2 October 1879, ibid.
3   Letter to the Reverend Barnes, Coutts and Co.
4   25 July 1880, Harrowby Mss.
5   4 July 1880, ibid.
6   Ibid.
7   10 July 1880, Windsor, Royal Archives L14/56
8   18 July 1880, Windsor, Royal Archives. Add. A12/544.
9   Harrowby Mss.
10   Ibid.
11   Ibid.
12   Ibid.
13   July 1880, ibid.
14   10 August 1880 B-C.
15   British Library, Gladstone Papers.
16   22 September 1880, *Disraeli; Letters to Queen Victoria*, vol. III, p. 146.
17   On 20 September 1880, Clara as the next heir, in accordance with the wishes of Thomas Coutts to Money. *Punch* seized the opportunity;

> *Money takes the name of Coutts*
> *Superfluous and funny!*
> *For everyone considers Coutts*
> *Synonymous with Money!*

18   Moore, *Memoirs*.
19   Teck.
20   Nutting, *Gordon*.
21   Ibid.
22   The papers relating to the leasing of Chantilly by the Baroness are in the Chantilly archives, Musée de Condé.
23   Teck, p. 156.
24   Windsor, Royal Archives Z210/21.
25   Pope Hennessy.
26   Although she spent a lifetime improving the lot of women in certain respects, Miss Coutts

took no part in the suffragette movement and was strangely reluctant to encourage women to take part in public life. Despite her support of Florence Nightingale she could still write; 'If females are to enter on a medical career and are to study with men either the latter will retire or barriers of common decorum must be broken down.' Letter to Sir Sidney Lee, 1891 (Bodleian).

Chapter Ten. THE NOBLEST SPIRIT WE SHALL EVER KNOW: 1893–1906

1   Furniss.

2   Compton Mackenzie, *My Life and Times*, London 1963, p. 289.

3   General Pasquali Paoli, the Corsican patriot, died in exile in London in 1807. Soldier, philosopher and democratic ruler of Corsica from 1757 to 1758, Paoli had been visited by Boswell, roused British support for his cause and had obtained a loan from the Edinburgh branch of Coutts Bank. Sir Francis Burdett had greatly admired him. The Baroness owned the churchyard in St Pancras where he was buried and when she was making this into a public garden she returned his remains to Corsica.

4   Musgrave, p. 365.

5   Mrs Twining's Journal, Westminster Public Library.

Index

Page numbers in italics indicate illustrations

Index

Index

Index